95

The Mode in Costume

THE
MODE
IN
COSTUME

By

R. Turner Wilcox

the first

Garment

NEW YORK

CHARLES SCRIBNER'S SONS

1948

Foreword

"He is only fantastical that is not in fashion."
Anatomy of Melancholy, ROBERT BURTON, 1577–1640.

THE WEARING of clothes being a necessity, the individual owes it to himself to display in the front he presents to the world, the most pleasing exterior possible. Wearing apparel therefore, should be artistic in color and design, charming and flattering according to the fashion and the circumstance.

The idea which prompted the execution of this work was to place before the student a study of the mode in civil costume of all ages. I have endeavored to portray and explain, as simply as possible, for each period, the prevailing design of costume worn and, wherever available, to give the information regarding origin, actual dates, fabrics, colors and accessories.

To produce a handbook of the mode in all the important periods and for the reader's convenience, under one cover, I found a task of considerable proportions, requiring the utilization of wide information acquired over many years of study and work in this field.

I have confined my research to the original contemporary sources, such as medals, coins, sculpture, tapestries, pictures or decorations extant of the various periods. My aim has been to simplify, especially in ancient costume, the basic garments by avoiding the use of unnecessary foreign names. In many cases, I find that authors of works on this subject do not always agree on the meaning of terms which are, very often, of singular importance.

The calamity which befell France in 1940 has stopped the exportation of the designs of the French couturiers to the women of America, for a time at least. This furnishes an opportunity to the designers of the United States to display their abilities in this field. Some progress, undoubtedly, has been made, but the production seriously lacks the authority and prestige of the famous names of the French Couture.

Talent of no mean caliber is at work on the problem of creating that which for so many years was a matter of copying and adapting. To supplant the work of the French couturiers will take time and any success will be grudgingly admitted. It is hoped the problem of the production of "exclusive" fabrics will be more easily solved due to our American quality manufacturers.

While maintained contact with London should take care of the style features of masculine clothing, the United States Government limitations on the "Victory suit" and overcoat will force the designers in men's apparel to mark time for the duration of this war.

R. T. W.

May, 1942
Tenafly, New Jersey

Foreword—1948

ORE THAN four years of the German Occupation effectively shut Paris off from the rest of the world, four years in which American designers were compelled to stand on their own feet. Working under the limitations in design and fabric imposed by Washington's L85, our designers truly found themselves and produced lovely, wearable and functional clothes. Meanwhile, the Haute Couture hoping and working for the Day of Liberation, gallantly plied their creative talents for the good and continuance of the French fashion industry. And despite "blood, sweat and tears" and scarcity of materials, our valiant English cousins carried on, producing and shipping to America a few of their inimitable tailleurs, models of perfection as ever.

Now in 1948 in this world of closer neighbors, we realize that Paris still carries the torch of fashion, yet at the same time the brilliant designers of London, New York and California continue to create equally individual creations, each fashion center affording inspiration to the other.

This after-war world is a changed place. So is the world of fashion and it seems fitting in this history-making period that we record 1947 in "The Mode in Costume" by adding another chapter to the original work.

R. T. W.

ix

Table of Contents

CHAPTER TWENTY-ONE

CHAPTER TWENTY-TWO

CHAPTER TWENTY-THREE

pumps · gaiters · mourning · wigs · cocked hat · the Androsmane · Holland hat · Quaker hat · jockey hat · neckcloth · canes · Europe follows French feminine mode · fashion dolls · whalebone corset · bustle · black silk lace · blonde lace · change to simplicity · sacque · description of various styles of gowns · riding habit · lingerie frock · robe à l'anglaise · fichu · sheer cottons · baby headdress · hedgehog headdress · powdered hair · face painting · the dormeuse · mob-cap · thérèse · caliche · straw hats · pelisse · children's dress

CHAPTER THIRTY-TWO

THE FRENCH REVOLUTION 1789–1795   220

Simplicity · less class distinction · English influence · standard masculine costume · appearance of trousers · pantalons à pont · carmagnole · sans-culottes · liberty cap · cockade · frockcoat · tight breeches · boots · wigs · hats · muscadines · patriot · feminine costume · chemise à l'anglaise · hats and caps · sandal slippers · lace factories demolished · trend toward Ancient Greece and Rome · ready-made clothes

CHAPTER THIRTY-THREE

DIRECTOIRE 1795–1799   228

Use of classic Greek and Roman design · the incroyables · exaggerated neckcloth · culottes · colors · blond wigs · sans-culottes discarded · "dog's ears" · Brutus cut · hussar breeches · two watches · single eyeglass · pumps · classic white · sheath or chemise gown · scarfs and muffs · cashmere shawl   Spencer jacket · reticle and sabretache · the merveilleuse · wigs · antique oil · the bob · feminine bonnet · classic footgear · artificial flowers

CHAPTER THIRTY-FOUR

THE FRENCH CONSULATE AND FIRST EMPIRE 1799–1815   236

Origin of the mode · pantaloons and trousers · stockinet and nankeen · the habit · greatcoats · polished tall hat · gaiters · pumps · the sock · English jockey boot · hussar boot · military boot · Brutus hair-cut · chemise gown · mameluke sleeves · Betsies · muslin pantaloons · corset waist · spen-

The Mode in Costume

Chapter One

Egyptian

3000 TO 525 B.C.

THE GARMENTS of the Egyptians were few in number. Because of an even, warm climate, they were made of cotton and linen. The upper class wore a fine transparent muslin, similar to that of contemporary East Indian make, woven from flax grown in the rich mud flats of the Nile. The predominant color was white, but all colors, both brilliant and somber, were worn, color, however, being more ancient.

The first and principal garment of the men was the *schenti*, or loin cloth, which was a long scarf wrapped around the hips and held in place by a tied belt or girdle. When worn by high dignitaries, it was finished in front with a pleated apron. The pleats radiated from the low corner of the apron upward toward the belt, representing the rays of the sun, the emblem of Uraeus. From 1500 to 332 B.C. a long apron like a wrap-around skirt was worn and over that a transparent coat, the hems of which were often edged with fringe. The emblem of Uraeus, attached to the girdle, hung in front. Pleats were a distinct decorative feature of the costume of this later period.

I

Women wore a straight, narrow-sheath gown, which hung from under the breasts to the ankles and was held up by either a single shoulder strap, or one on each shoulder. In early Egypt only the priests wore sandals; the feet of the others were bare. Sandals had soles of leather, papyrus or sometimes wood and were held on by a couple of straps.

Both sexes shaved their heads for such reasons as religious ordinance, cleanliness and heat, but hair and beards were left to grow when in mourning. The rich wore wigs of false hair, wool or palm-leaf fiber, while the poorer classes wore skull caps of felt. Wigs were really a protection against the rays of the sun, the foundation being a porous fabric, to which human hair or sheep's wool was attached. Heavy bonnets of cotton, linen or wool, striped or embroidered, were worn for the same purpose. The ornaments were significant of rank or office, such as the lotus, meaning abundance; the asp, royal power; the sacred feather, emblem of the ruler. The headband with hanging ends in back was worn by men and women. Women often added flowers to their headdress, a favorite being the lotus.

Women used two colors of kohl for the eyes, green and black. They outlined the veins of the chest in blue, painted their lips with carmine, colored their cheeks with red and white and tipped their fingers with orange henna. They made general use of perfumes and ointments. The men wore no beard or mustache, but the pharaohs and high dignitaries wore the *postiche* or false beard, with which a woman, if queen, also adorned herself. In the examples which exist, the *postiche* was attached to a chin strap, gold no doubt, which was part of a frame or cap worn under the wig or bonnet.

The later period was one of great extravagance, dating from 1500 to 1150 B.C. Men and women wore earrings, pendants, necklaces, bracelets and anklets in pairs, also jewelled girdles. They were encrusted with cabochons of turquoise, carnelian, coral and lapis lazuli. Pearls and amber were used and beads fashioned of many stones, of various shapes. The deep flat collar of strung beads was especially favored. The exquisite

jewelry of the Egyptians has never been surpassed in design or workmanship and the clasps of those pieces extant usually function as perfectly as
when made. The signet ring and the jewelled girdle date from ancient
Egypt.

In this later period, tunics were gorgeously embroidered. The Egyptians practised the art of embroidery, done with gold thread made of
strips of the metal, beaten and rounded. The Greeks, however, are supposed to have been the first to make a gold thread fine enough to be
used with needle. Sandals, too, became more elaborate, of soft leather
dyed purple or crimson, embossed with gold and enriched with precious
stones. There was also an Oriental style of sandal having long, turned-up
toes. Others were of plaited palm, painted vermilion and ornamented
with gold. It had become improper to go barefooted in the streets.

The umbrella was in use as a protection against the sun and the fan
of feathers or papyrus for cooling the air. Both had long handles and
were carried by bearers, that position being one of honor. Umbrellas
and fans were permitted only to persons of rank.

Egyptian

schenti or
loin cloth

embroidered
sheath gown

white
sheath gown

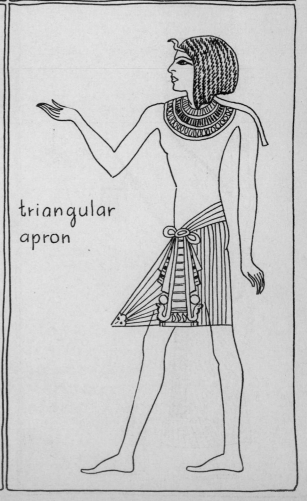

triangular
apron

RTW

Egyptian

viceroy

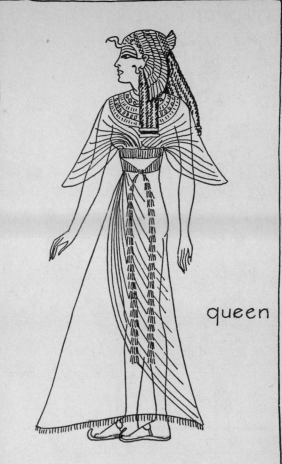

queen

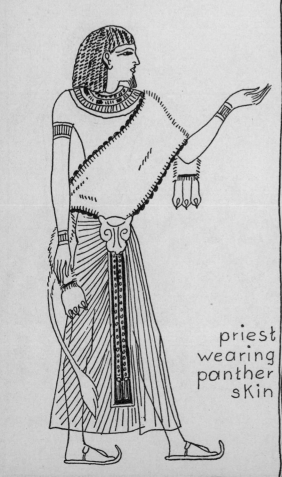

priest
wearing
panther
skin

king in
long
apron
and coat

RTW

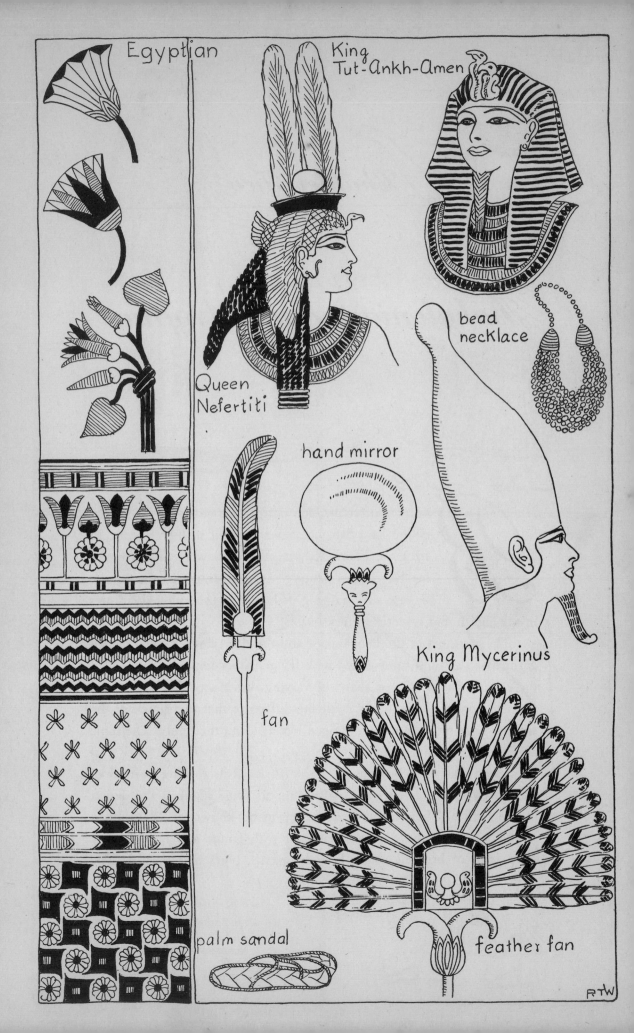

Egyptian

King
Tut-Ankh-Amen

Queen
Nefertiti

bead
necklace

hand mirror

King Mycerinus

fan

palm sandal

feather fan

RTW

Chapter Two

Babylonian and Assyrian

1500 B.C. TO 550 B.C.

ABYLONIAN civilization dated back nearly as far as that of the Egyptian, but never reached so high a state. In 1917 B.C. Elam, Assyria and Syria were united under the Babylonian Empire. Assyria conquered the empire in 1250 B.C., reaching its height in the mingled cultures in the eighth and seventh centuries B.C.

The costumes of the Babylonians and the Assyrians consisted of two garments, a straight tunic edged with fringe, either long or short, called the *candys,* and a fringed shawl of varying dimensions. Both men and women wore the same outfit, with the difference that the shawls of the women were more ample and draped loosely about the figure. The tunic appears often with a set-in sleeve.

Linen was used, but the principal fabric seems to have been wool elaborately embroidered with separate motifs founded upon the design of the rosette. Their embroideries came to be known as "Babylonian work." Garments were always trimmed with fringe and tassels. They were fond of brilliant colors in reds, greens, blues and purples. The purple candys embroidered with gold was reserved for the king. His hood was of wool decorated with embroideries and jewels, sometimes finished with a row of small feathers around the top. Jewelled tiaras were worn by high dignitaries.

The men wore their hair and beards long, done in carefully arranged tight corkscrew curls and are known to have powdered their hair with gold dust. Men and women wore jewelry of gold and silver in the form of earrings, necklaces and bracelets set with pearls and other precious stones. Their sandals had a sole of leather with heel straps or a heel cap, a ring for the large toe and laces tied around the ankle. The Greeks termed their footgear "miserable" as compared with the rest of the costume. Soldiers wore a buskin knee-high of leather laced from toe to knee. Umbrellas were used as a protection against the sun, but were permitted only to persons of rank, the same being true of fans. Both were carried by bearers.

Little is known of the feminine costume. Women led a most secluded life and are not represented in the bas-reliefs or sculpture, which have come down to us.

Babylonian and Assyrian

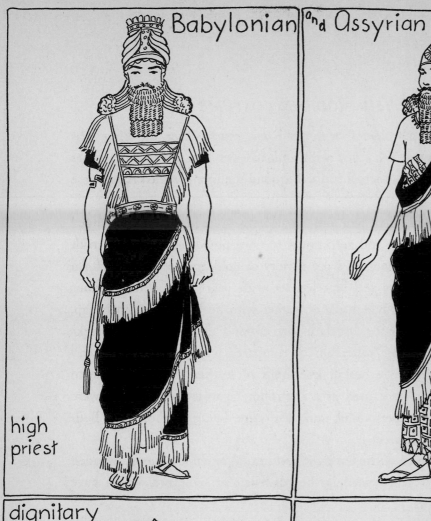

high priest

King

dignitary

attendant

RTW

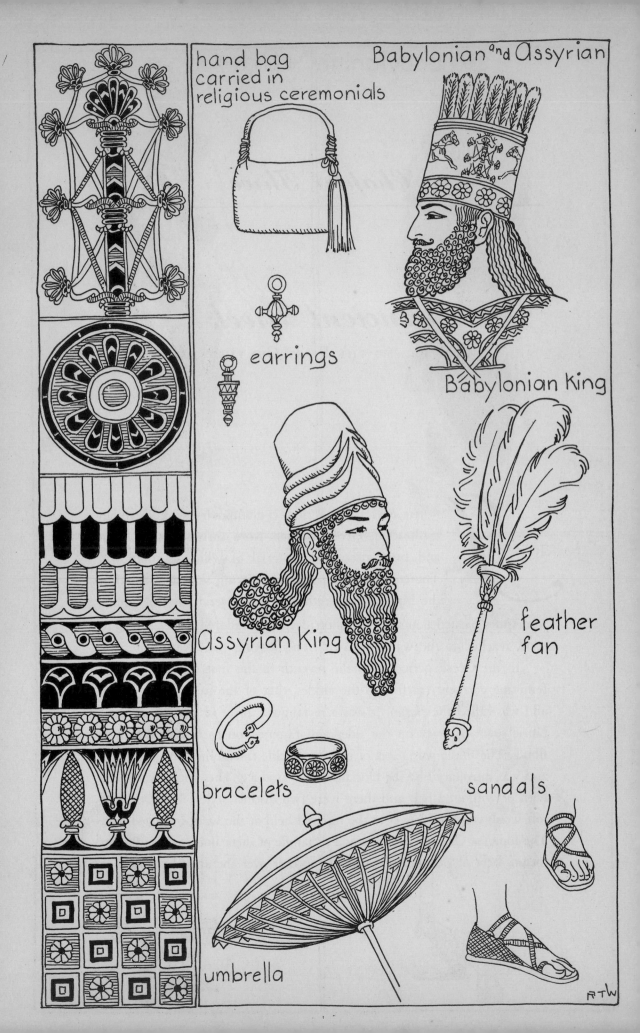

hand bag
carried in
religious ceremonials

Babylonian and Assyrian

earrings

Babylonian King

Assyrian King

feather
fan

bracelets

sandals

umbrella

RTW

Chapter Three

Ancient Greek

1500 B.C. TO THE FIRST CENTURY B.C.

IN THE Mycenæan Period, contemporary with Egyptian civilization, Greek women wore corsets, also a sewn and fitted dress, the material of which is unknown. The colors were bright. The flaring skirt was fitted at the hips, ankle-length and had several rows of ruffles, sometimes pleated flounces. The short decorated tailored jacket in bolero style, reached to the waist, open in front, leaving the breasts bare.

In the Greek period from the seventh to the first century B.C., the feminine garment reached to the ankles, that of the men to the knees, and was called the *chiton*. It was a rectangular piece of woolen or linen fabric sewn partway up the sides and fastened on each shoulder by a fibula. The fibula was a sort of clasp or buckle resembling our safety pin and was introduced by the Dorians about 1100 B.C. The chiton was worn with or without a belt and there were two distinct styles. The Doric, of soft wool, was folded over at the top and held at the waist by a tied belt. The Ionic, of Oriental origin, was a rectangle of sheer linen or fine Indian cotton, later of silk, but was caught together over the arms by fibulæ or buttons forming loose sleeves when belted. Too, there was a chiton with a short sleeve.

Men of action fastened the chiton on the left shoulder, leaving the right arm free, and sometimes wore a second belt around the hips, creating a second bloused section between the two belts. Women often bloused their tunic in the same fashion. Men retained the long chiton for ceremonial occasions.

A garment worn by women over the chiton was the peplos or peplum. It was a rectangle of woolen fabric of variable size, unsewn and fastened on the shoulders. It was draped like the chiton. The bloused section called the kolpos or deploidion, was carefully arranged in artistic folds which were weighted with lead pellets.

The *chlamys,* a light summer mantle, was originally worn on horseback. Later, it became the cloak of young men, made in expensive material and worn over the chiton. It was a rectangle about one by two yards in dimension and of woolen material, with small weights at the four corners to prevent its blowing. A clasp fastened it on the shoulder or in front and it was used as a protection against cold and rain, also serving as a cover when sleeping.

The *himation,* or cloak, was worn by both sexes. It was composed of a piece of fabric about one and a half yards by three in size, draped about the figure, usually over but one shoulder. Young men and philosophers are pictured using it as their sole garment, in which case it appears securely fastened at the waist by a belt. Women too wore it, often without the chiton underneath.

A sign of mourning in Greek costume was the unbelted trailing garments of either sex, presumably of a brownish hue.

Pleats were a favorite decoration and were made by wetting the garment in thin starch, twisting it carefully, then laying it in the sun to dry. In the earliest period woolen fabric was employed, later linen appeared, and in the latest period there was pure silk, also flax and silk combined.

An important article of dress worn by women, even when sleeping, was the *bandelette,* a tape or ribbon which, while most decorative, acted as a support to the breasts. It was sometimes worn under, but usually outside the chiton.

Both sexes were greatly addicted to the use of perfumes, and oils and essences were freely applied to the body.

It is recorded that men wore beards until Alexander's time. They wore their hair cut short, often held in place by a band tied around the head. Women wore their hair long, sometimes frizzed or in corkscrew curls, or parted in the middle and drawn into a chignon at back of the neck. They fastened their hair with hairpins of bone or ivory, which were plain or mounted with gold. They also had a spiral type of hairpin of gold wire. They were naturally blond, but often made use of wigs, dyed their hair and wore rich sheer veils. The veils were occasionally floating or, again, wound in the hair. Too, they dressed their hair with perfume, flowers and colored ribbons, wore jewelled tiaras and crowns of gold or silver wire, also the caul or net. The Greek bride wore a long sheer white veil attached to the back of her headdress, which was ornamented with pearls. Another bridal headdress was a wreath of violets and myrtle.

Some of the Tanagra statuettes have large hats with wide brims, set on the head over the veil. From Phrygia in Asia Minor came the "Phrygian bonnet," revived now and then down the ages, notably in the French Revolution, as the cap on the figure of "Liberty."

The Phrygians are credited also with being the first people to make gold wire into strands thin enough to use with needle for embroidery, and are believed to have taught the art to the Egyptians. Greek women of the later period were noted for their skill in weaving and embroidery, the borders, necks and armscyes of their garments being richly decorated. The handwork was executed in wool or linen.

When Greek men travelled, they wore, with the chlamys, a hat of felt with a broad brim, as protection against heat and rain. It was secured by a chin strap, which permitted the hat to hang down in back, when not in use. This hat was called a petasos.

Felt was also used for cloaks and caps. Wool or hair matted together while moist was the means employed then, as today, in its manufacture.

Men and women wore sandals, having a sturdy leather sole, held on the foot by leather straps. The *cothurn,* which was the shoe of the actor, had a thick cork or wooden sole. Buskins, also worn, reached to the middle of the calf and were laced in front. They were usually lined and ornamented with skins of small animals, the heads and claws of which hung over the tops. It was the custom among the early Greeks to remove their footwear upon entering the house. At a later period, all classes wore sandals, boots and shoes. In the Periclean Age, men's sandals were ornamented with gold, while those of the women were adorned with colored embroidery and gold; in fact, sandals became a very costly part of the costume. The Greeks are known to have shaped the soles to conform to the right and left foot.

Earrings, necklaces, bracelets and rings of the classic period were artistic and of beautiful workmanship. Beads of various stones enamelled with gold were used and the exquisite stone cameos of that time have never been equalled.

Umbrellas were used by Greek women as shade protection and fans as a cooling device. The long-handled fans were carried by bearers, but women carried dainty ones in the hand. The hand mirror was usually of thin bronze slightly convex, one side polished and the reverse ornamented with an incised decoration. Silver was also used and they are known to have made glass mirrors coated with tin.

Ancient Greek

Ionic chiton

chlamys and broad brimmed hat

king in himation and long chiton

chlamys and double girded chiton

RTW

Mycenaean
1500 B.C.

Ancient Greek

long tunic
himation
and hat

Doric
woolen
chiton

Ionic
linen chiton
himation

RTW

Ancient Greek

umbrella

mirror

fibulae

wig

caul

bracelet

sandal

earrings

buskin

Venus

Phrygian
bonnet

sandal

peacock
feather
fan

FTW

Chapter Four

Ancient Roman
The First Century B.C. to the Fifth A.D.

During the first three centuries of this period, the principal garment of the Romans was the *toga,* which was worn by both sexes. The feminine wrap later took the name of *palla.* Its use was the same as that of the Greek himation, but it differed in shape, the Greek wrap being a rectangle and the Roman mantle, when folded, a semicircle.

The toga was much larger than its Greek predecessor, being about two and one half by six yards long, making the draping of it heavier and more complicated. It was of wool and draped thus: an end was laid against the chest, then carried over the left shoulder, around the back and brought under the right arm to the front, again over the left shoulder to tie in the back, which arrangement left the right arm free. The draping of the toga became an art, with its straight-hanging folds, each one weighted with a pellet and, when the folds were in place, each had its name.

The ordinary citizen wore a plain white toga. Magistrates, priests and boys up to sixteen years old of the upper class wore the purple-bordered toga. The embroidered purple toga worn with the gold-embroidered tunic was the ceremonial dress of magistrates and generals and became the traditional costume of the emperors.

The origin of the word purple is the Latin "purpura," the name of a shellfish which yielded the famous Tyrian dye and was not violet but a deep crimson color.

Later, both sexes wore a tunic corresponding to the Greek chiton, underneath the toga or palla. Under that, men and women wore an undergarment reaching to the knees, similar to a shirt. It was made of wool for men and linen for women.

Over the undertunic, women wore the *stola,* a long, straight robe reaching to the feet. It hung straight or was bloused over a belt or girdle and had short set-in sleeves. The stola was usually fashioned of linen or soft, light wool, giving way later to silk and very sheer costly fabrics from the East.

Heliogabalus was the first Roman emperor (218 to 222 A.D.) to wear silk. In 533 A.D., looms were set up in the palace for the weaving of silk, but the raw material was imported from the East.

A wide purple band, called the *clavus,* insignia of rank, ornamented the center front from neck to hem, of the senator's tunic. The tunic of the knight bore narrow bands. The feminine tunic often had an embroidered band at the neck and the hem. Like the custom of the Greeks, the unbelted tunic of either sex signified mourning.

The art of embroidery was an art of great pride among Roman ladies. It was usually executed in wool, and for special costumes gold thread was added. Gold was lavishly used in the imperial periods.

Romans wore their shoes indoors and out, but did remove their sandals when dining. Their footgear was based upon Etruscan design. There were sandals, a short socklike foot covering, boots, and the buskin or *cothurnus.* These, in the later period, became elaborate and costly among people of wealth and rank. They were made of fine leathers, colorfully dyed and decorated with gold, silver and precious stones. Women generally wore the sandal or soft shoe. Men added to their height by means of a wedge placed inside the buskin at the heel.

Roman men were fastidious in the care of their hair and beards. Barber shops existed in their main streets, but shaving did not become the style until 454 A.D., when a group of barbers was imported from Sicily. From 68 A.D. to about 268, the nobles powdered their hair with gold dust on festive occasions. The hair of the women was usually parted in the middle and drawn into a chignon at the nape of the neck. It was waved and tightly curled.

Blond hair was much admired and desired and it is known that they wore wigs of that color made of hair bought from the northern Gauls. Too, they dyed their hair black or chestnut with soap imported from the Germanic tribes. Cauls of gold and silver net interspersed with pearls and other gems were worn by the women. They also wore veils, but for a general head covering draped themselves with a fold of the palla. Roman brides wore a flame-colored veil, while the Christian bride donned one of white or purple.

Beauty patches on the face were indulged in by the Roman women. The use of perfume by men and women probably surpassed that of any nation of all time. It was available in liquid, solid and powdered form and was applied not only to their persons, but to all articles and personal possessions with which they came in contact.

Umbrellas were used as a protection against the sun by the women and were later adopted by the men. The lady of early Roman period was cooled by a fan carried by an attendant, but later small fans were carried by fashionable women.

In the earlier period, jewelry consisted of wrought gold ornaments with engraved gems, which later developed into artistic and exquisite pieces. The Romans made use of many precious stones such as diamonds, rubies, sapphires, emeralds, pearls being favorites, set in rings, earrings, necklaces and bracelets. Their jewelry had not the refinement of that of the Greeks, being heavier and given more to display. The hand mirror of polished metal with incised ornamented back was usually disk-shaped.

Ancient Roman

Senator
white toga
purple bands
and boots

Knight
white toga
and tunic
purple bands
and sandals

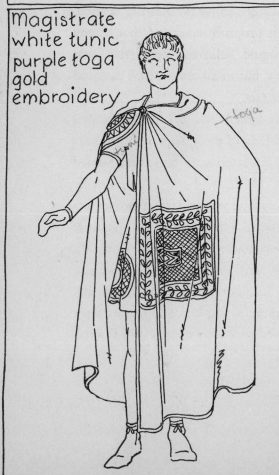

Magistrate
white tunic
purple toga
gold
embroidery

High Rank
white tunic
purple toga
gold
embroidery

RTW

Ancient Roman

under tunic
stola
palla

under tunic
stola
palla

purple stola
gold
embroidery

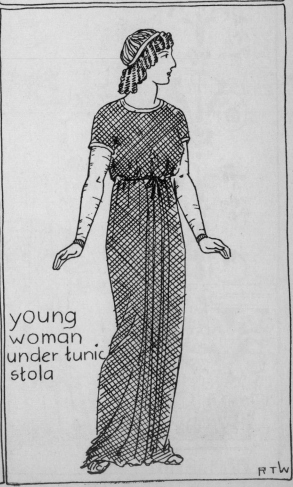

young
woman
under tunic
stola

RTW

Ancient Roman

sandal

plummed helmet

hair pins

sandal

ring

wig and necklace

earring

buskin

soft leather shoe

fibula

corselets with kilts

RTW

Chapter Five

Ancient Persian

550 B.C. THROUGH THE CRUSADES

THE PERSIAN costume, while originally a continuation of the Babylonian and Assyrian mode, furnished many striking and different features. The *candys* of wool or linen was worn, also of silk imported from the East. But this candys was a shaped and sewn garment with flowing sleeves, which fell into set pleats at the back of the arm. The skirt was drawn up into the belt in center front or at the sides, forming carefully arranged pleats, somewhat like the Egyptian robe.

Under it was worn a shirt, drawers and stockings, which were also shaped and sewn. It is the first time that underclothes are noted and it is also the first encounter with tailored garments and a definitely set-in sleeve.

Only high dignitaries were permitted to wear the candys, which the king gave as gifts. His were of bluish purple, ornamented with white and silver, while people of inferior rank wore garments dyed red. This color was called "Sardian red" from a dye made from the blossoms of the

24

sandix tree. Later, they had silk and woolen robes of all colors, but the predominant Persian colors were red, yellow and dark blue. Royal purple, dark blue and white appear to be the royal colors. Brown was the color of mourning.

Sashes were important, the king's being of cloth of gold. The king's wives wore golden girdles with a bag attached holding their "girdle money." The wives of some of the kings were allotted the revenue of entire cities for "pin money," as we term it today.

One decoration shows a king with a purple stole or shawl embroidered with gold thread and ornamented with precious stones. Later, the candys appears to have been replaced by a coat worn over trousers, surely the forerunner of today's standard civil costume for men.

Garments were elaborated with beautiful and colorful embroidery. Appliqué work was originated by the ancient Persians, serving in place of the all-over needlework. It was carried into Europe as a result of the Crusades and became very popular there.

A soft shoe was worn, always of yellow leather, shaped and covering the foot to the ankle, where it fastened by means of straps and buttons. In a later period, the shoe was heavily embroidered with pearls and other jewels. Gloves were known, and the gorgeous parasol and fan with long handles, carried by attendants, were only for royalty.

Their jewels were handsome, of heavy gold with colored enamels, set with pearls and rare gems. Stones were polished in cabochon form. There were earrings, bracelets and necklaces, especially the signet ring, symbol of authority. They had exquisitely wrought boxes and bottles of alabaster to hold their elaborately prepared perfumes and cosmetics. Girls, at the marriageable age of fifteen years, were given earrings. Also at that age, boys and girls were obliged to wear the sacred girdle or cord.

The men wore their hair and beards long, both meticulously fashioned in tight curls, and they dusted their hair with gold powder. Royalty wore headgear in the form of a tiara, miter or toque of white felt or striped in blue and white. Both the miter and tiara are of Persian origin, the miter being originally a turban or conical hat. Another head covering was the chincloth, seemingly of white linen, wrapped about the head and neck, extending up over the chin.

Few records of sculpture exist of feminine dress, women having led an entirely secluded life. In a bas-relief of the fifth century B.C., a queen wears the tunic and full trousers, known to us at a later period, which would lead us to believe that such had always been the costume of the women.

royal
body
guard

Ancient Persian

king in
purple
candys
blue and
white
striped
tiara

embroidered
coat and felt
mitre

embroidered
candys

RTW

Ancient Persian

umbrella

Nobleman

feather
fan

white
felt
toque

warrior

soft shoes
of
yellow leather

white
felt
toque

R T W

Chapter Six

The Northern Europeans
THE FIRST CENTURIES A.D.

O F THE Northern Europeans there exists little documentation except that furnished us by some coins, a few figurines and bas-reliefs. Only their arms and jewelry have survived the climatic conditions of their tombs.

The "Northern Barbarians," as they were called, wore a garment like that of the ancient Persians, a kind of drawers or breeches, shaped and sewn, rather like tights, which was later adopted by the Roman soldiers. Originally, it was made of skins, held around the waist by a belt and held close to the leg above the knee by cross-gartering of thongs or bands. Such a garment, no doubt, was the result of necessity for protection against severe climate. They are known to have worn a shoulder covering, a rather small square of leather or wool, folded diagonally like a shawl.

The women wore a long or short tunic with petticoat or kirtle of coarse woolen cloth. Their wrap was a square blanket fastened on one shoulder or in front with a clasp or buckle. A belt just below the breasts held the tunic in soft folds.

By the time the Romans penetrated into the northern parts of Europe, they found people there wearing trousers, a short belted tunic with sleeves, a cloak or mantle and perhaps, in winter, a cap of fur. They were proficient in weaving and dyeing. They wore squares of heavy woolen cloth in blue or black, rough on one side. Tunics and trousers were bright-colored, striped and checkered, red being the predominant color.

Long hair was a source of great pride to the Northern women and was worn flowing or hanging in long braids. The hair of the men reached to the shoulders. The women are known to have worn wigs, as the remains of brightly colored wool and silk wigs have been found in the catacombs. Red hair was a favorite of the Gauls and they resorted to dyeing to attain that color.

Many pieces of their jewelry have been found, most artistic and decorative in design, in fibulæ, buckles, armlets, necklaces or torques, hairpins, fashioned of bronze, occasionally a gold piece. The collar, or torque, was unique to the Northern tribes. It was heavy, of bronze or bronze and gold, and usually represented the wealth of the wearer. These collars were often taken as spoils by the conquering Romans and, in turn, handed out as rewards to the soldiers. Use was made of ivory for pins, and beads were made of brass, jet and amber from their own coasts, while they bought glass from Southern merchants.

After being conquered by the Romans, both sexes wore the tunic, short for men, long for women, in white, red, green or violet, decorated with bands of color. We learn from the Romans that the women wore white tunics ornamented with a purple design and that they were woven and dyed by the wearers. The wrap which followed Roman lines was sometimes trimmed with contrasting colored strips of cloth.

Important in the costume of these Northern tribes was the wearing of a real undergarment by the women, a sort of shirt of thin material, usually white. The Romans, who themselves were given to much bathing, were impressed by the Northerners' cult of cleanliness.

Footgear was simple, of moccasin type and sandals with straps by which to fasten them, also boots of undressed leather with wooden soles.

These boots reached almost to the knees and were decorated with pleasing designs.

Men had bonnets of leather or wool, while the women wore kerchiefs, utilizing mostly, however, a fold of the palla as a headcovering.

Still later, Byzantine influence became evident in the use of luxurious fabrics. Men wore, over their long breeches, a short tunic with long sleeves, belted at the waist, and a mantle fastened on one shoulder. They wore gloves too, in mitten style, without fingers.

The women wore two tunics, the under one of woven thread with long sleeves, which is the first noted body linen, or, as later called, lingerie. The outer tunic was long and straight, of rich fabric, cut with flowing sleeves and a train and often embroidered with gold and precious stones. Then, a mantle fastened on one shoulder or in front, and a scarf covering the head and shoulders. The head covering was the result of their adoption of the Christian religion, since women were compelled to cover their heads upon entering the church, as a sign of humility.

Jewelry had become works of art, usually intricate, in gold and silver encrusted with pearls and precious stones. There were clasps, buckles, necklaces, bracelets and rings. Girdles were embroidered with gold and decorated with gems.

Northern Europeans of the first Centuries A.D.

German-
linen and
woolen fabrics;
bronze jewelry

Gaul-
fur cap-plaid
and striped
woolen-leather
breeches and
moccasins

Frank-
fur jumper-
woolen tunic-
leather breeches,
moccasins and
cross-gartering

Briton-
plaid woolen
tunic-woolen
mantle-gold
jewelry

RTW

Chapter Seven

Byzantine
FOURTH CENTURY TO THE MIDDLE AGES

BYZANTIUM made two important contributions to the mode. In the third century A.D., Syrian weavers developed the weaving of patterned fabrics by the use of shuttles. Then, under Emperor Justinian, who reigned from 527 to 565, the process of raising the silkworm from the cocoon was established in the Occident. Under his patronage, eggs of the silkworm and seeds of the mulberry bush concealed in their hollow bamboo staffs, were brought from China by two Persian monks.

Byzantine costume revealed both Greco-Roman and Oriental influence, combining Roman drapery with the gorgeousness of the East, in heavy silks, damasks, brocades and cloth of gold. Due to the Christian religion, the body was now entirely concealed. Both sexes wore a long, straight tunic with long sleeves. It was made of silk or linen and confined at the waist by a girdle. Girdles were handsome and costly, of leather or small plaques of gold linked together and encrusted with colored stones.

Men of quality draped themselves in a rich mantle or dalmatique, reminiscent of the Roman toga, semicircular in shape. On the left front

33

edge was placed the clavus, insignia of high dignitaries. It was a large decoration, rectangular in shape, fashioned of jewels and gold embroidery. Women wore over their tunic a stola or palla, using a fold of the palla as head covering. Men and women fastened their mantles on the right shoulder with a gorgeous jewelled fibula or clasp.

The materials used in the masculine costume were usually of solid color with embroidered contrasting bands of color, while the feminine costume employed patterned fabrics. But the garments of both sexes were heavy with the weight of elaborate embroidery encrusted with precious stones.

Eventually, beneath the tunic, was worn an undergarment, short and made of linen or thin silk, really a shirt. The long tunic evolved into the *gunna,* or gown. Of a later period, was a short feminine garment, termed *juppe,* worn over the long tunic or robe. The sleeves were usually long and in dolman style.

Women enveloped their hair in a coif of silk or a network of pearls, a style later adopted by Medieval Europe. Pearls were plentiful and much used in company with diamonds and other gems, but later, bits of glass and even tiny mirrors were added to their embroideries. Their goldsmiths wrought beautiful jewelry, surpassing that of Italy. There were rings, bracelets, brooches, buckles and earrings of elaborate design. A favorite motif in earrings was birds in pairs. Oriental perfumes and incense were lavishly used.

Sandals were still worn, but the foot covering of the rich was a soft boot reaching to the ankle. It was of dyed leather with a rather long pointed toe. These shoes were bright in color and embroidered with gold thread and pearls.

The Byzantine mode became more sumptuous with the centuries and its influence is evident through the Medieval and Renaissance periods of Europe. It was the foundation of Russia's costume and survives today in the vestments of her church.

Byzantine

princess in
white tunic-
green mantle
lined with purple-
cerise boots-gold
and jewelled embroidery

Emperor
Justinian
6th C.

white tunic-
purple mantle-
cerise boots-
gold and jewelled
embroidery

emperor in
white tunic-
purple mantle
lined with green-
cerise boots-gold and
jewelled embroidery

Empress
Eudocie
5th C.

RTW

Byzantine

Queen

sandals

fibula

Emperor
11th C.

Emperor
9th C.

short tunic
or "juppé"
12th C.

soft leather
boots with
jewels

patterns of mantles

RTW

Chapter Eight

Italian Medieval or Gothic

HISTORIANS place the Middle Ages as the period between the fall of Rome, A.D. 476, and the fall of Constantinople in 1453. Others designate the period between the tenth and eleventh and the fifteenth centuries, as the flowering of the Gothic Period.

With the end of the Dark Ages, men and women were still wearing the Greco-Roman costume showing its Byzantine influence, but which, due to the teachings of Christianity, tended more and more to conceal the figure. In fact, the ecclesiastical mode definitely affected both style and color of clothes.

At first was worn the *bliaud,* a tunic with long sleeves, reaching to the knees on the men and to the feet on the women. Over that the *pallium,* or cloak, fastened in front by a large brooch or buckle. The men wore long, fitted and sewn stockings, a contribution of the Northern Barbarians. These stockings or tights were held up by a belt around the waist and were cross-gartered from the knees down. Later, the man's bliaud lengthened to the ankles.

37

By the eleventh century, the bliaud and mantle were worn by both sexes. The *chainse,* or undertunic, was made of wool, linen, hemp or silk, fastened at neck and wrist by buttons or tied with tassels. Later, it became really a piece of lingerie and was made of sheer washable fabric, with an embroidered edge showing at neck and wrists. Over that was worn the bliaud or long tunic, alike for men and women, reaching to the floor. The gown either hung straight or was belted with a plain or jewelled girdle and had long sleeves.

The fabrics had become rich and heavy, handsomely embroidered, fur-trimmed and fur-lined for cold weather. Ermine was the preferred pelt, but a fur called *miniver,* or *menu vair,* was also used extensively by fashionable people. It was gray and white, in small skins, and was a species of Russian and Siberian squirrel, also called *petit-gris.*

With the thirteenth century, the full overtunic of the men had shortened to the knees and by the latter part of that century, young men were wearing their tunics "shockingly" short. The tunic either hung straight or was belted, with a skirt of only a few inches below the waist. Hip-length stockings or tights were worn, made of bias material, usually red with gold and jewelled garters, accompanied by soft leather shoes.

Fabrics were dyed scarlet, green, blue and purple, of which there were fine linens, handsome brocades, embroideries and velvets. Sicilian brocades of the twelfth and thirteenth centuries were the finest in the world. All kinds of fur continued to be used, ermine being the favorite. Dull black cloth was worn for mourning, with tunic and mantle banded with white. The woman wore a white gauze cap, over which she draped her mantle.

Both sexes wore sumptuous loose full mantles. A particular masculine style was a long full cape with no opening except that for the head. The feminine tunic invariably had a train and many attempts were made to regulate the length of it.

The masculine head covering was a hood and shoulder cape in one. The hood, or *chaperon,* always had a point and this point, or *liripipe,* grew to all lengths over the years, to where it was worn wrapped about the neck or arm, or left to hang in back. Many arrangements of draping it about the head evolved. Later, the liripipe was draped over a padded roll, turban in shape, called the roundlet. In the second half of the fourteenth century, the liripipe, as well as other garments, was ornamented with "petal-scalloped" or castellated edge. The long hood was permitted only to the noble, the commoner was compelled to content himself with a very short one.

Men also wore skullcaps, peaked bonnets and bonnets with rolled brims and a long feather. This is the first appearance of the feather in modish dress. Felt bonnets were often worn over the hood. Men wore their hair moderately long with a deep fringe over the forehead.

A later style of feminine robe, which appeared in the early fourteenth century, is important, as being the cause of the second advent of the corset, its first appearance being noted in prehistoric Greece. It is also noteworthy, as being a real frock instead of a tunic. This was a gown with snug-fitting bodice, from which flowed a full trailing skirt. It created a vogue for a slim figure and both lacing and dieting were resorted to, to acquire the necessary silhouette.

The principal head covering for women in the Middle Ages was a piece of fabric, either cotton or linen, square, oblong or circular in shape, hanging to the shoulders or below. It was a continuation of the palla and was known as the *couvrechef,* "headrail" or "wimple." Crowns were placed over it. Crowns, by the way, were but signs of wealth and position in those days, and did not become insignia of rank until the sixteenth century. In the twelfth century, the hair was often worn flowing. Blond hair being the desired color, women sat for hours in roofless belvedere towers atop their houses, bleaching their hair in the sun. False hair and cosmetics were also used.

Then came the chinband in the next century, a fold of white linen which passed under the chin, fastened by pinning to a band around the forehead. Sometimes, the chinband went completely round the head. In another style, the headband was stiffened, forming a low crownlike or toque type of headdress. Sometimes, the toque had no top.

In the fourteenth century, the hair was dressed close to the head, usually parted in the middle in Madonna style, sometimes with a coronet braid. Small caps, nets and cauls of exquisite filigree work were much used, covered with sheer veils of silk or linen, shot with gold, which hung to the shoulders. The hennin and its many variations appeared in the latter part of the fourteenth century, to last a hundred years or more, and was the invention of Medieval Italy.

The hennin was a long-pointed conical headdress. The *escoffion,* a very ugly style, said to have originated in England, had two horns. Veils of different lengths, sometimes long enough to reach the floor, hung from these strange bonnets. The hennin was held on the head by means of the frontlet, to which the bonnet was fastened. The frontlet or ring which showed on the forehead was part of a cap of wire netting worn under the bonnet. The frontlet was covered with silk or black velvet and with gold, when worn by nobles. Veils alone were often worn. Elaborate stuffed rolls, turbanlike in shape, of Byzantine origin, were worn by Venetian ladies.

In the early thirteenth century, the Crusaders, returning from the East, brought beautifully embroidered costume accessories, which gave rise to a great vogue for such decoration. Pouches, bags, shoes, girdles and gloves were richly embroidered by ladies, who were proud of their accomplishment. In the same period, the Persian art of appliqué was copied. In the fourteenth century, pearls and spangles were added to the colorful embroidery.

In the fourteenth century appeared parti-colored clothes for men, which idea women later copied. The garment was divided into halves or quarters and each section was of a different contrasting color, even each shoe and stocking varying in color. Later, they took to dividing the costume diagonally and, by the end of the fourteenth century, men and women were wearing the coat of arms of both sides of their families appliquéd or embroidered on their costumes.

Shoes of both sexes were soft and pliable, having pointed toes and covering the foot to the ankle. They were works of art, executed in scarlet or violet velvet, even cloth of gold, ornamented with colored embroidery, strips of gold and sometimes encrusted with gems. Later, they were also fashioned of very soft leathers. The toes of men's shoes grew to such lengths, being stuffed too, that they finally reached a point, where they were held up by fine chains attached to the knees. These shoes were called *poulaines*. Also called poulaines were the clogs, or pattens, made of wood and worn to protect the soft shoes. They had very thick soles of wood or cork and a heel about an inch high. Pattens appeared about 1377, lasting into the eighteenth century. The *chopine*, adopted principally in Venice, came from Turkey. It was of wood, a stiltlike affair, painted and gilded.

Among the accessories were embroidered gloves of leather, occasionally ornamented with jewels and often with a single gem on the back. They were worn first by the men and later adopted by the women. The scented glove of Eastern origin appeared in Venice in the eleventh century and the vogue lasted for several hundred years. The handkerchief, a very costly accessory of display, was in the possession of the fashionable wealthy only, and usually that person owned but one.

Fans, of the hand-screen design, were imported from the Orient in the twelfth century and became generally used. Ostrich, parrot or peacock feathers were fastened to handles of ivory or gold set with precious stones.

It was a period of heavy massive chains and jewelled belts. From the belt or girdle hung a purse or pouch, from which wealthy people of both sexes scattered coins or alms to the poor. Jewelled daggers were also suspended from the belt.

The making of silk in Italy dates from 1148 at Palermo. Other beautiful silks came from the Orient and cotton from Egypt. Typical of the period were costly materials in diapered pattern with repeated motif, principally of conventionalized flower design.

By way of the ports of Venice and Genoa, Oriental luxuries reached the courts of Europe, Italy being thus the first to feel the effects of the more refined culture of the East. Venice reached its height of prosperity about 1400, with the Venetian mode influencing all Europe. However, it is recorded that in the fourteenth century Venice imported yearly a fashion doll from Paris.

The making of glass mirrors on a commercial scale was first developed in Venice in the fourteenth century, and from then on to the middle of the seventeenth century, when large mirrors were made, fashionable men and women carried small pocket mirrors in little cases of silk or ivory.

In the Middle Ages, the limit of one's extravagance in dress was specifically determined by one's position in society. Rich clothes were worn only by nobility. About 1476, the cost of robes, buttons, belts, jewels and furs, also the length of trains, were regulated by sumptuary laws, which held until the early part of the sixteenth century.

Italian Medieval or Gothic

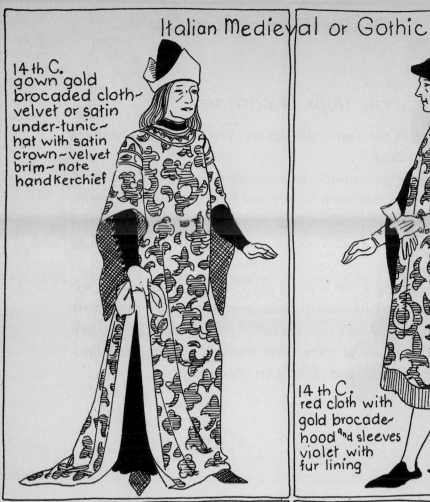

14th C.
gown gold
brocaded cloth-
velvet or satin
under-tunic-
hat with satin
crown-velvet
brim-note
handkerchief

14 th C.
red cloth with
gold brocade-
hood and sleeves
violet with
fur lining

15 th C.
fur lined velvet
tunic-cloth
under-tunic-
jewelled belt-
parti-colored
stockings

15 th C.
red velvet
cape lined with
green brocaded
velvet-tunic blue
and white brocade
red cap and
stockings

RTW

Italian Medieval or Gothic

13 th C.
brocaded
robe~purple
mantle with
embroidery
and jewels

13 th C.
bridal robe of
brocade-gold or
silver spangles-
pearl necklace

14 th C.
jewel embroidery-
sleeves fur lined-
brocaded
under-tunic-
stuffed turban

14 th C.
wimple and hennin-
brocaded robe-
flowing sleeves~
fur collar

RTW

Italian-Medieval or Gothic

wimple

turban with moiré leaves-11th C.

chinband of linen folds-12th C.

13th C. chinband and toque of white linen folds

net of gold cord and pearls over silk bag-12th C.

man's hood or chaperon 14th C.

15th C. two-horned hennin

14th C. wooden patten

14th C. man's hat with feather

lady's chopine

15th C. man's velvet hat

15th C. man's boot

RTW

Chapter Nine

French Medieval or Gothic

THE FRENCH medieval scene opens with men and women still wearing clothes of Roman origin, consisting of two tunics and a mantle for both sexes. The undergarment, or chainse, reached to the ankles, had long, straight sleeves and was usually belted. Over it men and women wore the bliaud or bliaut which exposed the sleeves and neck of the undergarment. Then a mantle fastened in front or on the right shoulder, leaving the right arm free. Later, the women held the ends of the mantle in the hands and the wraps of both sexes were often entirely pleated. The bliaud, origin of blouse, was sometimes ornamented with a handsome jewelled girdle.

In the thirteenth century, the chainse finally developed into the chemise or body garment, made of soft wool or linen, really the beginning of lingerie, but in saffron color. For a long period to come, it showed at the neck and wrists and was no doubt made principally of batiste, a closely woven sheer fabric which appeared in the thirteenth century. Batiste was named after its inventor, Batiste Chambray, but unlike the cotton batiste of today, was of very fine linen thread.

Later, an extra garment, the surcoat, appeared. It was derived from the armor covering worn by the crusading knight to eliminate the glare of the sun on his armor, when in the East. The original covering hung straight, front and back, reaching to the knees and was caught at the sides. There was a hole for the head to pass through. His lady's surcoat was also short and sleeveless, with wide armholes and was worn over the bliaud. It was fastened by means of buttons on the shoulders. In cold weather, men and women wore a short jacket or doublet of fur or fur-lined between the chainse or body garment and the outer tunic, and over that the mantle.

Men wore beards and their hair shoulder-length until the tenth century, when beards disappeared and the hair was bobbed with a long bang over the forehead, but shaved quite high in the back. In the following centuries of the period, it appears to have been worn moderately long, with the bob the prevailing style.

Women parted their hair in the middle and dressed it in two hanging braids, to which they often added false hair for length. The head covering consisted of a square of sheer colored linen or cotton and was known as the *couvrechef* in French, the wimple in English. Veils were required to be worn in church, women being forbidden to enter bareheaded. Crowns were worn by all members of the upper class, and not until the sixteenth century were designs settled to designate the rank of the wearer. Women wore the crown over the wimple.

In the thirteenth century, the surcoat took the place of the bliaud for both sexes. That of the man reached a point below his knees, hung straight or was belted, had short sleeves or none. In the fourteenth century, it shortened to the knees, while the sleeves lengthened considerably, sometimes almost reaching to the floor. These sleeves hung over the hands, or had openings halfway up from which the arms protruded. The long sleeves were often in knots at the ends. With the longer surcoat, a man wore long, sewn and fitted stockings, which were usually red and fastened under the surcoat by lacings with points.

The lady's surcoat of the thirteenth century was a long full robe touching the floor, belted at the waist. The lady copied the very long sleeves of her lord and often they were really false sleeves attached to the shoulders of her dress. The fantastic sleeves of both sexes lasted well into the sixteenth century. "Petal scalloped" or castellated edges on all garments became very popular.

In the fourteenth century, the feminine surcoat opened at the sides, revealing a fitted dress underneath, known as the *cotehardie*. The cote-hardie was either laced or buttoned in center front from neck to below the waist and had long tight sleeves with a row of buttons from elbow to the little finger. With it was usually worn a low-placed jewelled girdle, which showed in the side openings of the overdress.

Men also wore the cotehardie, of which the masculine version was a tight-fitting tunic buttoned down center front, having also the same long sleeves with buttons. Like the woman's dress, it too had a low-placed girdle.

The surcoat disappeared in the fifteenth century, women then wearing a real dress called *la robe,* in which the fitted bodice with tight sleeves was joined by a belt to a full skirt.

The man's surcoat was replaced by a jacket, under which he wore the *justaucorps,* or *pourpoint,* a sort of body coat, quilted and closed by lacings either back or front. The pourpoint originated as a garment worn under armor and was made with or without sleeves. It was also worn as the jacket proper and its vogue lasted from the thirteenth to the seventeenth centuries.

Shoes of the eleventh, twelfth, thirteenth and fourteenth centuries were of velvet and soft leather fastened by a jewelled button or buckle, often ornamented with embroidery, strips of gold and gems. As in Italy, pattens were worn to protect the soft sole. The stiltlike chopine of Turkish origin adopted by Venetian women was also worn by French ladies.

In the middle of the fourteenth century, shoes *à la poulaine* became the style, lasting until 1480. Their long, pointed toes grew to such lengths that it became necessary to hold up the stuffed points by gold chains attached to the ankles or knees. Noblemen were permitted toe lengths of two feet, gentlemen one foot, while the common man could have but six inches beyond his toes. They originated in Cracow, Poland, and became fashionable at all European courts. The French called them *poulaines* after Poland and the English *crackowes* after Cracow.

Due to the influence of the Christian religion, all during the thirteenth century, women's hair was more or less concealed by the wimple and neckcloth or gorget, which covered head and neck. Variations of these medieval headdresses survive today in many religious orders.

Then followed a small crownlike toque worn over a headband and chinband, all of white linen. The hair was dressed Madonna style, parted in the middle and drawn into a chignon. Following that period, the hair was parted down the center back, plaited and the two braids dressed over the ears in wheel fashion, or wound in loops at the sides of the face, covering the ears. The neckcloth or gorget was fastened to the hair over the ears with pins and the headcloth draped over it.

A most decorative style, the reticulated headdress or golden net caul, reminiscent of the Byzantine fashion, appeared in the fourteenth century, lasting until the middle of the fifteenth century. In that style, a low metal band or jewelled crown held the cauls of gold braid or wire set with gems with which the hair was covered. Cauls were also fashioned of gold braid, the checkered openings filled in with crimson silk. In this period of the golden net caul and hennin, both of which entirely concealed the hair, the short hairs at the nape of the neck were shaved off. Eyebrows were plucked to give a fine line.

In the fifteenth century, turbans were worn, which, too, concealed the hair. They were large stuffed rolls over which the wimple was sometimes draped. These stuffed rolls were also used to form some shapes of the hennin, principally the heart-shaped style. The hennin was brought to France by Isabella of Bavaria in the latter part of the fourteenth century and its vogue lasted a hundred years. There were many styles of the hennin, invariably draped with a veil, floating or with wired edge. They became so extravagant in size that the authorities found it necessary to regulate the height according to the social position of the wearer.

Women wore a huge cloaklike cape, which in winter was lined with fur. Of men's cloaks there were several styles, principally a voluminous cape, with collar and fastened on one shoulder. The *houppelande,* which originated in the Low Countries, was a long, full robe with long, full, flowing sleeves, held in folds at the waist by a leather or jewelled belt.

Men wore hoods, toques, chaperons and felt hats in sugar-loaf shape and with brims. Feathers as hat ornamentation first appeared in the Middle Ages, peacock plumage being favored. The cowl, or capuchon, was attached to the cloak, but the chaperon was originally the hood attached to the shoulder cape. Its point, which began to lengthen in the latter part of the thirteenth century, grew until, in the fourteenth century, it was wound round the head, and by the fifteenth century the pipelike tail, or liripipe, sometimes reached the floor. Eventually, the liripipe became merely a trimming added to a real hat or turban. The turban, or stuffed roll, was called *roundlet* and, when trimmed with the liripipe, was known as the *chaperon turban*. Dashing young men often slung the chaperon turban over their shoulders, instead of wearing it on their heads.

Parti-colored clothes became the style, with the entire costume being divided into sections of contrasting colors. Ladies and gentlemen of the fourteenth and fifteenth centuries wore their coats of arms emblazoned upon their costumes, stamped into the fabric in gold and silver leaf and enamels. Such costumes bore the name of *cottes historiées*.

Small silver bells, that odd form of ornamentation, were in vogue in the fourteenth and early fifteenth centuries. They were suspended from leather belts, jewelled girdles, around the neck, and were worn by men and women.

Both men and women wore heavy massive chains and jewelled belts. For a time, around 1300, women replaced gloves with mittens. The fashion of wearing gloves spread and several small French towns specialized in the making of them. They were made of doeskin, sheepskin and hareskin. Perfumed gloves were most fashionable, especially violet-scented ones, which appeared around 1400. Walking sticks were carried by men in the fifteenth century.

The principal fabric was cloth of Scotch wool, woven in Flanders and England, but there were also gorgeous silks from the Orient and Italy. Louis XI, in 1466, first established silk weaving at Lyons. Velvet, the greatest favorite, appeared in the thirteenth century and was woven in Paris. The tapestries of the Saracens were imitated and, as in Italy, the vogue for diapered patterns prevailed. Ermine was the costliest fur, but marten and miniver were much used. The idea of ornamenting white ermine with the small black tails originated in the twelfth century.

French queens of the Middle Ages wore white for mourning, but the Spaniards had been using black since 1100. In that feudal era, once a year at a stated time, the seigneur of a castle made gifts to the noblemen attached to his estate, of cloth or costume. The gift was called *livrée,* which is the origin of our word livery, or uniform of a servitor. The law governed the amount of one's possessions in wearing apparel, also the size of a cloak and the width of trimming. Nobles were permitted to own hoods with long liripipes, while the commoner was compelled to content himself with just a hood.

We read that in the thirteenth century, Paris was already giving proof of its great flair for the creation of artistic clothes and that in the fourteenth century Venice imported annually a French fashion doll. The small waxen mannequin attired in the very latest style was exhibited to the Venetian ladies. This method of "fashion-journalism" lasted to our own Colonial Period, when we read of "fashion dolls," or "fashion babies," coming to New York or Philadelphia by way of London. The thirteenth century is considered the most brilliant period of the Moyen Âge. The French Medieval Period is supposed to have reached its end with the reign of Louis XI, 1461 to 1483. An establishment for the making of silk under royal patronage was decreed by Louis in November, 1466.

Many luxuries reached the Western World through contact with the Orient during the Crusades, such as the cotton plant, with its name of Arabic origin and the Arabian invention of cotton paper, replacing parchment. Satin and velvet, with their names of Byzantine origin, and the knowledge of embroidery and carpet weaving came from the East. Toilet articles, such as rouge and glass mirrors instead of polished plates, were first used in the Orient. The revival of the custom of wearing beards by the end of the Middle Ages was a direct influence of Arabian contact.

French Medieval or Gothic

King-crimson
mantle-gold
cloth bliaud-
white chainse
gold embroidery
9th C.

surcoat over
chainse-
skullcap-
13 th C.

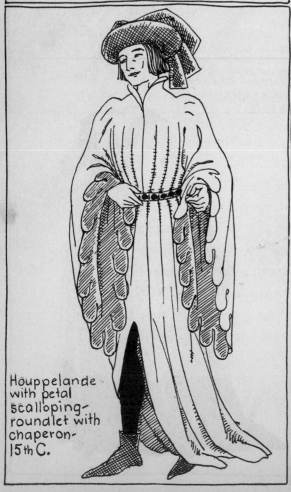

Houppelande
with petal
scalloping-
roundlet with
chaperon-
15th C.

Brocaded
cloth jacket-
fur trimmed-
jewelled necklace-
roundlet with
chaperon-
15 th C.

RTW

French Medieval or Gothic

white bliaud with
wide gold girdle-
crimson chainse-
purple mantle-gold
embroidery-cord belt-
9th C.

surcoat with false
sleeves-miniver
fur-cotehardie with
jewelled girdle-
14th C.

surcoat with coat-
of-arms-cotehardie
with jewelled girdle-
reticulated headdress-
early 15th C.

azure blue flecked
with gold-crimson
velvet trimming-gold
brocaded stomacher-
black velvet hennin-
15th C.

RTW

French Medieval or Gothic

parti-colored
hennin-15th C.

white linen
toque and
chinband
12th and 13th C.

man's chaperon-turban
14th C.

shoe 13th C.

man's sugar-loaf hat with
feather, jewels and
cord ~ 15th C.

wooden patten
15th C.

hennin with white
under-cap-black
velvet fold-15th C.

man's white felt hat-
peacock feathers-red
bandeau crossed with
gold braid   15th C.

small bonnet with wired
veil ~ 15th C.

reticulated headdress-
wimple over golden net cauls-
15th C.

reticulated
headdress-gold
braid over crimson silk - stuffed roll with jewels-14th C.

shoe and wooden patten
15th C.

RTW

Chapter Ten

English Medieval or Gothic

I N THE early part of this period, the Britons, both men and women, were still wearing three important garments, the stola or cotte, the bliaud or overtunic, and the palla or mantle, all reminiscent of Greco-Roman style. But they also wore, next to the body, a piece of lingerie, a garment of thin white material, either wool or linen, called a *shert,* or camise. The bliaud, bliaut or bliaus, is the origin of the blouse and the camise of the chemise.

The feminine bliaud or overtunic, a sleeveless garment worn indoors, was often long, but sometimes reached only to the knees, below which hung the long underdress, or cotte. The masculine tunic stopped halfway below the knees, showing his chausses or long thick stockings with feet, which were cross-gartered with leather thongs.

Men and women wore loose cord or leather belts. The men wore low leather shoes fastened at the ankles, the women soft shoes of either leather or fabric. Women were accomplished in weaving and embroidering and the tunics of both sexes were ornamented with bands of needlework at the neck and hem. Men wore simple hoods or skullcaps, while the women concealed their hair under a scarf or "headrail" of linen or cotton. It was circular, square or oblong and was wrapped about the neck like the Persian or Roman chincloth. A crown, if worn, was placed on top the headrail.

With the coming of the Normans, costume, while remaining about the same in style, became richer in fabric, to which were added costly silks, furs and jewels. The first princess style of dress appeared in the time of William II in 1100. An opening in the center back, reaching from the waist to between the shoulder blades was laced, not tightly, but just enough to eliminate the wrinkles around the diaphragm. A cord girdle was added, on which hung purse, keys and mirror.

The coiffure then changed, the hair being worn parted in the middle with long braids, to which false hair was often added for length and finished with ribbons wound about. The headrail developed into the wimple of fine white or colored fabric, held on the head by a snood or metal circlet. Later appeared the chinband and small toque of stiffened white linen. Sometimes it was crownless, with the wimple drawn through and draped in folds.

There was a long-lasting vogue for diapered fabrics, patterned with designs in lozenges, crescents and stars. The clothing of nobility was made only of costly cloths, silks and finest linens, richly embroidered. So much gold tissue was worn that it became necessary to lay thin paper between the folds to prevent tarnishing and that is the origin of our "tissue paper."

Gloves with jewels on the backs were worn by the men. Their long loose drawers gave way to more fitted hose in gay colors, cross-gartered with gold bands. It is interesting to note the leather belt with buckle worn by men and women, with the long tongue left hanging in front. The length of the yard measure was established in the reign of Henry II, 1154 to 1189, by the length of the King's arm. In that period, men's tunics were fastened at the neck by means of small gold studs.

In the twelfth century, a new garment appeared for women called the *pelisse*. It was a loose coat reaching to the knees, had flowing sleeves and fastened at the waist. In fabrics, there were wools woven in Flanders, brocades from Venice and, as on the Continent, ermine was the favored fur.

Between 1199 and 1216, the *surcoat* was adopted in England by men and women, copied after the panel of fabric worn over the knight's armor. Surcoat was the original name for the garment, the cotte or coat being the dress underneath. The surcoat was held in place by a cord girdle or belt. The cotte eventually became the petticoat, while the surcoat developed into the dress.

Gloves were made of wool and leather, and ladies carried theirs tucked into their belts. The shoes of both sexes in this period were of fabric or leather, often embroidered. Toward 1200, women dressed their hair up and adopted the chinband, to which the wimple was pinned, all of sheer linen.

In the early part of the thirteenth century, the *cotehardie* took the place of the surcoat. For men, it was a tight-fitting jacket buttoned down center front. It had long, tight sleeves which buttoned from elbow to the little finger and was finished with a jewelled belt placed low on the hips. The now long, fitted stockings or tights were fastened under the jacket with laces and points.

In the fourteenth century, parti-colored clothes appeared and lasted a half century. At the same time, the toes of the soft, plain or embroidered shoes grew to very long points, which were stuffed and stiffened. Pattens were worn outdoors to protect the soft soles.

In the latter part of the thirteenth century, appeared the *liripipe,* or hood with tail. In the fourteenth century, men wore the draped turban of the Continent with its very long tail, which was either wrapped around the neck or left hanging in the back. By the end of that century, the liripipe became part of the folds of the turban, looking very much like a cock's comb, thence the term "coxcomb," designating a dandy. That ornament dwindled in size, becoming finally, an insignia, the remains of which we have today in the cockade on the coachman's hat. Skullcaps, tall-crowned felt bonnets with narrow rolled brims, were in style too, often the bonnet worn over the hood. The roundlet, the evolution of the chaperon turban, was adopted by Englishmen in the fifteenth century. They also copied the Continental fashion of wearing it slung over one shoulder, holding the liripipe in one hand.

The masculine haircut was usually moderately short, but, in contrast to that style, some men wore their hair cropped short like a priest's and the back of the neck shaved.

There were several styles of cloaks, long and loose, square or circular, with or without hood, wide at the neck or buttoned with two or three buttons. Some had collars and lapels of fur. There were also men's hats with fur brims. Nearly always the masculine costume was finished with a black leather belt, from which hung a triangular pouch and dagger.

At that time there was little change in women's costume, which consisted usually of three garments: the cotte, or robe of cloth with long, tight sleeves and high at the neck; a tunic over that, having shorter and wider sleeves and fuller skirt, of which one or the other had a train; worn over the two was the surcoat, and around the throat a gorget of sheer white material, to which the wimple was pinned.

The hair was done in braids, which were looped up on either side of the face. Later, the wimple was replaced by cauls of various shapes, nets of gold thread or braid interspersed with jewels. This style is known as the golden net caul or the reticulated headdress. Any hair that showed on the back of the neck below the caul was plucked; even eyebrows were plucked in those days and rouge was in fashion.

In the fourteenth century, the *houppelande* came from the Low Countries and was adopted by men and women. It was long and voluminous, belted at the waist, often fur-trimmed and occasionally fur-lined. Young men wore a short version of it, but the various styles of the houppelande were in rich fabrics, sometimes elaborately embroidered. In the same period, edges of garments were petal-scalloped and castellated. Later, the houppelande was belted into evenly arranged pleats.

The heavy gold chain of the period has survived as a badge of office, worn today by mayors, judges and various orders. Large thumb rings were worn, and masculine and feminine costumes were ornamented with heraldic designs stamped on the cloth and velvet in gold, silver and colored enamels.

In the fourteenth century, the underdress with low-placed girdle, the cotehardie, became the mode, also the various styles of the hennin. The tall hennin was called the "steeple headdress" and the two-horned one the *escoffion,* which is said to have originated in England. As on the Continent, the hennin was fastened to a tiny skullcap worn underneath with the frontlet showing on the forehead. The frontlet was of black velvet and was permitted only to persons having ten pounds a year or more. Then came colored wimples after centuries of only saffron or white having been used.

Along with the more elaborate hennins came the higher-waisted gown with fitted bodice, while men adopted short tunics with full sleeves and the broad shoulders of Venetian influence. The long-pointed masculine shoes, called in England "crackowes" after the town of their origin, Cracow, Poland, lengthened to such a degree that, in 1463, an ordinance was passed permitting persons of rank to have points but two inches beyond their toes.

Small silver bells were a fashionable adornment in the late fourteenth and early fifteenth centuries. The jester's costume of parti-colored clothes, hood with short cape, castellated edges, tinkling with bells, has come down to us intact, as the dress of that period.

English Medieval or Gothic

king-10th C.-
white tunic-
red and blue
embroidery-red
mantle and
stockings-gold
braid cross
gartering-black
shoes

yellow surcoat
over white tunic-
red embroidery-
leather belt with
long tongue-yellow
leather shoes-
12th C.

crimson cloth
houppelande
over white
camise-leather belt-
white chaperon turban-
green stockings-
brown leather shoes-
14th C.

bagcap with jewel-
jacket of orange
brocaded cloth-
green velvet sleeves-
alternating green and
orange stockings and
shoes-15th C.

RTW

English Medieval or Gothic

blue headrail-
red mantle-green
bliaud-gold
embroidery-white
chemise-
9th C.

white linen wimple
and gorget-jewelled
circlet-gray mantle-
diapered gold cloth
bliaud-white chemise-
13th C.

jewelled caul-
violet surcoat
over green cote-
hardie-jewelled
girdle-buttons on
sleeves - th 14 C.

green hennin and
wimple over jewelled
caul-green velvet
overdress with
ermine-brocaded
silk underdress-
15th C.

RTW

English Medieval or Gothic

chinband wimple and toque - 13th C.

man's shoe - 14th C.

headrail drawn through crownless toque - white linen - 13th C.

dress laced in back - 11th C.

pelisse - 12th C.

sugar-loaf hat worn over hood - 14th C.

jewelled circlet - headrail - 14th C.

a haircut of the 15th C.

wired veil - jewelled cap - 15th C.

man's money pouch worn on belt - 14th C.

cylindrical cauls of reticulated headdress - 14th C.

crackowe and patten - 14th C.

woman's bag worn on girdle - 14th C.

chaperon turban - 15th C.

jewelled reticulated headdress - 15th C.

RTW

Chapter Eleven

Flemish and German
MEDIEVAL OR GOTHIC

THE FLEMINGS were skillful weavers, their craft dating from 900. Tapestry weaving in Europe originated in their city of Arras in the fourteenth century. They produced beautiful patterned leathers which rivalled those of Spain. They wove woolen cloth from English and Scotch wool, which was worn by all the other countries and sent to the East in exchange for the luxuries from those regions.

In the thirteenth century, the long tunic and mantle were still worn in the Low Countries. The tunic reached to the ankles on the men and was full-length on the women. Men wore their hair long, curled at the ends, while that of the women was long and flowing.

By 1300, the same development in the tunic as that in the neighboring countries had arrived. The women's tunic gradually changed into a robe, which was important as a German style, because it was worn over a corset. It was a fitted dress with flowing sleeves and unadorned neck and was worn over a complete undergarment, the chainse or chemise.

63

About the middle of the fourteenth century, the cotehardie appeared. For men, it was a short, fitted tunic, reaching halfway down between thigh and knee. It buttoned down center front and had long, tight sleeves with buttons from elbow to the little finger. The women's cotehardie resembled that of the man, except that the skirt lay in folds on the ground. Over it was worn the surcoat with large armscye, exposing to view the jewelled girdle at the hips.

The man's tunic changed into the *pourpoint,* a quilted jacket, short of skirt, the body laced either front or back and worn with long, fitted stockings or tights. When the pourpoint was sleeveless, it was worn under the jacket. The later carefully pleated tunic worn by all fashionable Europe originated in Flanders.

Because of the colder climate, fabrics were practical and heavy, richly patterned, but not distinguished. There were silks, brocades, velvets and cloth of gold, also their own beautiful woolens. The Flemings had developed the weaving of linen and cotton to a high degree, producing sheer veiling, muslin and delicate gauze, which were used for headdresses.

The hair was now dressed close to the head, a favorite style being long braids coiled on each side of the face, then, draped over that arrangement, the wimple, which in Germany and Flanders was most intricate and of many styles. Cauls and circlets of gold were worn too and crowns were placed on top of the wimple. The gorget enjoyed its vogue, worn pinned to the wimple.

Men wore hoods, the draped or chaperon turban and hats with brims. Men and women wore the soft, fitted shoe of leather or fabric like those of the other countries and used pattens in the streets. Both sexes were fond of many finger rings, worn also on the thumbs. The women did not use cosmetics. Fashionable people of the Low Countries, in the late fourteenth and early fifteenth centuries, adopted the fad of utilizing small silver bells as ornamentation on their clothes.

This people liked brilliant colors. They wore the parti-colored costumes of the period and surpassed all the other countries in their use of petal-scalloped or castellated edges of garments. A peculiar style of the fifteenth century was the silhouette with a straight back and what we might describe as a bustle worn in front over the stomach.

People of the Low Countries did not wear their clothes with the same style as their neighbors, their figures being heavier and shorter of waist. They did not have that innate feeling for the mode, so that their costumes became over elaborate and bulky.

Despite that fact, certain German styles did influence the northern countries. They furnished an important garment to the rest of Europe in the houppelande, a mode which lasted until the sixteenth century. Their adoption of that fantastic style of slashings and puffings in the last quarter of the fifteenth century, spread to the other courts of Europe, reaching its peak between 1520 and 1535.

The starching of sheer fabrics used for caps, wimples and collars originated in Flanders. In the fondness of the inhabitants of the Low Countries for excessive ornament, not only in dress but also in architecture, can be seen the foundation of the baroque or rococo period of the seventeenth and early eighteenth centuries.

Record has it that steel needles were made in Nuremberg in 1370.

Flemish and German- Medieval or Gothic

embroidered bliaut or tunic- leather belt and shoes- jewelled circlet-12thC.

red cloth cape- fur collar and lining-blue tunic-leather belt- yellow stockings- green shoes-gold circlet with jewels- 13thC.

cotehardie or jacket with buttons- castellated edges- ermine on sleeves- jewelled belt- chaperon-embroidered shoes-14thC.

sugar-loaf hat- brocaded cloth houppelande with long sleeves- 15thC.

FTW

Flemish and German-Medieval or Gothic

bliaut or tunic
with leather belt-
jewelled circlet-
12th C.

diapered gold
cloth surcoat
laced in front-
blue cotehardie
with gold braid
and embroidery-
jewelled circlet-
13th C.

diapered cloth
cotehardie over
white tunic-
reticulated
headdress of gold
braid and silk-
14th C.

mantle with cord-
gown with full
sleeves-turban with
jewel and
castellated edged
tabs-15th C.

RTW

Flemish and German-Medieval or Gothic

gold crown-
white linen cap
and chinband-
12th C.

Shoe of gold strips
and pearls-
11th C.

jewelled circlet-net
of crocheted wool or
knotted cords of silk,
gold or silver-13th C.

woman's belt
with and purse
keys-
14th C.

toque and chinband
of embroidered linen
.13th C.

turban of red
and white linen-
jewel and
heron plumes-
bell trimming
on dress-
15th C.

leather boot
11th C.

turban of white
linen-jewel and
gold braid-15th C.

roundlet with
chaperon-15th C.

reticulated headdress-
gold braid
and pearls-
15th C.

hennin and
gorget-15th C.

tunic and
baldric with
bells-15th C.

shoe with straps-
14th C.

man's felt hat
with feather-
15th C.

RTW

Chapter Twelve

Italian Renaissance

THE RENAISSANCE in Europe originated in Italy, brought about by the decline of Greco-Roman influence and the undertaking of the Crusades. It began in the thirteenth and fourteenth centuries, was fully under way at the beginning of the fifteenth, its height being about the middle of the century and its climax about 1500. At its height, there had existed no parallel except that of the Roman Empire in its greatest glory.

It affected men's costume more than women's. The feminine mode of the early part of the period was of a religious or so-called "conventional" style. Because printing began to be used in Europe about the middle of the fifteenth century, we have much authentic material.

The masculine costume consisted of a shirt, tunic or doublet and hose. Over the doublet was sometimes worn a garment called *pourpoint*, jerkin or jacket and sometimes a robe, called a gown. The shirt or body linen was made quite full, gathered at neck and wrists, the gatherings edged with fine embroidery in gold or red and black silk. This decoration, of ancient Persian origin, came from Spain and was known in Europe as Spanish blackwork.

The neck was either round or V-shaped, square neck predominating from 1500 to 1525. Then came the small turned-down collar, followed by the ruche of Spanish origin, which developed into the ruff in the second half of the sixteenth century. The doublet was a short tunic, jacket-like with sleeves, originally tight, but later tight over the forearm and puffed above.

Slashings appeared in the last quarter of the fifteenth century, lasting until the middle of the seventeenth century. That style originated among the Swiss soldiers, was adopted to an extreme degree in Germany and definitely marked the costume of France and England. The sleeves of the doublet in this period were often slashed and paned, revealing the shirt of rich material. Panes were strips of fabric used vertically over puffings, and these strips were, in turn, ornamented with slashes edged with stitching or gimp.

Wings, or puffs at the shoulders, masking the junction of sleeve and shoulder or the armscye, appeared in the second half of the sixteenth century.

The jerkin or jacket was now a rather short, full tunic, which either hung loose, or was belted into carefully arranged pleats. It had square or round neck, often long full sleeves. Sleeves were frequently detachable from doublet or jerkin, as were fronts or vest pieces, called stomachers.

The man's gown, which opened in front, varied in length, usually had long full sleeves and was made with or without collar. It was lined with rich fabric or fur. Voluminous cloaks were the fashion, both short and long, capelike or circular in cut. They were draped about the figure or simply hung from the shoulders and usually had broad collars.

The men wore fitted and sewn tights, which reached from waist to toe and were made of cloth or silk. Parti-colored hose were worn to the end of the fifteenth century. The short puffed trunks attached to the long stockings or tights were called trunk hose and were in fashion from 1575 to 1595. Trunk hose and codpiece were secured to the doublet by points or lacings. The codpiece was a decorated bag which held the sex piece and continued in fashion until 1580. It was of fabric, usually silk and often elaborately embroidered. From 1560 on, trunk hose were usually slashed or paned, revealing a full, padded silk lining.

Knee breeches followed in the 'seventies, tied below the knee with fringed or tasselled ribbon garters. Such breeches were known as "Venetians."

Footgear with long, pointed toes was replaced by a soft heelless shoe with broad toe. During the period of slashings, these broad toes were also slashed. Boots of varying height were worn until 1510.

Men's hair ranged in length from moderately short to shoulder length with a fringe over the forehead, occasionally in ringlets. Toward the end of the sixteenth century, mustache and beard reappeared.

The masculine head covering was principally a small toque and the béret-crowned hat with plume or jewel. The béret, in its various styles, which was to last a long time and be worn all over Europe, originated in Italy. It was made of felt, cloth, velvet and silk and was first a circular piece of fabric, drawn up on a string or band to fit the head. The tiny bow on the inside leather band of the man's hat of today, is a survival of that string. The béret was ornamented with a jewelled or embroidered band, sometimes a jewelled necklace being used. Brims of hats were sometimes laced with points as trimming.

Points were little metal tags or aglets attached to strings, ribbon, yarn or leather used as lacings and were a definite feature of the period. All parts of the costume were fastened in this manner. For ordinary wear, they were of metal, later they were made of gold and silver and set with precious stones. Points appear to have served for three centuries.

The gown of the lady of Renaissance Italy was artistic in design and rich in fabric. She made use of handsome brocades, embroidered velvets, satins, damasks and pearl-sewn cloth of gold. The Renaissance is sometimes called the "Pearl Age." From the East came gems and rare stones, cloth of gold and silver tissue; from Russia and the North furs such as sable, ermine, vair, marten, lynx, fox and lambskin; from Rheims rich brocades, while Venice made gorgeous silks and velvets.

The bodice of the gown was snug and short-waisted, which brought about the wearing of a heavy-fitted linen corset. The petticoat or "la robe" was of costly green or crimson satin or velvet. The early sleeves were long and tight, later puffed and slashed to reveal the sheer full lingerie undergarment. Necks were round, V-shaped, more often square. The ruff was adopted in the second half of the sixteenth century. Mantles or cloaks were fastened by brooches or cords and tassels.

Sewn stockings were held up by a garter above the knee, while shoes were of the same style as that of the men. The beginning of the heel can be seen in the thick wedge sole attached to the soft shoe, which appeared in the sixteenth century. When a belt or girdle was worn, it was jewelled and held a money pouch, a rosary, sometimes a feather fan and even a dagger.

The hair was worn off the forehead, parted in the middle and drawn into a chignon at the nape of the neck, although early in the period it was dressed in a hanging braid wound with ribbon. In another style, the parted front hair was cut short to below the cheek, curled and left to hang like a bob. The thin gauze or voile veil floating from the back of the head was a favorite fashion, too; ribbons, cauls and caps were worn. Brides wore their hair flowing, parted in the middle and crowned with a wreath of flowers.

False hair, especially blond color, was much worn, also wigs made of white and yellow silk. A favorite was a single jewel which hung in the middle of the forehead attached to a fine chain. That headdress is known to us as the ferronière.

Earrings appeared and became a popular adornment. Jewelry was ornate in design. There were heavy gold chains, strings of pearls and belts of gold and silver filigree. Buttons and clasps were fashioned of gold, silver, enamel, amber, crystal and pearls. Jewelled feathers were worn on men's hats, both sexes wore diamonds and rubies and gold and pearl embroidery.

From antiquity to the sixteenth century, all garments carried some touch of embroidery, Italy now holding the foremost position in this form of decoration. Gloves, hats, shoes, even furs carried decorative handwork, and men's clothes were embroidered in gold and silver or edged in fine red and black stitching. With the advent of the steel needle from the Orient, introduced into Europe by the Moors, embroidery became finer and more elaborate. All fabrics were decorated in colored silks, gold, silver, pearls and other gems.

During this period, the invention of lace took place, and while sparingly used before the seventeenth century, eventually ornamented every article of clothing for both men and women. Before the middle of the sixteenth century, the word lace designated tapes, cords and narrow braids, which were used as trimming and also served to lace together various parts of the costume. Laces were made of two to fifteen strands twisted together. The first lace with pattern was made of these twisted threads, usually white linen. Lace of fine and delicate pattern seems to have been an evolution of embroidery, the design cut out and edged with the buttonhole stitch. It appeared in Italy and Flanders about the middle of the sixteenth century.

It is noted that from the middle of the sixteenth century, both men and women used sunshades which were called umbrellas, even to carrying them on horseback. "Dandies" carried small thin canes, like the "swagger sticks" of today.

Fans, of Oriental origin, returned to vogue. Feather fans and small flag-shaped ones were fashionable in Venice. The flag fans were small squares of plaited straw, linen, parchment or silk, painted or embroidered in colors and attached to a slim ivory stick. Small flat muffs of brocade, silk or velvet were carried by Venetian ladies around the end of the fifteenth century. The possession and use of handkerchiefs became more general, both men and women carrying this accessory of embroidered silk or cambric. Most exquisite ones were adorned with drawn work, leaving very little of the original fabric.

Women made use of cosmetics, perfumes and lavender water and whitened their bare chests. The making of perfume in Europe originated in Renaissance Italy, founded upon the knowledge brought back from the Orient by the Crusaders. René, an Italian perfumer, opened the first perfume shop in Paris about 1500.

Italian Renaissance

satin gown with
velvet collar and
lining-doublet with
lacings over white
shirt-jewelled
necklace-slashed
sleeves-velvet cap-
parti-colored tights-
embroidered gloves-
gold chain-
late 15th C.

cloak of
silk brocade
with velvet-silk
tunic-slashed
velvet hat-silk
tights-velvet
shoes-16th C.

slashed satin
pourpoint and
trunk hose-fur
collared mantle-
velvet hat-black
leather shoes-sword-
gold chain and
buttons-16th C.

cloth mantle
with buttons-
brocaded tunic
and Venetians-
sword-silk hat-
late 16th C.

RTW

Italian Renaissance

embroidered
moiré over
brocaded velvet
petticoat-silk
voile-feather
fan-late
15th C.

silk robe over
brocaded petticoat-
voile scarf-silk
fringe-embroidered
beret-1st half 16th C.

lady of
Mantua-
cloth cloak
with voile
scarf and
jewel-brocaded
gown-2nd half
16th C.

beret and gown
of brocaded crimson
damask-slashed
velvet sleeves-
shirred yoke of
fine linen-feather
fan-1st half 16th C.

RTW

Italian Renaissance

crown with pearls-late 15th C.

late 15th C.

Pearls and silk voile-late 16th C.

man's hat of braid-15th C.

flag fan of plaited straw-16th C.

man's felt hat-15th C.

lady of Lombardy-braids in rolls-silk voile scarf-16th C.

young woman of Piedmont-braided coiffure-16th C.

late 16th C. fringed muff of brocade

wedge sole-beginning of heel-16th C.

"trembling cap"-net over silk voile-edged with pearls-late 16th C.

Points-paned trunk hose-codpiece-middle 16th C.

fabric boot fastened on inside of leg-pearls-late 15th C.

silk fan-ivory handle-16th C.

RTW

Chapter Thirteen

German Puffs and Slashes
The First Half of the Sixteenth Century

*S*LASHINGS originated in the costumes of the Swiss soldiers after 1477, when they won their battle against the Duke of Burgundy and mended their ragged uniforms with strips of tents, banners and furnishings left behind in the flight of the Burgundians. It became a fashion and was indulged in to the extreme by the Germans, especially the soldiers, mercenaries called Lansquenets. From them, the style passed to the rest of Europe, reaching its height from 1520 to 1535.

All articles of clothing, even gloves, shoes and stockings were slashed and paned, revealing puffings of contrasting fabric and color. The high waistline prevailed in both masculine and feminine dress. Narrow shoulders, a small tight waist and full hips were the characteristic features of the feminine silhouette, while the masculine effect was broad to squareness.

An exaggerated fullness over the abdomen, below the tight waist, was affected by the women. The underskirt was of heavy contrasting fabric and color, either edged with a wide band of embroidery or bands of velvet. Under that, several linen petticoats were worn. The body garment consisted of a shirt.

Under the large hats, men often wore a cap, while women wore either caul or cap. Hats were ornamented with jewels, embroidery and that great favorite, the ostrich plume. Brims were slashed. Instead of a cap, the man often resorted to a chinstrap or string to hold his hat in place. The string also enabled him to drop his hat to the back of his neck and there the hat was often carried.

Women drew their hair tightly off their faces and invariably concealed it beneath a caul or cap, while men featured theirs in waves and ringlets.

The fronts of shoes were square, of a much broader width than the foot. Daggers, swords and rapiers in ornate cases were suspended from belts. A woman, too, carried a small dagger in company with a decorative bag attached to the end of the girdle. Both sexes wore many rings on various fingers and heavy gold necklaces around their necks. The women used no cosmetics and were not addicted to the use of perfume.

Rich and heavy fabrics, in wool and brocades from the Orient, were used to make the evenly arranged organ-pipe folds of tunic and robe. The supremacy of the English woolen weavers caused the Germans to turn to the weaving of linens and cottons. They produced sheer gauzes, veilings and muslins of exceptionally fine textures.

German Puffs and Slashes

scarlet with white
puffings-gold décolletage
and belt-full white
yoke-jewelled
girdle with dagger
and bag-scarlet
béret hat-white
plumes-gold caul
and necklaces-
1st half 16th C.

tunic with
velvet bands-
jewelled clasp-
doublet over white
linen shirt-paned
breeches-ribbon garters
with beads-parti-
colored stockings-béret
hat with plumes-
dagger and rapier-
1538

young woman in pale
blue-bodice with
white puffings and
red embroidery-red
band at neck-blue
cape lined with
violet-violet apron-
black velvet bands-
hair in pigtail wound
with silk-red béret
hat with green
and white plumes-
gold and pearl
necklaces-
1st half 16th C.

soldier-doublet
with paned and
slashed sleeves-
waistcoat with
scallops-paned
and slashed breeches-
slashed codpiece-
ribbon garters-parti-
colored stockings-hat
with plumes-brim
in two pieces-sword-
early 16th C.

RTW

German Puffs and Slashes
1st half of the 16th Century

hat with rolled velvet edge-ostrich tips

coif of gold striped tissue over crest shaped cap

béret with slashed brim-ostrich plumes

flat béret attached to seed-pearl sewn caul-ostrich plume with pearls on spine

velvet hat with shallow crown-brim in two halves-attached to cap

felt hat with castellated edge and slashes-attached to cap-chin strap

velvet béret with tiny gold loops under brim

lady's bag of pleated silk and jewelled frame

béret hat with gold embroidery-attached to seed-pearl sewn caul

béret with castellated edge-net caul-ostrich plumes-chinstrap

shoe with slashed heel

hat with castellated edge-satin threaded through slashes

shoe with strap and buckle

RTW

Chapter Fourteen

French Renaissance
The Valois

CHARLES VIII—1483-1498
LOUIS XII—1498-1515

IN THESE two reigns, the Renaissance in France was taking root to reach full bloom in the reign of François I. By this time, it had already existed for one hundred years in Italy. The French mode of the sixteenth century was inspired by the Venetian mode of the fifteenth century, but was not as restrained and elegant. There were, however, the same heavy silks and satins, velvets and jewelled embroidery, metal braids, ribbons and costly furs.

Men wore the long tights reaching to the waist, the pourpoint or doublet which now had a low neck, usually square, worn over a full sheer lingerie shirt. The tights were often parti-colored, in silk or cloth of gold appliquéd in velvet or passementerie.

There were two styles of cloaks, both were full and had large openings for the arms to pass through. The long one, reaching to the ground, had long hanging false sleeves and the body was sometimes confined by a girdle around the waist. The shorter one, too, hung loose, reaching to a point below the knees. Both had lapels or wide collars and were often fur-trimmed and fur-lined. Hats were rather flat in béret style, soft-shirred crowns with brims of varied shape, turned up and frequently ornamented with a jewel and a plume.

The predominant style in women's dress appears to have been a snugly fitted bodice, under which was worn a fitted corset of heavy linen. There were two variations of this mode, Italian and French, the difference being in the sleeves. Those of the Italian gown were long and fairly slim, broken by small puffs, while the French sleeves flared into wide, turned-back cuffs. The neck of the bodice was usually square. The full skirt flared out from the waist on a straight line, opening over a petticoat of contrasting, heavy, rich fabric to which embroidery and jewels were added. Other ornamentation consisted of wide bands of fur, velvet and embroidery. Under this there was a foundation petticoat of taffeta-covered canvas. The wide-flowing sleeves showed their linings of fur or velvet. Later, sleeves of many puffs came in, wide at the top and tight at the wrists. Elaborate necklaces, strings of pearls and the jewelled pendant or cross attached to a fine, black silk cord were of the period. Jewelled girdles with a long end hanging in center front were worn, from which hung rosary or mirror.

The shoes of both sexes were soft, in leather, silk or velvet, with a round toe which finally became square. A buckled or buttoned strap served as fastening. Metal or gold points attached to laces were used to secure the different parts of the costume.

Men wore their hair in a bob to a line just below the cheek. Women dressed theirs in the Italian or Madonna fashion, parted in the middle and drawn back into a chignon at the nape of the neck. Over it was worn a hood with hanging folds at the sides and the back. The curtain or loose back piece of the hood was called the "fall," and the narrow side pieces "lappets." The favorite hood was of black velvet, embroidered and lined with red or white. The cap, or "coif," worn under the hood, was either sheer white or gold tissue, usually edged with a narrow frill. Many variations of the hood developed with the eventual pinning up of the fall and the lappets. The hair was concealed in silken cases

Ladies of rank wore enveloping mantles of rich fabric, caught together at the neck by buckles, brooches or cords with tassels.

French Renaissance

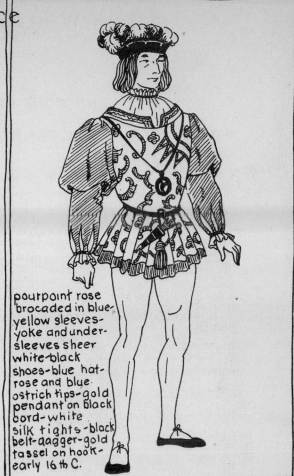

Crimson velvet
gown-gray fur-
false sleeves-gold
satin pourpoint-gold
necklace-black
velvet hat-white silk
tights-white shoes-
end of 15th C.

pourpoint rose
brocaded in blue-
yellow sleeves-
yoke and under-
sleeves sheer
white-black
shoes-blue hat-
rose and blue.
ostrich tips-gold
pendant on black
cord-white
silk tights-black
belt-dagger-gold
tassel on hook-
early 16th C.

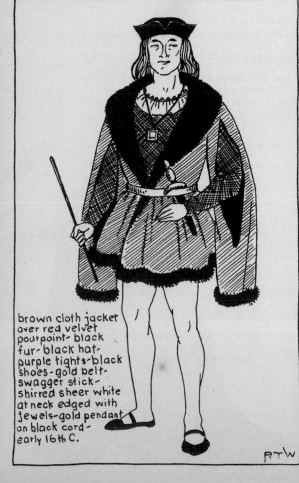

brown cloth jacket
over red velvet
pourpoint-black
fur-black hat-
purple tights-black
shoes-gold belt-
swagger stick-
shirred sheer white
at neck edged with
jewels-gold pendant
on black cord-
early 16th C.

brocaded gold
cloak-fur-lined and
edged-white shirt
and sleeves embroidered
in gold-gold, red and
black embroidery at
neck-red tights with
blue and gold bands-
black shoes and hat-
gold chain-early 16th
C.

FTW

French Renaissance

Italian style-
peacock blue moire-
under dress beige
brocaded in red-sheer
beige puffs-jewelled
necklace, headband
and ornament-
late 15th C.

French style-
gold brocade with
ermine-red velvet
underdress-black
velvet neck-edged
white frill-black
velvet "fall" with gold
braid-sheer white
coif-gold chain girdle-
gold braid on petticoat-
jewelled necklace-
early 16th C.

silk gown with velvet
petticoat-overskirt
lined with brocade-
brocade oversleeves-
lingerie yoke and
undersleeves-velvet
bands with pearls-
pearl necklace-
white coif
with black
velvet "fall"-
early 16th C.

orange velvet bodice,
slashed puffs and
cuffs-lingerie yoke
and puffs-gold beads
and heavy gold chain-
blue silk skirt over
brocaded petticoat-white
cap-Flemish influence-
early 16th C.

RTW

French Renaissance

felt béret with brim-late 15th and early 16th C.

girdle of strands of yarn with pearl knots-16th C.

caul with jewelled band-velvet lappets-jewel on head-16th C.

jewelled girdle-16th C.

hood of tapestry and silk-large jewel-velvet lappets-sheer wired peak-late 15th and early 16th C.

cap with bound strands of yarn-velvet lappets-embroidered edge-16th C.

felt hat-jewels and crenellated edge-early 16th C.

lady's "hand bag" or small satchel-velvet with embroidery and pearls-early 16th C.

rose velvet band with jewels-hair bound with ribbon-early 16th C.

hat of brocade and felt-late 15th C.

felt hat with wired ostrich plume-jewelled ornament-late 15th C.

RTW

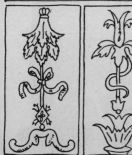

Chapter Fifteen

French Renaissance
The Valois

FRANÇOIS I—1515-1547
HENRI II—1547-1559

broad square silhouette

WITH the reign of François I, the French Court became definitely established and by its brilliancy revealed its Venetian origin and influence. The mode for both men and women was decidedly broad and square with much slashing in all parts of the costume. Colors were in a lighter vein than those of Italy, sky blue and white, lilac tones, rose, gold and silver being much favored.

The embroidered low-neck chemise or shirt of the man was shirred into a higher neckline, finishing in a narrow frill, the beginning of the ruche in France. The full sleeves were gathered at the wrist. The pourpoint, or doublet, had a low square neck, a fitted body and very full puffed and slashed sleeves, which were tight at the wrists. Early in the century, the pourpoint was skirtless, but later developed a short skirt often with scalloped or crenellated edge. The jerkin or jacket, really a tunic wrap, in this period was voluminous but short, with huge flowing sleeves that sometimes had wide turned-back cuffs. Occasionally it had hanging false sleeves or, again, puffed sleeves to the elbow with deep, tight cuff.

Trunk hose, stuffed or bombasted with horsehair, bran or other padding, became very short. They were paned and slashed, of different fabric from the stockings, but trunks and stockings were often made in one. Trunks or breeches were called upper stocks, while stockings were known as nether stocks. When trunks were fashioned of pieces or strips placed vertically, the English term for the strips was panes, thus paned breeches. Stockings were parti-colored, one plain and the other striped with garters and ribbon bows worn just below the knees. The codpiece attached to the trunks was still prominent and elaborately embroidered. In fact, the entire costume was decorated, slashed with puffings of different materials of contrasting colors showing through the openings. The puffings were also embroidered and the edges of the slashings finished with braid or gimp of silk, gold or silver.

Jewelled swords were worn at the side. Hats were the same for both men and women, the béret crown with narrow brim and trimmed with a white feather, which might have been ostrich, peacock or wool imitation of feathers. The same shapes in straw were worn in the summer.

The masculine undergarment was of finest linen, white with delicate black embroidery, known as Spanish blackwork. The outer garments were in colors of white, rose, sky blue and soft yellow, while at court functions, white and cloth of gold were worn. Men wore beards and mustaches, with their hair bobbed short.

The hoop came to France in 1530 with Eleanor of Castille, the second wife of François I. It was a petticoat of heavy canvas, with the lower part a wicker hoop covered with heavy taffeta. It flared out from the waist to the ground, creating a conical shape. The cotte or robe opened over an elaborately embroidered petticoat of rich fabric, under which was worn the hoop, women wearing for the first time three skirts.

Also an innovation, was the corset, or bodice, called the *basquine,* separate from the skirt and of different material and color. It was very tight, usually with low, square neck, which now curved upward across the front. Under it was worn the fitted corset of heavy linen, while steel rods were added to the bodice itself. Sleeves, which were often separate from the costume, were puffed and slashed and elaborately ornamented.

A distinctive feature of both men's and women's costume was the full sheer guimpe, or chemise, which appeared above the square neck of tunic or bodice. The jewelled girdle with long end in front, as worn by Catherine de' Medici, was really a rosary with a mirror at the end.

Women gathered their hair into a chignon at the back of the head. They parted it in the middle, over which were worn lovely caps of sheer gauze or linen, cauls of gold threads and jewels and nets of pearls. In the style known as "la ferronière," so called after "la Belle Ferronière," mistress of François I, a jewel hung in the center of the forehead, suspended from a fine chain around the head. In this period, the ornate jewelled gold necklace was popular.

Men and women wore squared-toed shoes of soft Spanish leather, silk or velvet. The toes were slashed and the feminine shoe ornamented with embroidery and jewels. Ladies wore stockings in crimson or scarlet with an embroidered or cut edge which rose three inches above the knee. Garters above and below the knee held them in place.

The Venetian mask of black velvet lined with white satin was the fashion for both sexes. Women wore them outdoors to protect their complexions and make-up and to the theatre to conceal their identity. There was a small mask which covered the upper half of the face. A larger one covered the entire visage, held in position by means of a button attached to the inside, which was inserted between the teeth.

Fabrics were indeed gorgeous with embroideries and jewels, patterned cloths, brocaded silks and velvets. Trimmings consisted of wide bands of contrasting colored cloth, embroidery or fur, such as sable, marten and ermine. Scarfs of fur were finished with head and claws encrusted with jewels and were worn throughout the entire sixteenth century. Other ornamentation was of gold and silver in thread lace and rosettes. There were also plain heavy silks, satins and velvets, velvet being the favorite.

The beginning of the supremacy of France in perfumes dates from this reign, François I encouraging the celebrated Italian perfumers to establish themselves in France.

With the reign of Henri II, the Protestant influence and severe restrictions in the use of silks and velvets, came a sobering of the mode. More somber colors and a great deal of black was worn. The broad silhouette disappeared, the Spanish style of bombast or padding taking its place. The distinctive features were the high collar, long wasp waist and padded hips. The first silk knit stockings, a Spanish invention, were worn by Henri II.

The man's pourpoint, or doublet, still embroidered and braid-trimmed, became high-necked with the narrow ruche of the chemise showing above the collar. Sleeves lost their extreme fullness, but were still tight at the wrists. The short skirt of the doublet opened in front, revealing the codpiece. Trunk hose became shorter and fuller, were still padded, while stockings knitted of silk or wool were better fitting. The soft shoe, still slashed, conformed more to the shape of the foot. Sword and pouch or money bag were worn in the belt. Pockets, inserted in the trunks, appeared in the latter part of this period.

The style of hat remained the same, with the brim a bit narrower. The hair was worn short with mustache and clipped beard. The long gown or robe continued to be worn, but the short circular cape of cloth or velvet was newer.

Catherine de' Medici, wife of Henri II, is credited with bringing to France the steel corset in the form of the stomacher. The stomacher, which was the outer bodice, was fashioned of splints of ivory, steel, mother-of-pearl or silver covered with fabric and heavily embroidered with gold, silver and jewels. Under it was worn a garment of heavy linen, reaching from chest and underarms to the waist, tightly laced in back.

The basic design of the robe had changed little, except that the neck rose high, as did the men's, finishing with the narrow ruche or frill, also at the wrists. This narrow ruche of Spanish origin and the beginning of the ruff was also introduced into France by Catherine. Narrow thread lace now began to edge these frills.

When hats were worn, they were of the same béret style as the men's. The small and very becoming cap of the period was of sheer gauze with wired edge, its characteristic feature being the dip over the forehead. It is known as the "Marie Stuart cap," but Catherine seems to have established it as the "widow's cap." The hair was parted in the middle, drawn over puffs, pads or wires at the temples and rolled into a chignon at the back. A contemporary painting of Mary Stuart in her mourning headdress of white, portrays her with a cap to which is attached a gorget, or *barbe,* biblike in shape, of pleated sheer white linen.

Crimson satin was a passion of Catherine's, but after the death of the King, she never relinquished wearing black for mourning.

The vogue for paint, powder and perfume grew and Catherine, like François I, encouraged the settling in France of celebrated Italian perfumers. Perfumed gloves of fine leather were introduced to the court by Count Frangipani and manufactured at Blois after the Italian model. They were named "gants à la frangipane." Knitted silk gloves were also worn.

The shoes of Mary Stuart and Catherine de' Medici are the first shoes made with high heels in the modern fashion, that is, the heel in pedestal form, separate from the sole.

Men and women wore a great deal of jewelry, even the men adorning themselves with earrings. Pearls and other jewels were freely sewn over both masculine and feminine costumes and women added jewels to their coiffures. Both sexes wore gloves, carried needle-worked handkerchiefs and, throughout the Renaissance Period, made free use of cosmetics to enhance their appearance. The art of "face-painting," if we could call the use of white lead and vermilion such, was introduced into France by Catherine. Drawn and cut-work ornamentation appeared about the middle of the sixteenth century. It was executed in white thread upon white linen. The fact that linen became sheerer and the handwork closer and finer, explains the origin and evolution of lacemaking.

French Renaissance

page in rose cloth
jacket-gold and
purple embroidery
on skirt-gold pourpoint
with blue embroidery
white linen shirt with
blue and gold neckband,
white tights-black
fur collar-black felt
hat-1st half 16th C.

blue gown-
shoes and puffings-
rest of costume
white-white lingerie
shirt-gold embroidered
band-chain -sword-
1st half 16th C.

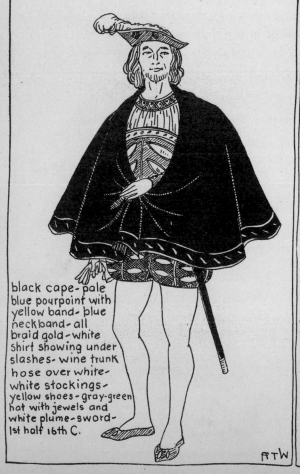

black cape-pale
blue pourpoint with
yellow band-blue
neckband-all
braid gold-white
shirt showing under
slashes-wine trunk
hose over white-
white stockings-
yellow shoes-gray-green
hat with jewels and
white plume-sword-
1st half 16th C.

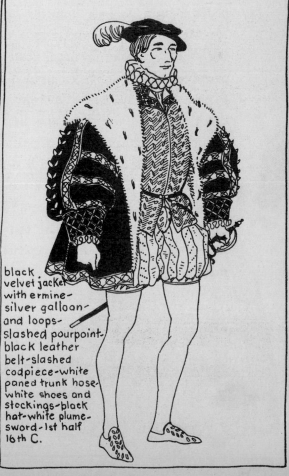

black
velvet jacket
with ermine-
silver galloon-
and loops-
slashed pourpoint-
black leather
belt-slashed
codpiece-white
paned trunk hose-
white shoes and
stockings-black
hat-white plume-
sword-1st half
16th C.

RTW

French Renaissance

gown of dark red and silver- "wings"-bow knots- pearls in hair and sewn on bands- embroidered gauze cap-middle 16th C.

black velvet and brocade with bag and mirror-gold cloth cap with white gauze- 1st half 16th C.

crimson brocaded satin- petticoat white with gold embroidery-white gauze-pearls-jewelled girdle-feather fan- cap with pearls- 1st half 16th C.

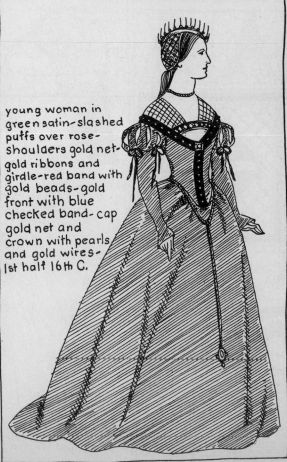

young woman in green satin-slashed puffs over rose- shoulders gold net- gold ribbons and girdle-red band with gold beads-gold front with blue checked band- cap gold net and crown with pearls and gold wires- 1st half 16th C.

FTW

French Renaissance

la ferronière-
gold chain with
jewel-early 16th C.

black felt hat-cap
gold braid over rose-
pearls-white feathers-
middle 16th C.

gray leather shoe-
inverted pleat and
jewel-1st half 16th C.

braids and pearls-
middle 16th C.

net of gold   ribbon
over red   velvet-
jewels and   tassel-
1524

black velvet trimmed
with gold-1st half 16th C.

black velvet trimmed
with gold-white
feather-1st half 16th C.

white linen cap with
pearls-metal frame-black
velvet fall-early 16th C.

slashed leather
shoe with pearls-
middle 16th C.

black velvet-pearls-
white ostrich tip-
middle 16th C.

white mourning cap
with wimple and gorget-
band with pearls-1560

slashed white fabric
shoe-1st half 16th C.

RTW

Chapter Sixteen

French Renaissance
The Valois

Charles IX—1560-1574
Henri III—1574-1589

Under Charles IX, men's costumes changed slightly, the Spanish influence still dominating the mode in the padded or bombast style. The long-bodied, small-waisted pourpoint or doublet became really a corset. It had stiffening, a busk in center front and the skirt of the garment was short. Sleeves were still tight at the wrists and padded, but not full. The embroidered linen shirt was still worn with a turned-down collar showing above the neck of the doublet. Buttons fastened the doublet down center front. The newly invented watches were carried in the pockets inserted in the trunk hose. Pockets were also inserted in the doublet sleeves.

Also worn were Venetians, which were breeches, full at the upper section of the leg, tying or buttoning below the knee. The codpiece embroidered with gold thread and jewels was still seen, but in the 'seventies, began to disappear, to be entirely gone by the 'nineties.

Gowns, cloaks and jerkins developed wings or shoulder puffs. An unusual jerkin worn by soldiers was the *mandilion,* short and wide with hanging sleeves, a garment which later became part of livery. The short Spanish cape continued in fashion. An interesting note in men's costume is that after 1565, the long robe and the flat béret cap continued to be worn only by elderly men and city people, eventually becoming the uniform of professional classes.

The soft crown of the béret grew high over a wire foundation and a narrow rolled brim appeared. The hat was fashioned of velvet or silk with a small standing plume, the crown encircled by a cord or perhaps a jewelled band. This toque was adopted by both men and women. The hair was worn short, beards were cropped and pointed and mustaches were the style. Pearl earrings were worn by both sexes.

Women now wore the Spanish hoop, called verdingale or farthingale, a petticoat of graduated hoops, or the French cartwheel which was a padded bolster tied around the hips. The corset-shaped bodice was high-necked with a ruff. Puffs and wings ornamented the shoulders and false or hanging sleeves were worn.

The hair continued to be dressed simply, off the face, parted in the middle and slightly rolled or puffed at the temples. Powdered hair was in vogue during most of the second half of the sixteenth century. The desired hue was black with a lighter shade showing through, blonds tinting theirs to gain the effect.

Caps ornamented with pearls and other gems were worn, also a hat of the same style as that of the men, narrow brim with béret crown, trimmed with a feather and jewels.

Masks of black velvet continued to be worn out of doors and to the theatre. They were to last well through the eighteenth century, passing from people of quality to the bourgeoisie. Later on, masks were worn as a protection against the winter cold. Green silk ones, covering the entire visage, were used on horseback to shield the complexion from the sun. Such a mask was held in position by a button clenched between the teeth. The wearing of them persisted to the time of our American Colonies.

When riding horseback, women wore, under the gown, a kind of doublet with upper house, called *caleçons,* rather resembling the union suit of today.

Small muffs came into fashion in this reign, with colored furs being reserved to ladies, black only permitted to the bourgeoisie. The wearing of velvet was forbidden to the lower classes.

The period of Henri III was marked by an extreme decadence and degeneracy in the character of the fashionable men at court. In fact, Henri III has come down to us as the synonym for effeminacy and profligate living. Men used cosmetics and perfumes, and slept with masks and gloves to soften the skin. They plucked their eyebrows and mustaches to make a fine line. Both men and women used violet-scented powder in the hair and wore much jewelry, including earrings.

The doublet developed an ugly shape in front, called the peasecod-belly, a busk down the center front and a stuffed-out hump protruding over the belt. Men are supposed to have worn a corset. The skirt of the doublet was quite short, the neck high and finished with a ruff, sleeves still puffed, slashed and tight at the wrists. Sleeves were finished with narrow ruches or lingerie cuffs, but the neck ruff, following the Spanish fashion, had grown much larger. It was now starched, its edge wired, and was tied in front with the strings left hanging.

Trunk hose became so short that sometimes they were only a short puff below the waist, but the space from there to the knee was covered with a garment called *canions.* Canions were breeches conforming to the shape of the leg, usually made in many rows of slashed puffs. With them were worn stockings reaching halfway up the leg, gartered conspicuously at the knee with ribbons having fringed ends.

The béret crown rose still higher, supported on wire, but another style was also worn by Frenchmen during the 'eighties. It was a sort of bonnet with very narrow rolled brim, shirred crown, the whole worn on the back of the head. In center front was perched an ornament of small feathers and jewels.

The hair was short and brushed up at the temples like the feminine coiffure. Mustaches and cropped, pointed beards continued in fashion.

Henri III is supposed to have disliked beards. Men wore pearl earrings and carried their pocket mirrors in their breeches pockets.

Capes and cloaks were of all styles and lengths. The short Spanish cape sometimes had a cowl in back, while the French cape of three quarters and knee length had a collar or shoulder cape. Capes were worn in any manner possible, over both shoulders or just hanging from one shoulder, then again draped diagonally across the back and held in front.

Shoes were still slashed, but in a smaller design. They conformed to the shape of the foot, covering it to the ankle. Pantoffles, or pattens, which had a cork sole and a piece over the instep, were worn over these shoes outdoors. A style of shoe, no doubt inspired by the chopine, had a second sole or platform placed under the sole and heel of the shoe. A portrait of Henri III pictures him wearing such a pair of shoes with red heels. Cork soles appeared in this period, often being placed between the sole and upper leather. Boots of Spanish leather, preferably white, rose above the knee and were fitted to the leg. They were held up by narrow straps and sometimes fastened down the leg by means of buckles or buttons. The tops were often turned down in Spanish fashion and the edges cut in tabs or scallops. A low, flat heel began to appear.

Along with gloves of leather, there is mention of knitted gloves of silk.

The Spanish style persisted for women with the corseted bodice, busk and long point in front and the large ruff, starched and with wired edge. Under the bodice was worn a veritable instrument of torture, the *corps piqué*, or "stitched body," which, according to description, seems to have been a corset fashioned of wooden splints covered with heavy linen.

The hoop skirt went to the extreme in shape. The Spanish skirt with its petticoat of graduated hoops was conical in silhouette, while the French was drum-shaped because of the padded bolster set on the hips.

A feature of this period was the *conch,* a shell-like wrap with large wired wings, rising above the shoulders in back, framing the face. It was fashioned of sheer material and hung to the floor. The style of waving the hair in small, tight curls came in and the center part gave way to a pompadour dressed over pads or wire frames, ending in a flat bun in the back.

Hats followed the masculine style, along with jewelled caps, which were still the mode. Shoes were like those of the men.

Collars and cuffs were now being edged with lace and Catherine de' Medici is noted as having had handkerchiefs of silk or linen edged with gold lace. Henri III introduced lace-making to France by bringing to his court Venetian pattern makers of lace and linen needlework. The cartwheel ruff was changing into a fan-shaped lace-edged collar, open in front, where it rose from a low décolletage which exposed the bosom, sometimes the entire bosom. The velvet mask continued in use by both sexes.

During the second half of the sixteenth century, all modish European women wore the same cloak, with slight variations. It was a simple flaring coat with collar and short puffed sleeves, reaching to the hem of the skirt. It fastened only at the neck, flaring open in front, and was made of elaborately embroidered or brocaded fabric, the edges often finished with wide braid.

The vogue for small muffs continued. Fans of plumes attached to decorated sticks or handles came into fashion. To Catherine is accredited the introduction into France of the folding fan. It was of Spanish origin and came by way of Italy. Both men and women used this fan of heavily scented leather. In this period of needlework, men vied with women in the art of embroidering their gloves and shoes.

French Renaissance

jacket with "wings", velvet bands, buttons and loops-slashed pourpoint-paned trunk hose-cod-piece-béret with brim-sword-1560's

all black-cape with heavy gold braid-white collar with lace edge-white wrist frills-trunk hose-canions-rapier-béret-2nd third 16th C.

paned pourpoint banded with gimp-and buttons-paned trunk hose-ruff-small béret with feather and jewel ornament-rapier-last quarter 16th C.

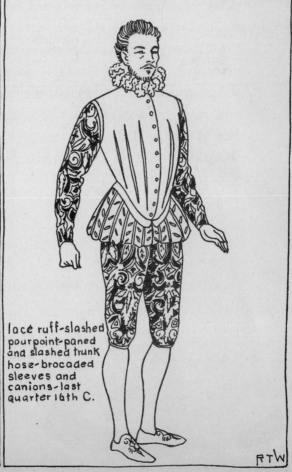

lace ruff-slashed pourpoint-paned and slashed trunk hose-brocaded sleeves and canions-last quarter 16th C.

RTW

French Renaissance

mourning costume-
Catherine de Medici-
white frills-conch
of sheer fabric-
wings and cap wired-
3rd quarter
16th C.

heavy silk with braid-
wings and hanging
sleeves-lace edged
ruff, frills and
handkerchief-
jewelled buttons-
brooch and chain-
pearls and
aigrette in hair-
2nd third
16th C.

cloak of embroidered
cloth-fur border-
bands of galloon-short
sleeves-gown of
velvet and brocade-
edged with beads-
2nd half 16th C.

embroidered satin-
sheer white yoke
and collar-edged
with lace ruff-
knotted string of
pearls on bodice-
cap over hair
tightly curled-
1575

RTW

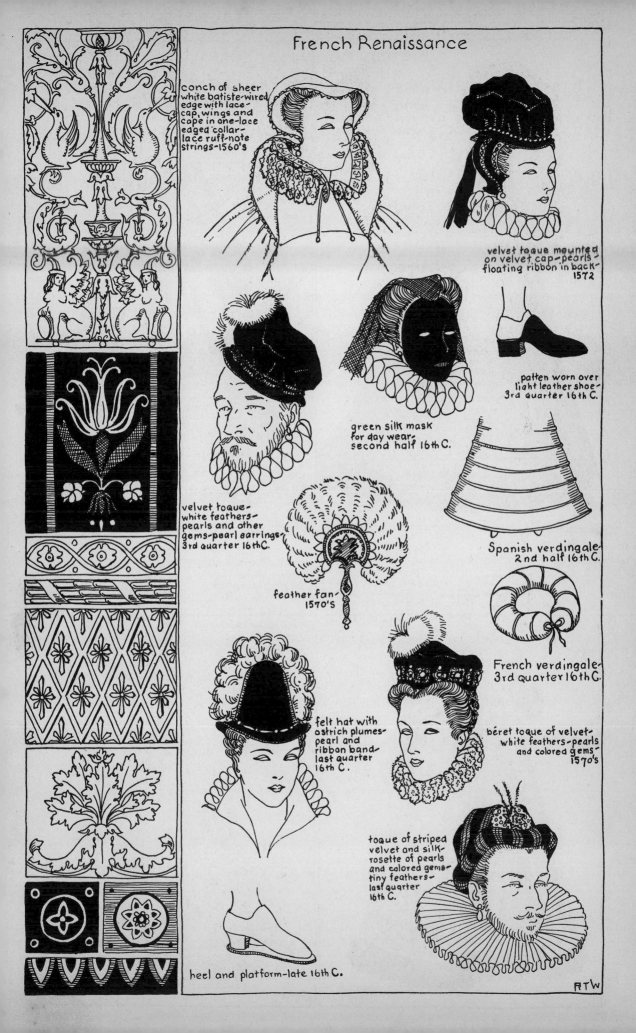

French Renaissance

conch of sheer white batiste-wired edge with lace-cap, wings and cape in one-lace edged collar-lace ruff-note strings-1560's

velvet toque mounted on velvet cap-pearls-floating ribbon in back-1572

velvet toque-white feathers-pearls and other gems-pearl earrings-3rd quarter 16th C.

green silk mask for day wear-second half 16th C.

patten worn over light leather shoe-3rd quarter 16th C.

feather fan-1570's

Spanish verdingale 2nd half 16th C.

French verdingale-3rd quarter 16th C.

felt hat with ostrich plumes-pearl and ribbon band-last quarter 16th C.

béret toque of velvet-white feathers-pearls and colored gems-1570's

toque of striped velvet and silk-rosette of pearls and colored gems-tiny feathers-last quarter 16th C.

heel and platform-late 16th C.

RTW

Chapter Seventeen

The Hispano–Moresque Period of Spain

THE SARACENS, by the middle of the eighth century, had conquered the entire Near East and settled in North Africa, Southern Italy and Spain. They ruled Spain for the next eight centuries. The Saracens, or Moors, were a people who had absorbed the culture of the other civilized countries, and thereby kept alive during the Dark Ages the development of art and science. They were the teachers of Medieval Europe and their period in Spain is known as the Saracenic or Hispano-Moresque. The influence and richness of their design are revealed in the arms, armor, jewelry and fabrics of the Gothic or Medieval and Renaissance Periods. Steel needles were introduced into Europe by the Moors.

In the earlier examples, their costumes were simple and voluminous, of plain wool, designed to protect them from the heat by covering the body almost entirely. As with other nations, the basic costume seems to have consisted of two garments or tunics, a long, straight, sleeveless one, ankle-length, called the *gandoura,* and over that another, more ample, with long, flowing sleeves. The outer tunic was drawn up and bloused over a girdle, shortening its length, thereby revealing the under one. Attached to the masculine outer tunic was a hood. The whole garment is known by the name of *burnous* and is still worn by the Arabs. Over their hoods, the men wore twisted turbans. Both sexes wore trousers.

That costume remains practically the same today among the Arabian peoples of the desert. Later, the Saracenic mode combined Arabian of the desert with Persian. During the Middle Ages, the costume was fashioned of gorgeous fabrics in cloths, silks, damasks, metal brocades, gauzes and sheer muslins in lovely colors.

The coat of Persian origin became, ultimately, almost regulation for men. It was of varying length, with long, straight, narrow sleeves. Sometimes the sleeves reached to the knees in length. A crushed, wide, soft sash usually accompanied it and trousers were worn underneath. The coat, of varied length and cut, worn over trousers, was also a feminine mode. Trousers were in three styles—long, straight ones slightly shaped to the leg, petticoat trousers, long and flaring, and very full ones, gathered at the ankles. The long, straight, feminine ones were of silk embroidered from knee to the ankle.

Women wore a short, full, pleated skirt or a scant one, just covering the knees, with the trousers or pantaloons showing below. Sometimes they wore a long robe or tunic like a candys, with a wide sash tied at the hips. When in public, baggy pantaloons covered feet and legs to the waist and an enveloping mantle concealed the body and head. It also covered the face, either having slits for the eyes or being worn just below the eyes.

Men and women wore sandals and slippers of soft leathers, colorfully dyed. A portrait of a Persian lady of the late sixteenth century pictures her wearing a short skirt about twelve inches from the floor, revealing embroidered trousers, below which appear well-fitted soft-leather boots with heels and pointed toes.

The women colored their fingers and toenails with henna, used rouge and darkened their eyes with kohl and indigo and were fond of perfumes. Both sexes adorned themselves with ornate jewelry.

Spanish blackwork, that fine black embroidery stitching combined with gold and silver thread which enjoyed such a long and tremendous vogue during the sixteenth century, came from the Moors and was, no doubt, of Persian origin. It edged the neck and wrists of the white linen or batiste shirts of the fashionable man of all the European courts.

The Christian Spaniards of the Middle Ages wore the costume of Medieval Europe, similar to that of Italy, but revealing the influence of their Oriental rulers in its color and decorative motif, employing much red, black and white.

Moorish or Saracenic Spain

Turkish Moorish-
dark green turban-
green tunic over
yellow-violet scarf,
yellow fringe-yellow
leather shoes em-
broidered-leather
shoulder strap
with jewels

Arabian Moorish-
blue shawl over
red pill-box cap-
yellow brocade
pleated skirt-red
pantaloons

Persian Moorish-coat
of painted, brocaded
or embroidered silk-
loops and buttons
at sides-vaile under
garment, turban and
gorget-jewelled
headband-moiré
trousers embroid-
ered to knee-dyed
leather boots

African Moorish-
woolen burnous-
loops and
buttons-dyed
leather boots

RTW

Moorish or Saracenic Spain

Knight in red surcoat-
gold buttons-white
cotehardie-undersleeves
striped red and black-
yellow bands-white
tabs at neck-white
stockings-jewelled
yellow leather shoes-
13th C.

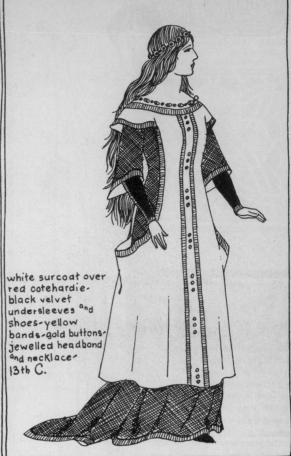

white surcoat over
red cotehardie-
black velvet
undersleeves and
shoes-yellow
bands-gold buttons-
jewelled headband
and necklace-
13th C.

matron-
brocaded gown of
gold cloth, silk or damask-
white head cloth and
gorget-black mantle-
soft shoes and chopines-
16th C.

a toga-like
mantle of dark
green cloth-red
cap-brown
leather boots and
shoulder strap-
15th C.

RTW

Arabic inscription from the Alhambra—"There is no conqueror but God".

Moorish or Saracenic Spain

Persian Moorish— young woman—gold brocade—voile scarf with fringe—jewelled gold disques

Arabian Moorish—front and back of shawl with pleats

Persian Moorish— young woman—gold brocade—white feathers—jewelled ornament

African Moorish—white cotton turban

African Moorish— young woman— draped band with silk tabs resembling feathers

Persian Moorish— married woman—white linen or cotton gorget— draped velvet turban and bonnet

RTW

Chapter Eighteen

Spain of the Sixteenth Century

By THE eighth century, Spain was almost entirely conquered by the Saracens, who ruled the land for the following eight centuries, stamping their Moorish civilization upon the Christian native. Eventually, bit by bit, the Spaniards regained their country, but the centuries of intercourse with the Moors, who possessed a much higher culture than any of their contemporaries in Europe, produced a remarkable character, which was individual in living, art and dress.

Their style was elegant and distinctive and it influenced, not a little, the mode of the other countries. They gave to Europe the ruche, the ruff, the short cape, the corset, the hoop, the bombast style of the padded doublet and trunk hose, followed by the unpadded trunks or breeches. Silk knit stockings were a Spanish invention and for a long time surpassed those of other countries.

They contributed also that great note of smartness in any period, the wearing of black in rich fabric. Black was the color for the general occasion, color being reserved for festive events. Black for mourning had been worn by the Spanish from the twelfth century, which custom was unusual, as the wives of most European kings wore white in like circumstance.

Despite the hoop, slimness of body for both men and women was the desired form and we read of the French resorting to diet to accomplish the "Spanish figure."

In the first half of the sixteenth century, men wore the elaborately embroidered doublet with short skirt and puffed sleeves over an embroidered lingerie shirt. The narrow ruffles or ruches which finished neck and sleeves showed at neck and wrist. After the middle of the century, the tiny neck ruffle became a fully developed ruff; then, in the 'eighties, a huge cartwheel, starched and wired. Later, narrow lace edging appeared. The width of the fashionable ruff was about a quarter of a yard and the frills contained eighteen or nineteen yards of fine linen lawn or Holland cambric, a luxury for the wealthy only. A frame of fine wire covered with silk thread was worn under it, the edge of the ruff being wired also. Ruffs were starched in various colors, blue, green, with yellow being a favorite and worn over Europe.

The general style of sleeve had moderate fullness, tight at the wrist with puffs or wings masking the armscye. Later in the century, bishop and leg-of-mutton shapes were paned and slashed, as were trunks and hose.

Trunk hose were bombasted or padded to great bulk with rags, bran, wool, almost anything that could be used for stuffing. Canions appeared, covering the leg from the trunks to the knee. Venetians were knickerbockers tied or buttoned below the knee. French breeches reached to the knee, conforming to the shape of the leg, but were divided into horizontal rows of puffs. The short, full unpadded breeches were known in England as "Spanish slops," and the full unpadded breeches reaching to the knees, as "full slops." Knitted stockings appeared during this period.

The typical hat of the period, worn by both men and women, was of velvet or satin with béret crown, which grew very tall toward the end of the century. It was trimmed with jewels and a tuft of feathers, usually small ostrich tips with aigrettes. The hair was worn fairly short by the men, accompanied by mustache and clipped beard.

The shoes of both sexes were shaped to the foot, reaching to the ankle with fronts pierced in various designs. Pantoffles and chopines covered them for street wear. Men also wore a high, fitted boot and, before the end of the century, a low heel came into vogue.

Until after the first half of the sixteenth century, men wore a cloak just covering the trunks. It was a gorgeous garment of velvet or brocaded fabric with full sleeves in many puffs. The winter cloak had wide collar and revers faced with fur, which also lined the wrap. Later, the short cape became universally worn, of cloth with taffeta lining in summer and of velvet or cloth, fur-lined, in winter. The cape often had hanging sleeves. The high collar of doublet or cape when worn open, with fronts folded back in revers, now showed the nick or notch which survives today.

The dagger or rapier was carried, attached to the belt, gloves were part of the costume and dandies sported a rose behind the ear.

Women wore the corseted bodice, deeply pointed in front, and the bell-shaped hoop of Spanish origin. Sleeves were full and flowing, over undersleeves of lingerie material with lace insertions and edgings. The gown was usually of black velvet or satin, ornamented with bands of embroidery or galloon. Lace-edged ruchings finished neck and wrists.

Also part of the costume were large jewelled brooches, ropes of pearls and knotted loops of ribbon with jewelled points. Both men and women wore heavy gold necklaces set with large gems. A favorite feminine ornament was the ornate brooch with pendant, also pearl earrings. Women wore cauls of gold wire or pearl strings set with jewels, over which the velvet hat with béret crown was placed. The hair was drawn off the forehead in pompadour fashion, waved or tightly curled, and dressed over a wire frame.

Gloves were carried, and invariably the sheer handkerchief edged with most exquisite lace. The embroidered and perfumed Spanish leather gloves were greatly desired by the fashionables of Europe. They surpassed those of Italian and French make in retaining the odor of the scent and were in demand for several centuries.

There were fans of feathers attached to ivory handles, folding fans of vellum and the fan of scented leather. The folding fan of heavily scented leather, of Oriental origin, was first used in Spain, passing to Italy and appearing in France in the reign of Henri III, 1574–1589. Sun-shades were in use by both men and women from the middle of the sixteenth century.

Spain of the 16th Century

silk béret hat
with jewelled
band-white
ruffs-cape of
woolen serge-
jacket with braid
and buttons-paned
trunk hose-silk
stockings-slashed
leather shoes-sword
and gloves-
last quarter 16th C.

béret hat with
ostrich tips-brocaded
silk coat-fur collar
and lining-galloon on
sleeves and skirt-
small puffs paned-
silk doublet-jewelled
silk tassel-paned
and corded canions
with codpiece-silk
stockings-embroidered
leather shoes-
1st half 16th C.

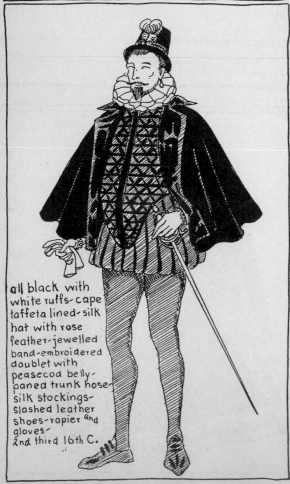

all black with
white ruffs-cape
taffeta lined-silk
hat with rose
feather-jewelled
band-embroidered
doublet with
peasecod belly-
paned trunk hose-
silk stockings-
slashed leather
shoes-rapier and
gloves-
2nd third 16th C.

all black with
white ruffs-cape
taffeta lined-
silk hat-pleated
crown with self
band-buttoned
doublet-paned
and slashed trunk
hose-silk upperstocks-
heavy netherstocks
with buttons-leather
shoes with heels-
rapier-gloves-
end of 16th C.

RTW

Spain of the 16th Century

velvet with bands of embroidery- shoulder wings- sleeves sewn with pearls- white frills at neck and wrists- jewelled belt- pearl necklace- velvet béret hat with jewels and feathers-1st half 16th C.

white velvet- bands of jewel embroidery- shoulder wings- hanging sleeves in back-ruff and frills with fine point lace- braid on under sleeves- jewelled headdress and brooches- pearl necklace- middle 16th C.

gold and rose brocade- hanging sleeves rose velvet with gold braid- sheer white ruff, cuffs and guimpe with lace- jewelled headdress and buttons- feather fan- ivory stick- 2nd third 16th C.

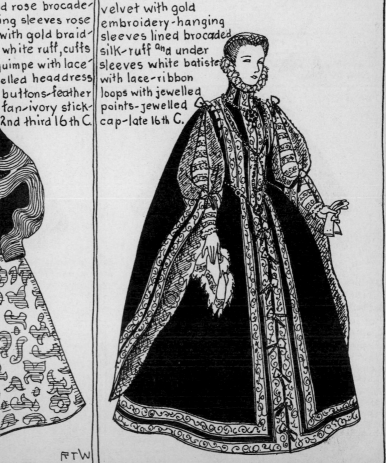

velvet with gold embroidery- hanging sleeves lined brocaded silk- ruff and under sleeves white batiste with lace-ribbon loops with jewelled points- jewelled cap- late 16th C.

FTW

Spain of the 16th Century

ribbon loop with ivory points-last half 16th C.

pearl bands and jewel-early 16th C.

velvet béret over jewelled caul-pearls, ostrich tips and aigrettes-2nd half 16th C.

cap of pearls with aigrettes-ruff of lace edged embroidered-lawn-wired supporting frame-late 16th C.

velvet béret with pearls and ostrich tips-1560

flat velvet béret-early 16th C.

"Spanish blackwork" fine stitching in black-sometimes red and gold added

folding fan of vellum or paper-ivory sticks-second half 16th C.

velvet hat-pearls and jewels-ostrich tips-1585

scented leather fan in permanent folds-ivory handle-middle 16th C.

man's embroidered money pouch suspended from belt-middle 16th C.

man's cloak with hanging sleeves-brocaded silk and embroidery-edged and lined with ermine-pearls on collar and front edges-1560

RTW

Chapter Nineteen

Spain of the Velasquez Portraits

V ELASQUEZ, who painted during the reign of Philip IV, 1621–1665, has left such magnificent portraits of this period, that his name has become definitely associated with the Spanish mode of his time.

The predominant color for both men and women was black in rich fabrics such as velvet and satin, ornamented with much gold and silver, often lightened by the use of white taffeta or lingerie fabric in the sleeves and about the neck. Cerise and vermilion were favorite colors too, with occasionally a costume of white. All-over embroidery of jewels, especially pearls, were lavishly used on the feminine costume, also ribbons, gimp and galloon.

To Philip is accredited the invention of the small, neat collar of thin lingerie fabric mounted over pasteboard. It flared out of the standing collar of the doublet, a sheer round, flat shape with pointed corners, open in front. This small flaring collar was known in English as the "neck whisk" and the lay-down style as the "falling band." Compared with the ruff, it was a tremendous change and improvement in comfort.

Men wore the heavy gold chain necklace and their shoe ties became large bows and rosettes, called shoe roses.

The bell-shaped hoop skirt was still being worn in the 1630's, with the long, pointed corseted bodice. The ruff too, was still the mode, and Velasquez painted a portrait of the Queen Marie-Anne, wearing a ruff of fur instead of lingerie material.

Later, the bell-shaped skirt changed to a hoop skirt of entirely different silhouette, flat front and back, but very wide at the sides. It spread abruptly out from the waist over hips, dropping as abruptly to the floor, creating a decidedly square outline, the width at the floor being as wide as the height of the figure. A circular peplum usually spread out from the waist.

The low, round neckline, horizontal from shoulder to shoulder, bateau-shaped, finished with a flaring bertha, a most artistic effect. In the center front of the bosom was usually placed a large ribbon rosette with an elaborate jewelled brooch.

The women wore many rings. A portrait of the Infanta Maria Théresa shows her wearing the two watches hanging from fobs or cords attached at the waistline. That style became popular later in the other countries, with the difference that the watches were worn, one on each hip.

The hair was dressed flat on top of the head, hanging to the shoulders in extreme fluffiness, continuing the broad width of the silhouette, when seen from back or front. Added to the coiffure, hanging plumes, rosettes and many bowknots helped to give breadth to the contour. Rosettes of ribbon adorned the wrists, and a costly, large, sheer lace-edged handkerchief in the hand completed the picture.

A contemporary writing tells us that when the women married they were permitted to wear high heels and use cosmetics. The Moorish fashion of being veiled in public was observed.

A later distinctive Spanish style, which did not appear until 1790, was the gown and mantilla of black lace. The black silk was imported from Chantilly, France, and called by that name. The high comb, shawl and fan of our day appeared in the nineteenth century.

Spain of the Velasquez Portraits

all black-sheer white "neck whisk" and cuffs-striped silk doublet-velvet "full Spanish slops"-pendant on moiré ribbon-shoulder wings-cloth cape-shoe roses- 1623

gold and pearl sewn black velvet with gold braid-shoulder wings and hanging sleeves-brown fox ruff-large brooch-necklace-jewelled buttons-lace edged handkerchief-1630

velvet with metal cloth and galloon-shirred sheer fabric yoke-jewelled rosette-brooch and chain-headdress in curls-bowknots-flowers-feathers-embroidered hanckerchief-1658

embroidered jerkin with hanging sleeves-over doublet metal tissue-embroidered lingerie "falling band" and cuffs- "Venetians" tied with fringed ribbons-silk stockings-shoe roses-beaver hat with plumes-rapier on sash-middle 17th C.

RTW

Chapter Twenty

Renaissance England
The Tudors

HENRY VII—1485-1509
HENRY VIII—1509-1547

WHILE SIGNS of the Renaissance were evident in the reign of Richard III, the true Renaissance is considered to date from 1485 to 1603, that is during the reigns of the four Tudors.

In the first years of the reign of Henry VII, the medieval mode was still in existence, with the long, fitted stockings and short tunics for men. The women were still wearing the towering hennin or the wired sheer linen arrangement over a cap. The gown was long and full with a slightly fitted bodice, belted high. Ofttimes, the one-piece princess gown was laced in back to give the fitted look.

With the Renaissance years, the masculine tunic, which was short, opened over a waistcoat or stomacher of gorgeous brocaded material. The waistcoat was sometimes laced across in front, or sometimes laced together in back. Above it, at the neck, showed the sheer linen shirt gathered into a narrow frill.

Over the waistcoat was worn the gown or long coat, with loose, full sleeves, slashed to show the tunic sleeve, which in turn was slashed again, revealing the white linen shirt. The long gown was usually belted. When the gown or coat was cut short, it was called a petti-coat. Jerkin was the term for the short fitted jacket.

The long, fitted sewn stockings of every color and design were worn along with the conspicuous pouch or codpiece, embroidered and tied with colored ribbons.

For men, the bob with bangs was the style in hairdressing, with the black velvet hat of béret crown, ornamented with feather and jewel. Shoes had become more practical in design, the same for both men and women, made of cloth, leather and velvet, often embroidered and with ankle straps. Black velvet bands and facings trimmed the costumes of both sexes. Gloves were beautifully embroidered, and in the girdle or sash were carried purse and dagger.

The bell-shaped canvas underskirt, forerunner of the hoop, came to England in this reign. The skirt proper was long and full. The bodice was still slightly fitted with low, square neck, filled in with shirred white linen. Sleeves were of all styles, but principally long, wide and flowing, revealing a contrasting lining and a tight undersleeve. These gowns were often lined with fine fur and draped up in back, held by a button or brooch at the waist, to show the fur. Sometimes the skirt opened in front over a brocaded underskirt, or again the bodice opened V-shaped over a stomacher of handsomely decorated fabric.

A peculiar style of headdress, of English origin, was worn until 1550. Because of its outline, it was called *gable* hood, *kennel* or *pedimental* headdress, and covered the hair entirely. Over a close-fitting cap of linen, gold tissue or velvet, which showed at the forehead, was placed a broad fold of black silk or velvet. This fold, or lappet, was wired into a gable point in center front and fell to the shoulders. The lappet was richly embroidered with jewels and often edged with gold. Over the top of the head and hanging in back, was the *fall,* usually of black silk or velvet. The hair was concealed in silk cases. In a later style, the fall or back piece was often tied back by strings with metal points which were attached at the sides of the headdress. Puffed silk turbans, embroidered with gold and jewels, were also the fashion. The *barbe* was also worn, a biblike pleated piece of white linen passing under the chin and attached to the cap at the side like a gorget.

Fabrics for the costumes of both sexes were covered with a pattern semi-Spanish in design. Gorgeous figured silks and brocades came from the Orient, velvets and gold cloth brocaded in velvet from Venice, silks and satins from Bruges, the finest linen from Ypres and cambric from Cambrai. There were domestic linens, also hand-blocked linens of great beauty.

Necklaces of gold, jewels and beads were worn and the purse continued to be carried in the girdle. A fine, black-silk cord was in vogue for beads, jewelled pendants and the cross.

In the time of Henry VIII, there were two distinct fashions for men, the very square style with padded shoulders, as portrayed in Holbein's paintings, and another, fairly slim. Both, however, were influenced by the German-Swiss fashion of slashings and puffings either in a moderate or extravagant manner. The slashed and puffed sleeves of the masculine and feminine costume grew very large, full and elaborate and an outfit often had several pairs of detachable sleeves. They were attached by means of lacings, with points.

The slimmer costume of the man had a short waistcoat, cut straight across the chest, short at the waist with shirt showing above and below. The space left between waistcoat and breeches was filled in with shirt, the two edges being laced with strips of leather or ribbon having metal points.

The style usually connected with Henry VIII had the long, fitted sewn stockings, slashed and puffed, slashed, square-toed shoes and the elaborately embroidered and slashed tunic of length between thigh and knee, held at the waist by a belt from which hung the dagger. Silk knit stockings from Spain are known to have been presented to Henry VIII. In the opening of the shirt appeared the embroidered and jewelled codpiece of the period.

The collar of the white shirt was either a narrow ruffle or a narrow straight piece, embroidered in black silk. The latter had strings which were either tied or left hanging. Ruffles showed at the wrists, and if the tunic, jacket or jerkin was open in front, the shirt front ornamented with "Spanish blackwork" was revealed. This black silk embroidery, often combined with gold and red stitching on white linen, was of ancient Persian origin and its vogue lasted for more than a hundred years.

The handkerchiefs of Henry VIII were of Holland lawn, edged with gold fringe from Venice and embroidered in red and white silk.

Men and women wore several rings on the thumb, first and last fingers of both hands and heavy jewelled necklaces around their necks. They carried the perfumed and embroidered gloves of the time.

About 1521, short hair came in with the cropped beard and mustache; in fact, this French style was rigorously enforced at the court of Henry VIII. The béret hat continued in vogue.

In women's costume, the skirt now worn over a larger hoop, opened over a handsome kirtle or underskirt of embroidered satin or brocaded velvet of a contrasting color from the rest of the gown or cotte. The bodice still had the low square neck, but the sleeves had very wide cuffs, sometimes turned back, which were of black or colored velvet, of fur or gold net.

The gable or diamond-shaped headdress which now permitted the hair over the forehead to show, had become much more elaborate, with the fall and lappets caught up on top and stiffened into shape. Then came the smaller hood, known as the French hood, which left the front hair uncovered. The back hair was always concealed in a bag of black velvet, called the *cale*. The bonnetlike fold of velvet or satin was placed over a small cap or coif of white linen or gold net, edged with embroidery, gimp or jewels. Women also wore the béret-crowned hat, with narrow brim like that of the man, but placed over the cap.

The ruffles of the chemise appeared at the wrists. Sometimes the bodice opened over a rich stomacher, which was occasionally crossed with lacings.

There were long capes, open in front, and voluminous cloaks with the large puffed sleeves, very much like the men's. Only the royal were permitted to wear genet, a species of civet; only those above the rank of viscount could wear sable and to wear martin or velvet one had to be worth over two hundred marks a year.

The first mention of a nightgown is of that worn by Anne Boleyn, which was of black satin trimmed with black velvet. Perfume was excessively used, even such accessories as gloves, fans and shoes being saturated with it. The perfumed leather fan mounted on a carved ivory stick remained the favorite.

Queen Catherine used pins imported from France. That useful article came from France till about 1626, when the manufacture of pins was introduced into England. The pin was a fairly costly gadget in those days, whence the origin of the term "pin money."

Renaissance England

full white shirt-red stomacher or waistcoat-blue jacket with slashed sleeves-particolored tights with codpiece-gown brocaded cloth-cloth collar-felt hat with jewel-leather belt and shoes-around 1500

velvet gown-slashed sleeves lined with ermine-jacket with ermine-felt hat with brooch-jewelled necklace-late 15th C.

German-English-white shirt-yellow jerkin and tights laced together-slashings and puffings-black velvet bands, hat and shoes-blue velvet gown-1st half 16th C.

velvet gown-satin revers with braid-cloth jacket-white shirt with Spanish blackwork-dagger with tassel-silk tights-codpiece-slashed shoes-velvet hat with feather and jewel -1540

RTW

Renaissance England

rose silk and velvet brocade-brown fur-gold galloon panel-shirred white neck with black velvet edge-jewelled gable-black velvet fall and lappets-around 1500

red velvet and gray blue brocade-wide cuffs of gold network-slashed undersleeves with embroidered frills-gable hood of white with black velvet, gold ribbon, pearls and emeralds-same jewels in necklace and girdle-1536.

dark green velvet-pearl sewn bands-embroidered white yoke and undersleeves-gold belt and buckle-cap sheer white with pearls and gems-gold brocade vestee-1539

cloth mantle with fur collar-cord and jewelled buttons-gable hood black velvet, gold ribbon, jewelled frame-2nd quarter 16th C.

RTW

Renaissance England

gable hood - black velvet lappets and fall - white cap - pearls and jewels - around 1500

man's shirt collar - Spanish blackwork and tie strings - 2nd quarter 16th C.

felt cap with jewelled ornament - late 15th C.

gable hood with pinned up lappets - black velvet fall - pearl trimmed - 1530 - back view to right

gable hood with pinned up lappets and fall - pearl sewn - 1528

black velvet béret - white plume - topaz ornaments - pearls on chains - tied shirt collar - Spanish blackwork - 1537

back view gable hood - lappets with square crown - front view to left

slashed glove - 1549

velvet béret with white plume over jewelled and embroidered cap - 2nd quarter 16th C.

sheer white cap - wired edge - seed pearls and colored gems - over embroidered coif - jewelled rosette with bead fringe - 1539

velvet béret - jewel and tiny gold loops - 1536

wrist frill - Spanish blackwork

white cap with gold framework - fluted ribbon next to hair - black velvet fall - 2nd quarter 16th C.

RTW

Chapter Twenty=one

Renaissance England The Tudors

EDWARD VI—1547–1553
MARY—1553–1558
ELIZABETH—1558–1603

URING THE SIX YEARS' reign of Edward VI, costume lost much of its ornamentation and slashing. The square outline of the masculine costume waned and shoes were designed more to the shape of the foot. The cloaks of men and women had hanging sleeves. Record has it that Edward VI was presented with a pair of silk stockings from Spain by one of his lords. The flat velvet béret with narrow brim continued to be worn, with the end of its vogue in sight for the fashionable world. It has remained the headgear of the Beefeaters of the Tower of London to the present day. Men and women wore velvet nightcaps.

The marriage of Philip II of Spain to Mary brought about the Spanish influence in dress. Men adopted the narrow-brimmed bag hat with shirred high crown, all of black velvet, the small ruff, the short mustache and the clipped beard. The short cape came in with its standing collar and the notch (its first appearance) at the junction of collar and front. Gowns or cloaks, too, had standing collars, hanging leg-of-mutton sleeves and a skirt length which covered trunks and doublet

126

skirts underneath. The vogue of the boot was in the making. Boots reached to the knee or stopped halfway up with turned-back cuffs.

Women's gowns had changed little, were simpler, with higher necks. Embroidered flaring collars were of linen or silk, usually white, sometimes with a wired edge. The hair was dressed simply, parted in the middle and knotted in the back, tending to be puffed at the temples. Hoods grew smaller, short at the sides and in back. The jewelled girdle with rosary or mirror at the end was worn, and small bouquets of flowers were carried in the hand or tucked into the neck of the bodice. The skirt flared open in front to show an embroidered or brocaded velvet petticoat of contrasting color. In jewelry, there were heavy gold chains, large jewelled pendants, rings and buttons. Gold and jewelled buttons by the dozens were worn by men and women.

In Elizabeth's time, the Spanish influence of the previous reign evolved into a definite style. Men wore Venetian breeches, full at the top, narrowing to the knee, paned, slashed or puffed, French breeches were tight, but done in horizontal puffs, and the short, full-padded trunk hose.

Trunk hose were the very short puffs which covered the thighs and were often made in one with the stockings. There is much confusion over the name "trunk hose." While the garment itself was of Spanish origin, there was a definite German influence in the mode at that time, and the name appears to be from the German, hose, or *hosen,* signifying drawers, breeches or trousers, thus "trunk hose." The later unpadded trunk hose were termed "Spanish slops," and the very full breeches bagging at the knees "full slops."

Pockets were inserted in the lining. Canions, those leg coverings which filled in the space between stockings and trunk hose, were also worn. Stockings which met the breeches at the knees were called netherstocks, and the breeches upperstocks. Stockings were of yarn, silk or wool, clocked at the ankles in various patterns, and in gold and silver thread. Clocks are the remains of the fitted seams, concealed by embroidery. Ribbon garters, tied just below the knees, held the stockings in place.

There was the fitted doublet with short skirt, and the "peasecod bellied" doublet of Spanish origin with its padded long-pointed projecting front. Both were slashed and embroidered. The Englishman appears to have adopted a less extreme version of the doublet with wooden busk and overhanging point than his Continental neighbor. At the neck there was a linen collar edged with lace, perhaps two small collars or a ruff. The small, detachable collar, which came from Spain and was worn by both sexes, came to be known as the partlet, or partlet strip. The doublet armscye was ornamented with wings, and the sleeves were tied into it by means of points.

The hair was short, accompanied by a trim mustache and beard, sometimes a beard with two points. Hats were of various shapes, narrow brims with high or low crowns, trimmed with bands of silk, wool, shirred lace, gold and jewelled chains and plumes. From this period dates the popularity of beaver felt for hats and the tendency toward the broad-brimmed Jacobean headpiece is apparent. Shoes became extravagant parts of the costumes, ornamented with embroidery, lace and jewels. They were shaped to the foot, tied with shoe roses and often had red heels. Boots reached to the ankles or to the knees, held up by leather straps.

Both men and women began to use lace, which is supposed to have been introduced into England by Catherine of Aragon. There were imported Italian lace and bone-bobbin lace made at Honiton. Large earrings were in fashion, worn principally by the men.

Gowns or cloaks and capes were worn, with a long, plain cape for travelling. The short Spanish cape for men was the most fashionable, often made of perfumed leather. Gloves, too, were made of perfumed leather, embroidered and fringed for both men and women. Although worn in Italy and France for several centuries and at the court of Henry VIII, the perfumed glove did not become the vogue in England until this period. The scented fan was taken up and perfumes were freely used.

In Elizabeth's reign the hoop or wheel farthingale and the ruff grew to exaggerated proportions, with the steel and buckram corset a definite feature of the mode. The corset consisted of two garments, an under one of buckram, which was laced tightly over the body, then a case of sheet steel, which opened on hinges at one side and was fastened by hooks on the other. It was perforated with a decorative design and encased in velvet. It sometimes formed the bodice proper, or was covered with the stomacher of the gown.

The Spanish ruff began as a cambric collar, became larger, more pleated and then wired. A wired support was called the *underproper,* or *supportasse.*

Handkerchiefs, which were still a luxury, and carried conspicuously by men and women, were of cambric or silk. They were trimmed with lace, some were stitched with blue, while others were fashioned of cut-work embroidery.

Calico, which came from Calcutta, India, was new in this period.

There were two styles of gowns, the exaggerated silhouette with long, pointed bodice and wheel farthingale, the other with moderate hoop and moderately fitted bodice. The skirt of the latter opened in front over a petticoat of contrasting color, richly embroidered and trimmed with gimp and fringe. Several linen petticoats were worn. Both styles had a low, straight décolletage with either a fan-shaped collar or a ruff. Sleeves were full, tight at the wrists and finished with lingerie cuffs or ruffles. False hanging sleeves and separate sleeves were the fashion, which were laced to the armscye with points.

The wired wings of the shell-like shaped wrap, which rose in back above the shoulders, were worn, with the long ends hanging to the floor. The very low décolletage, which bared the bosom, introduced by Catherine de' Medici, was also affected. In England, it was worn by maiden ladies, the queen wearing it in her later years. Quantities of pearls and precious stones were added to the costume.

Feminine hats, like those of the men, had brims and a feather, the crown encircled by a band or necklace. Lawn caps were of all shapes and close to the head. Velvet nightcaps continued to be worn. A particular style of bonnet is that known to us as the "Mary Stuart cap," of cambric and lace, wired into shape, its feature being the dip over the forehead.

False hair and wigs dressed with jewels, glass ornaments or feathers, were in vogue. Red and blond were the favorite colors, and in this period hair was often dyed red in compliment to the Queen's red hair, since Elizabeth set the fashion at her court. Powder and rouge were used. Little balls of scent, encased in gold or silver, sometimes enamelled and set with jewels, hung from girdle or rosary, also the fan and looking glass. The little ball was called a dry-scent box, or pomander. All accessories of costume, such as gloves, handkerchiefs, ruffs, fans and bags were scented. Beautiful feather fans were carried and the black velvet mask was worn in the street and to the theatre.

Elizabeth, like Catherine de' Medici and Mary Stuart, wore a slipper with a high heel. It is in this period that the low-cut shoe or slipper first appears, and "pumps" are mentioned for the first time. Shoes had cork soles, the uppers of leather or velvet, stamped with designs or embroidered in gold or silver. It is also stated that Elizabeth was the first Englishwoman to wear silk stockings. Perhaps silk stockings and the new heel were *la raison d'être* of the ankle-length gown seen in several of the Queen's portraits. From this time on, women began to wear the costly hand-knitted silk stockings, decorated with clocks in gold, silver and color. Red stockings were fashionable, worn with red or blue slippers.

The first knitting machine for stockings was invented by an Englishman, William Lee, in 1589. Ignored by Elizabeth and offered patronage by Henri IV, he established himself at Rouen with success. His workmen returned to England with the invention after his death and the assassination of Henri IV.

As on the Continent, chopines, pattens or clogs and pantoffles were worn over the shoes of both men and women, when outdoors. The Venetian chopine was less popular than the patten. Pattens and pantoffles were also used in the American Colonies. Chopines had stilts from four to as high as seven inches, pattens had wooden or cork soles, while pantoffles, with their cork soles, had only front uppers.

In this period, no person, unless of royalty, was permitted to wear crimson, except in underclothes, and the use of velvet, for sleeves only, was allowed the middle classes. In all, it was an era of great richness, extravagance and overdressing.

Elizabeth, in her many regulations pertaining to overdressing, issued a decree forbidding the wearing of "cut or pansied hose, or bryches, and of pansied doublets," which leads one to consider that the origin of the descriptive word "pansy" might perhaps be a result of this law and thus of early origin.

Renaissance England

doublet with buttons
galloon and embroidery
paned trunk-hose
with cutwork-silk
stockings-ribbon
garters-shoe-roses-
braided leather belts-
rapier-bag hat-
jewelled band-ostrich-
jewelled necklace
with pendant-1567

padded
satin doublet
with peasecod
front and buttons-
jerkin with paned
wings and skirt-
points untied-
knotted cord
round neck-
Venetians with
paned frills-slashed
shoes-sword
1572

bag hat with ostrich
and jewelled band-
neck ribbon with
pendant-mandillion
of velvet, taffeta and
gold braid-embroid-
ered doublet with
wings-embroidered
paned trunk hose-
wrinkled taffeta
canions-ribbon cross-
garters-pantoffles
over light colored
shoes-1575

black taffeta
doublet, trunk hose
and canions-cord-
ings-neck whisk
and cuffs with
point lace-
beaded belt-
jewel on cord-
beaver hat with
crêpe band-
pantoffles over
shoes-1597

RTW

Renaissance England

velvet gown-brocaded
undergown-sleeve
straps with jewelled
buttons-jewelled
girdle-jewelled
mirror on silk cord
black velvet hood
with white lawn
and pearls-collars-
embroidered
pearl sewn
gloves-1554

velvet gown-
embroidered and
jewelled petti-
coat-pearl sewn
galloon-cap, ruff,
yoke of white
lawn-white
plaid gauze
mantle with
wired edge-
point lace-
pendant on
ribbon-
jewelled
girdle with
mirror-
satin
slippers
1560's

rose satin cloak-
fox collar-gold
buttons-leather belt-
quilted yellow gown-
red sleeves-white
lawn yoke and ruff-
black felt hat-
crown in folds-
blue ostrich
1590

queen's gown-velvet with
jewels, pearls, gold braid
loops-oriental satin
petticoat, stomacher
and slippers-mantle
and ruff white
gauze, point
lace and pearls-
wired wings-
wig with jewels-
jewelled feather
fan-pearl
sewn gloves-
knotted pearl
necklace-
end of
16th C.

RTW

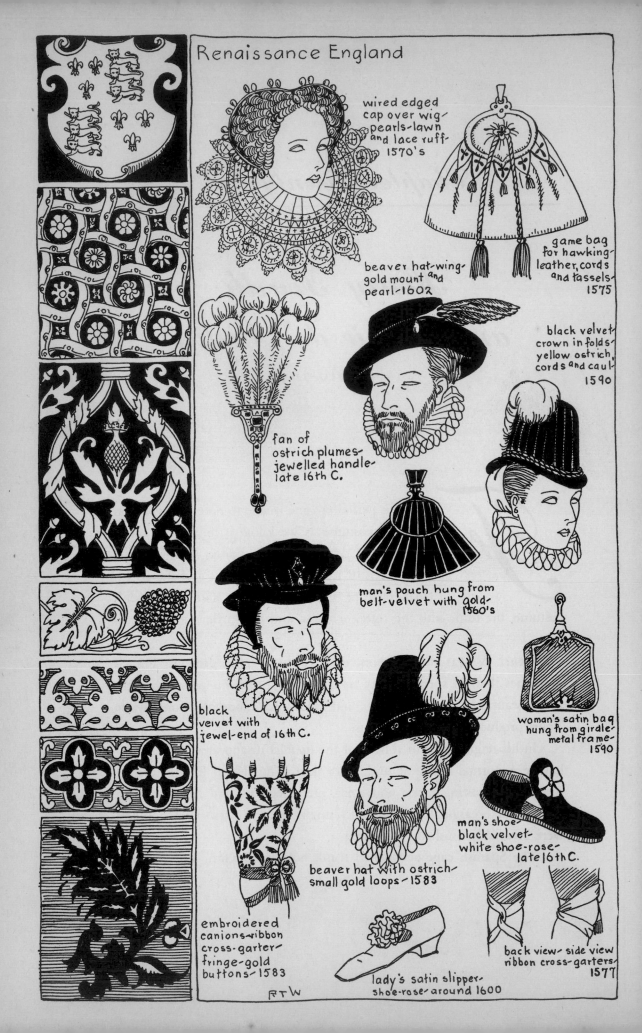

Renaissance England

wired edged cap over wig-pearls-lawn and lace ruff- 1570's

game bag for hawking- leather, cords and tassels 1575

beaver hat-wing- gold mount and pearl-1602

black velvet crown in folds- yellow ostrich cords and caul- 1590

fan of ostrich plumes- jewelled handle- late 16th C.

man's pouch hung from belt-velvet with gold- 1560's

black velvet with jewel-end of 16th C.

woman's satin bag hung from girdle- metal frame- 1590

man's shoe- black velvet- white shoe-rose- late 16th C.

embroidered canions-ribbon cross-garter- fringe-gold buttons-1583

beaver hat with ostrich- small gold loops- 1583

lady's satin slipper- shoe-rose-around 1600

back view-side view ribbon cross-garters 1577

RTW

Chapter Twenty=two

Henry Fourth
and Marie de' Medici

1589-1610-1617

F ROM this period on, one is able to note the evolution of men's costume as we know it today; the tunic, pourpoint or doublet into the vest or waistcoat, the justaucorps or jerkin into the jacket and the gown, cloak or cape into the topcoat; and in women's costume, the tunic into the cotte, or dress, and the kirtle into the petticoat.

Henri IV was more interested in furthering the growing French industries than in spending any time or thought on his personal wardrobe. Beautiful brocades, velvets and silks were made at Lyons, while Tours produced the heavy taffetas.

In his reign, the stuffed beak of the doublet disappeared, the doublet having a normal waistline and short skirt. The sleeves of the doublet were of contrasting fabric and color, often separate and laced on with points, but occasionally the doublet might be sleeveless. The shoulders were invariably finished with wings.

The Spanish cape and paned trunk hose were worn, also "Spanish slops" and "full slops." The full breeches reaching to the knees were tied with ribbon garters, which had lace ends, for lace was now in vogue for both men and women. Pockets were inserted in the lining of the breeches.

The courtier wore elbow-length gauntlet gloves of velvet or satin, silk or gold fringed, with backs embroidered or sewn with jewels. Riding gloves were of doeskin. Men's shoes now took on high heels and the front fastening of the low-cut shoe was covered with a huge shoe rose. High-dress boots of Russian leather were introduced, made by craftsmen who had been sent to Hungary to learn the art of dressing leather. These boots appeared in the salon and at balls. Turkish and Spanish morocco leathers were also used for boots. Leggings were in use, worn to protect the fragile and costly silk stocking. For country wear, they were of velvet with gold and silver embroidery; and of leather, for horseback riding.

The baldric, or shoulder sash of satin, was the fashion for both men and women, white being for the King only. The sword hung from a narrow leather belt. Henri IV is recorded as the first owner of an especially designed walking stick.

The costumes of both sexes were in all colors, but in subtle and beautiful shades, and for the first time we note that colors were given descriptive and fantastic names. The most distinguished masculine costume was of velvet.

Worn in the early part of the reign was a hat of felt with narrow brim and tall crown, ornamented with a band, jewel and plumes. Around 1600, from America came beaver pelts for the costly beaver hat with wide and rolling brim and crown of moderate height. Hats of castor, the European species of beaver, had been imported from Flanders before this period.

Henri IV permitted all styles of hair and beard. The hair was moderately short, with trim mustache and cropped beard. Lovelocks appeared, a long, plaited length of hair on one side, with a ribbon tied at the end.

The hoop, verdingale or farthingale grew to enormous proportions in this reign, spreading out straight from the waist, creating a cylindrical drumlike shape or, again, wide at the sides and flat front and back The hoop, or foundation-skirt was of canvas or heavy linen, with hoops of wood or steel. Over it and tied round the hips was placed the round bolster. Three elaborately trimmed and embroidered petticoats of contrasting colors were worn under the skirt proper.

Women wore the corset or stomacher to acquire the figure of the period. First, laced very tightly, was a bodice of heavy linen, over which was placed a steel case or garment, hinged on one side and fastened on the other by clasps. This "armor" was perforated in a most intricate design and encased in velvet. It sometimes formed the outside bodice or stomacher of the gown, in which case it was covered with elaborate embroidery.

To silk and jewel-encrusted embroideries were added lace and ribbons.

Lingerie ruffs, ruffles, bands and cuffs finished the neck and wrists of the bodice. The lace-edged ruff of the earlier part of the period opened into a standing fan-shaped frill, high in the back with low décolletage. This collar is known as the Medici collar and was accompanied by cuffs to match. The mantle of sheer material, with wired wings which rose above the shoulders continued to be worn and the false hanging sleeves were still in evidence.

Gowns for state occasions were intricately embroidered with gold, silver, pearls and other gems. Watches became the fashion, long ropes of pearls were worn, also pendant earrings and rings.

The riding habit of Marguerite de Valois, first wife of Henri IV, was of black velvet faced with cloth of gold, with which she wore a plumed hat having a diamond aigrette.

Marie de' Medici, second wife of the King, wore slippers of Spanish Moroccan leather, with high heels connected with the sole by a platform. With them she wore knitted silk stockings imported from Spain and Italy. They were red, orange or purple and embroidered with French lilies or the Medici crest.

Women dressed their hair high off the forehead, waved and rolled over a pad, usually in a heart-shaped silhouette. False hair was used, and for a while wigs were worn in blond and brown. Powder for wigs was used in the form of starch mixed with pomade and perfumed with violet or iris, violet for brunettes and iris for blonds. The hair was often sprinkled with jewels. The fashion of wearing a jewel on a fine gold chain in the middle of the forehead was originated by one of the mistresses of Henri IV, la Belle Ferronniére. The "Mary Stuart cap" was worn in its many versions.

Paint, powder and beauty patches adorned the feminine face. Beauty patches of black taffeta were the fashion, and in public the mask of black taffeta was worn, the velvet mask being permitted to women of quality only. Masks in those days served as a protection against the hot sun and were worn both when walking and when horseback riding. Embroidered and lace-edged handkerchiefs were carried.

From Italy came beautiful fabrics and laces, especially Venetian point, also the parasol, which did not become popular. From Spain and the Orient were imported perfumes, sachets and rare scents. During this reign there were periodic restrictions against the excessive importation of luxuries, which took money out of France.

The perfumed gloves known as "Frangipani gloves" continued in vogue. Like those of the men, satin and velvet gloves fringed with gold, silver or silk were worn by women at court and doeskin ones of elbow length for the hunt. Colored furs were permitted to the nobility only, while black was decreed to the bourgeoisie. Muffs were carried in the winter and fans in the summer. The latter were made of ornamented silk, sheepskin and goatskin, but the most fashionable and costly were of ostrich plumes mounted on gold, silver or carved ivory handles.

To assure the prosperity of the silkworm culture, Henri IV ordered extensive planting of mulberry bushes.

After the death of Henri IV, it is noted for the first time in history that the mode in costume was indulged in by the middle class.

Henri IV and Marie de Medici

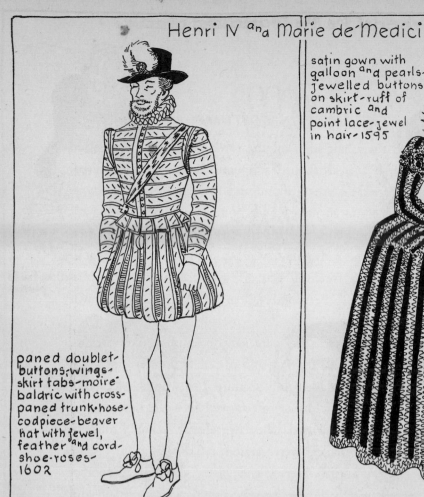

paned doublet-
buttons-wings-
skirt tabs-moiré-
baldric with cross-
paned trunk-hose-
codpiece-beaver
hat with jewel,
feather and cord-
shoe-roses-
1602

satin gown with
galloon and pearls-
jewelled buttons
on skirt-ruff of
cambric and
point lace-jewel
in hair-1595

taffeta with wheel
verdingale-wired fan
shaped pleated collar-
point lace-corded
puffed sleeves-contrasting-
colored corded petticoat-
pearl necklaces-
jewelled hair
ornament with
aigrette-late
16thC

doublet with
wings and remains
of hanging sleeves-
buttons-skirt tabs-
falling ruff-"slops"
Russian leather boots
with spur leathers-
baldric sash-sword-
beaver hat with
plumes-1st quarter
17th C.

RTW

Henri IV and Marie de' Medici

soldier's hat worn until 1600 - embroidery and ostrich plumes

tucked cambric cuff - lace edged handkerchief - pearls

felt hat with plumes

leather boot which buttoned to trunks - spur and spur leathers

beaver hat with jewels and plumes

heart shaped coiffure with topknot and a jewel

turned down collar attached to shirt

black velvet cap with pearls - white cambric ruff

embroidered and fringed doeskin glove

felt hat with applique motifs - cord - jewel - ostrich tips

man's leather shoe - cork sole and heel - jewelled shoe - rose

beaver hat - crushed ribbon band - ostrich tips

Chapter Twenty-three

Louis Thirteenth

1610–1643

T HIS is an important period in costume because, during it, France definitely established herself as arbiter of the mode. The first part of the reign was still given to elaboration and overindulgence in rich fabrics and embroideries, but with Richelieu's ban in 1625 against the importation of gold and silver cloth, galloons, passementeries and velvet brocades from Italy and Spain, costume took on a rich simplicity. Then followed, in 1633 and 1634, an edict against the wearing of gold or silver galloons, lace passementerie or embroidery.

Garments were fashioned of French fabrics, such as the plain but heavy satins and velvets and simpler patterned materials in more neutral tones. The new thread laces and embroideries began gradually to usurp the position held by rich embroideries. About this time, ribbon as we know it, a narrow band of silk with two selvedges, became fashionable. Lace, as a trimming, became very important, especially for the edge of the wide flat collar or falling band, known as the Louis XIII collar.

In the early part of the reign, men still wore the doublet with corseted body and the deep-busked point in front, shoulder wings and short skirt. A lace-edged ruff finished the neck and sleeves. The sleeves were usually slashed. In breeches, Spanish slops or full slops were worn, with ribbon garters tied at the knees and edged with points, lace or fringe. Trunk hose, except as livery for pages, had gone out of fashion. Pockets, which were vertical linings, braid-bound, were placed near the waist to either side of the front of the breeches.

With the seventeenth century came the development of the "Cavalier fashion," elegant in color and cut. The corseted shape was discarded and the doublet became a waistcoat with sleeves, while the ruff changed to a whisk, a falling ruff, a turned-down collar or falling band of fine lawn or cambric edged with lace. The sleeves and upper part of the doublet were often slashed, revealing the shirt, also of fine lawn or cambric. Occasionally, the doublet was buttoned from the neck to a few inches below, opening over the shirt. The doublet was often buttoned down center back. The shirt became of great importance, very full in body and sleeve, and of lingerie fabric. The shirt showed through a long slit in the back of the doublet and in the open front seam of the sleeve.

Neckpieces were tied in front with "band strings," which were cords or strings with tassels of yarn, silk or ribbon attached to the ends. A distinct style feature in neckwear was the falling band of sheer white fabric without the lace edge, made familiar in the portrait of Richelieu by Philippe de Champaigne. Bands diminished in size from about 1640.

The cravat, which was to enjoy such a long vogue from the next reign on, originated in this period. It appeared in 1636, a length of folded white linen, lawn or mull, tied loosely around the neck, its ends finished with lace. It was founded upon the custom of the Cravates, or Croats, serving in the French army, who wore a like fashion, a cloth muffled about the neck as a protection for the throat. A bow was added later. Dating from this period, the neck of the "well-dressed man" has never gone without a scarf or cravat in some form.

The baldric, or satin sash, tied from left hip to right shoulder, continued to be worn.

Ribbons and points now became ornaments instead of fastenings, large metal hooks and eyes supplanting them. However, points were functional and ornamental in the front closing of breeches. Brandenburgs, an innovation in both fastening and ornament, appeared in this period. They were horizontal strips of braid or loops with buttons or frogs, and originated on the jackets of the German Brandenburgers.

Breeches were moderately full, descending to below the knee, where they were tied with ribbons, or finished with a ruche of ribbon loops called *cannons*.

Short leather boots, of Spanish origin, with falling tops, became the fashion about 1625. They were of soft leather in very light colors, such as buff, beige, yellow, pale blue, a favorite being white. The fashionable stocking was of knitted red Milanese silk, and in winter several pairs were worn, one over the other. Worn between the boot and the silk stocking were boot hose of heavy linen finished with a deep, lace-edged or embroidered cuff. The cuff was turned down over the top of the boot, permitting the variegated colored loops or cannons of the breeches to show. Spurs were worn and the accompanying spur leathers grew in size and shape. Boots and spurs were not confined to the out-of-doors but were worn indoors and even at balls. Shoes with high red heels and red soles were in vogue and pantoffles continued in fashion. Shoes became long and narrow, with square toes, and took on very large and costly ribbon shoe roses centered with jewels.

Slightly longer capes, with a broad, square collar or none at all, were draped about the figure in every conceivable manner and were called manteaux instead of capes. Two cords, sewn inside the collar and tied around one shoulder, made it possible to hold the garment in place. The cassock, a loose greatcoat, had big sleeves, usually three-quarter length, with turned-back cuffs. Capes and coats had rich linings which were displayed by turning back the wrap.

The large felt or beaver hat, with sweeping or cocked brim, which style originated in Flanders, had one or more ostrich feathers with long flues, "weeping plumes," they were called. It was worn over waved and curled hair, parted in the middle and flowing to the shoulders. This style brought about the wearing of wigs, which were definitely accepted about 1600. The *cadenette,* or lovelock, a long curl or strand over one shoulder, was worn by the cavalier. It was often tied with a ribbon or a string with a rosette at one end. Hats were worn indoors until 1685. A large pearl earring often adorned the masculine left ear.

The beard, which had been banned by Henri III and again permitted by Henri IV, was worn by magistrates and ecclesiastics to Richelieu's time, who then authorized the wearing of a small chin beard only.

A long ebony stick with ivory top, often tied with ribbons, was carried by the King. The wearing of galloons, plumes, boots or spurs was not permitted the bourgeoisie.

The modish woman of the period wore a chemise, a corset, then several petticoats over the verdingale, or hoop. The hoop had grown smaller but continued to be worn until 1630. Over that was the gown, consisting of skirt and bodice or stomacher, with sleeves of light-colored satin or other fabric. And, over that, a robe or sort of redingote of darker or contrasting colored material, opened the full length in front. The robe usually had slashed sleeves showing the undersleeves. This robe was invariably worn until 1645. The outer robe was called *la modeste,* and when there were two skirts the outer one was called *la friponne* ("hussy," in English), the under one *la secret.*

An important style of the Louis XIII period was the looped-up outer skirt, adopted principally by the bourgeoisie. The overskirt was drawn up at the sides or sometimes drawn to the front and pinned in place.

The bodice of both robe and gown were in separate parts. The décolletage was low, straight across, round or pointed, with the moderate ruff or fan-shaped collar. From then on the gown changed, the hoop disappeared, the corset became less confining, with the bosom left free. The bodice was high-waisted, with a short peplum opening over a round-pointed stomacher and sometimes the bodice was laced in back. Wide lingerie collars and cuffs always finished the gown, and occasionally lace-trimmed aprons were added. The lace-edged collar or falling band was made popular by Anne of Austria, wife of Louis XIII.

The headdress, also introduced by Anne of Austria, had a fringe across the forehead, with the side hair cut short and hanging in ringlets over the ears, the remainder drawn to a knot at the back of the head. Out of doors, fashion decreed that the head be bare, only the bourgeoisie wearing hats. Veils and kerchieflike hoods of lace or dark-colored fabric were worn, sometimes tied under the chin. Hats, resembling those of the men, wide-brimmed and ornamented with plumes, were worn when hunting. An odd, cagelike hood of wired chiffon enveloped the head and shoulders, when in mourning. See Page 166.

Shoes were of satin or Moroccan leather, with high heels and usually worn with rose-colored stockings. Slippers developed flaps in front like the masculine shoe and were tied above the instep. New were pattens of crimson velvet with very thick soles, presumably of cork.

Capes were worn in winter, but the gowns were heavily lined with weight enough to require no wraps. Long kid gloves and fur muffs were in fashion. The vogue of the perfumed leather gauntlet continued. In this reign Marquis Frangipani, a descendant of Count Frangipani of "perfumed-glove fame," discovered that, by treating solid scents with alcohol, a perfume could be produced in liquid form. Beauty patches and masks of taffeta continued in the mode, with velvet still reserved to ladies of quality. Cosmetics were freely applied to the face, producing an artificial effect. The fan became very popular, in use by both men and women, the folding style being the favorite, hand-painted on vellum or silk. Jewelry was sparingly worn, while from the belt were suspended the small mirror and the perfume box.

The umbrella, of Italian name, fashionable in Italy at this time, does not appear to have been taken up in France until the next reign. It was carried by the individual whom it shaded, was of leather, folded, and when carried by horsemen was attached to the hip.

Louis XIII

slashed doublet-
falling ruff-
wings-buttons-
paned sleeves-
and breeches-
plaited leather
belt and straps-
fringed gauntlets
with braid-beaver
hat with plumes-
1620's

cavalier
wearing wig-
falling band tied with
bandstrings-slashed
sleeves-frogs, buttons
braid loops-breeches
tied with tasseled
strings-cannons at
knees-linen and
lace boot hose-spur
leathers with ribbon
rosettes-embroidered
gauntlets-1630's

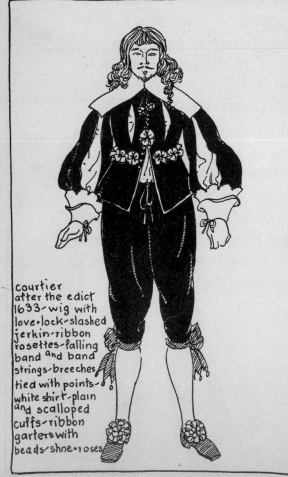

courtier
after the edict
1633-wig with
love-lock-slashed
jerkin-ribbon
rosettes-falling
band and band
strings-breeches
tied with points-
white shirt-plain
and scalloped
cuffs-ribbon
garters with
beads-shne-roses

slashed jerkin-
falling band-
wings-paned
sleeves-bowknots
with points-gimp
and buttons-leather
baldric-breeches tied
with points-slashed
spur leathers-fringed
braided gauntlets
beaver hat with
plume-love-lock-1630

RTW

three different fabrics-
tucked and embroidered
lingerie collar and double
cuffs-tied oversleeves-
paned undersleeves-
ribbon belt- button
trimming-rosette
on bosom-ostrich
tip in hair-velvet
mask-pearl
necklaces-
1620's

taffeta and brocade-
tucked and lace edged
lingerie collar, yoke
and cuffs-pinned up
overskirt-kerchief
hood-fur and
fabric muff-
necklace, rosary
and watch-
1620's

taffeta over satin-
slashed sleeves-
lingerie collar, yoke and
cuffs-shirred ribbon
on bodice and sleeves-
gimp on stomacher
and underskirt-
ribbon rosette on
bosom-knitted
cap-mirror-
vanity case-
1630's

cloth with lingerie
collar, yoke and
cuffs-slashed
sleeves-rosette
at bosom and
belt-cord with
bag-kerchief
hood-after
1633

RTW

Louis XIII

painted vellum fan

slashed felt hat with plumes

beaver hat with ostrich plumes-falling band-wig-love-lock with rosette

wig with love-lock and rosette-falling band with band strings

man's shoe and pantoffle-shoe-rose

first form of the cravat

felt hat-love-lock-falling band

hunting hat-beaver with ostrich plumes

hair dressed with ribbon bows

woman's striped silk slipper-red heel-red velvet pantoffle

red calotte or skullcap-falling band-band strings

braid and ringlets

head covering for street wear

cassock

embroidered linen boot hose-patten

pattern of circular cape-strings tied around shoulder

leather boot-extra sole-red heel

RTW

Chapter Twenty=four

England Under James First and Charles First

1603–1625
1625–1649

HE MODE of this period was founded upon French influence, brought about, no doubt, by the relationship of the English and French ruling class. Some of the wild extravagance of the preceding reign was now discarded.

The stiff doublet had a more normal waistline in position and girth, with a short skirt and shoulder puffs or wings. Sleeves were of self material or contrasting fabric and color, sometimes paned, finished with a turned-back cuff. The small ruff was still worn, but newer was a large collar of sheer linen or lawn-edged with exquisite lace, as were the cuffs. The rich embroideries were replaced by the new thread laces and white embroidery. The collar, or "band," was usually tied in front with strings or ribbons finished with small tassels, called "band strings." The pleats, or "pinches," of the ruff were often formed by pinning. Yellow starch from France stiffened the ruff or collar, but other colors were also used, such as red, blue, purple and green.

Breeches were very full, unpadded and bagging at the knees or sometimes moderately full at the top and tight over the knees, where they either buttoned or tied with ribbon garters, ending in a bunch of ribbon loops. Shoes with costly jewelled ribbon shoe roses were worn, but high, soft leather boots in pale colors and white were popular too. The knitted stockings were of silk, worsted and thread, yellow being a favorite color.

Mustache and hair were not as trim as in the preceding period, the hair being of moderate length. Beaver hats had been imported from Flanders for more than two centuries, but it remained for the beautiful pelts from America to create the tremendous vogue for the costly beaver hat. The style of this period had a tall, tapering crown with rolling brim of moderate width, ornamented with a band and plumes. The band was either cord, ribbon or a jewelled necklace. Men wore their hats indoors and out, at church and at table, and the custom held throughout the seventeenth century.

The full cape reached almost to the knees and embroidered gloves were worn. The sword hung from the belt and a new and important accessory was a small tobacco box with an inserted looking glass. Another new accessory was the gold-and-ivory-headed cane. Both sexes were lavish in their use of jewelry, wearing earrings and favoring diamonds and pearls.

The verdingale, vardingale, farthingale or Catherine-wheel made of whalebone, was still being worn along with the long and tapering waist. Sometimes, two Catherine-wheels were worn over the elaborately embroidered underskirt. The full drum-shaped hoop skirt cleared the floor, often ankle-length, revealing satin shoes with high heels and fastened with large shoe roses. Sleeves fitted the arm, ending in lace-edged cuffs and often there were long-hanging dummy oversleeves. Ruffs were still in evidence, but, when the neck of the gown was low in front, it usually had the wired, fan-shaped collar edged with lace. Sometimes the décolletage was cut below the bosom in England, a sign of maidenhood. Then came the round or "Dutch waist."

For both sexes there was a vogue for white in silk, cloth and velvet, and the first mention of an all-white wedding gown occurs at this time at the marriage of Princess Elizabeth to Prince Palatine.

The hair was dressed up off the forehead over a wire frame and sprinkled with jewels. In a variation of this style, the front hair framed the face in a small roll, held in place by a concealed band. Then the frizzled length was dressed over the high frame. In addition, false hair and hair dye were employed along with paint and powder, also patches of all shapes. "Patching the face" was the English expression for that practice. Masks were worn in public, and gloves, fans and small muffs were of this period.

Hats, when worn, resembled the masculine type, a rather stiff shape but very smart, with narrow brim and high crown, ornamented with ostrich plumes. The style is known to us as "postilion." Turbans trimmed with pearls and feathers are to be seen in contemporary portraits, also wide-brimmed hats of soft fabric with either lace or embroidered edge, which set on the back of the head, framing the high headdress in halo form.

The reign of Charles I is contemporary with the second half of the regime of Louis XIII, and, being under French influence in dress, costume became rich, simple and artistic. It was during that time that Van Dyck painted his beautiful and aristocratic portraits.

The man's costume of this period has come down to us under the name "Cavalier." Along with more serious political reasons, the Cavaliers scorned the Roundheads as being too soberly dressed and living too solemnly. The Roundheads disliked the long-ribbon-tied curls of their aristocratic friends and cropped their own hair close, to show their disapproval.

The tight and bombasted look disappeared, the waistline became normal. The doublet became a jacket, buttoned from the neck to over the chest, open from there down to expose a full sheer lingerie shirt. The long slit, down center back, and the open front seams of the jacket sleeves also permitted the showing of the shirt. With this style, half shirts or stomachers came into fashion. Points in bowknots, as an ornamentation, were placed around the waistline of the jacket. Over the jacket was worn the baldric, a satin sash or leather belt with jewelled buckles, reaching diagonally from right shoulder to left hip.

The falling band of sheer lingerie material, with its fine lace and embroidery, is a definite feature of the period and is known to us as the Van Dyck collar. The untrimmed band of the same shape was called a "playne band." These bands were kept in especially made decorated boxes which were called bandboxes.

Breeches were full to the knees where they were tied with colored ribbons and points. Or they were fairly tight to the leg, finished at the knee with loops or points. A new idea in trimming was the bunch of ribbon loops placed on different parts of the costume.

Shoes had square toes, medium heels and large ribbon ties or shoe roses. Boots had become popular for walking and were of soft leathers in light colors, with tops and cuffs in various styles. Boots had heels of moderate height and occasionally the added platform sole. Heel and sole were often red. Spurs and large spur leathers were worn or, again, just spur leathers for ornamentation. Over the falling tops of the boots hung the embroidered and lace-edged tops of the boot hose, linen stockings which were worn between the boot and the silk stocking. When boot hose were not worn, separate flounces or ruffles were attached at the knees, and sometimes boot cuffs were lined with elaborate frills.

Canes with heads of gold, silver or bone and further decoration of bunches of colored ribbons were carried. The hair fell to the shoulders, often in ringlets, and there were lovelocks tied with bows of colored ribbon. The lovelock introduced by Charles I was worn on the left side, a curl longer than the other ringlets. The trim mustache and the small "Van Dyck" beard were in vogue at the same time. Pearl earrings were worn by the smart masculine world. Jewelled buttons became very fashionable, being sewn even to handkerchiefs and called "handkerchief buttons."

Hats were in Cavalier fashion, of beaver and felt, wide brim with crown of normal height, or narrow brim with tall crown encircled by a jewelled band and with or without plumes. A ruling of Charles I finally prohibited the use of any fur but beaver to be fashioned into hats. This was probably intended as an aid to the North American colonists, to whom beaver was an important export.

Cloaks were short and capelike, draped in every possible manner, revealing rich satin linings. Ivory, light blue and pale green were the fashionable colors, but men were inclined more and more toward the wearing of black. Muffetees appeared in this reign, a pair of small fur muffs, one for each hand. They were also made of various colored worsted fabrics.

In women's costume, the ruff and farthingale disappeared along with the stiff-corseted silhouette. In that evolution came first, with the higher waistline, a loose overdress open in front over another dress which still retained its stomacher. Both garments were made separate in bodice and skirt, the whole tied with a narrow sash or belt.

Next, the stiffly boned stomacher and the overdress disappeared. The skirt was long and full, the bodice often low-necked and short-waisted with short peplum, the edge of which was straight, scalloped or crenelated. The bodice was more often laced in back. The original word was boddie, thus, later on, stays which were laced in back and fastened in front, were a pair of boddies and, finally, a bodice. Occasionally an overskirt was caught up at the sides or in front.

The neck was finished with the falling band, a wide collar which reached from neck to shoulder in width. It had square or round corners, was edged with lace or embroidery and was sometimes composed of two or three layers. Sleeves were full, reaching to elbow or wrist, finished with the sheer lingerie cuff matching the collar. When of elbow length, long kid gloves were worn, which, too, were often edged with lace. Also worn, and matching these lingerie accessories, were aprons of exquisite workmanship which in England were called *pinners*.

Women wore a capelike wrap resembling that of the men for winter, and there was the loose, short Dutch jacket, edged and lined with fur. Added to the latter, for warmth, were the long gloves and muffs. As with the masculine costume, bunches of ribbon loops or points ornamented the costume.

The coiffure was that made familiar by the portraits painted by Van Dyck of Queen Henrietta Maria, wife of Charles I. It had a fringe over the forehead and loose, short, hanging curls on either side of the face, with a bun on the back of the head. False hair continued in fashion and wigs came into vogue.

For horseback riding, women wore the soft leather top boot, safeguards or outer petticoats of red, gray or black homespun and large beaver hats. In public, they wore hoods or kerchiefs tied under the chin, or occasionally just hung a short veil over the head. The mask was also worn. Their shoes were of the same pattern as those of the men, but with very high heels and with huge shoe roses which were costly to have made. The perfume box and the small mirror hung from the girdle.

The manufacture of pins was introduced into England about 1626, pins until this time being imported from France.

brocaded
silk-doublet with
wings and tabs-lace
edged ruff and cuffs-
full slops-ribbon
garters-slashed shoes-
shoe-roses-satin cape-
brocade lining-sword-
jewelled belt and
strap-1st decade
17th C.

flowered silk doublet-
lace neck-whisk
over scalloped gorget-
wings-tabs-points
tied in bowknots
around waist-lace
cuffs-one boot
turned down show-
ing stocking-
sword on strap-
1614

black taffeta with
gimp-velvet wings-
lace edged ruff and
cuffs-ribbon bows
with points-Spanish
slops-wrinkled
canions-ribbon
garters-satin shoes
with taffeta ties-
pendant on
moiré ribbon-
1624

velvet jacket-
slashed
sleeves-
brandenburgs and
frogs-falling
embroidered band
and cuffs-band
strings-cloth
breeches tied in
front with points-
loops at knees-
embroidered linen
boot hose-boots
with platform soles
and spur leathers-
1630's

RTW

English - James I - Charles I

striped silk and gimp-
lace collar over
wired underproper-
lace cuffs - buttons -
long hanging sleeves-
tabs - lace edged
velvet hat - jewels
in hair - jewelled
baldric - shoe - roses
1st decade 17th C.

velvet with lace,
gimp and embroidery
hanging sleeves -
rosette on bosom -
apron - fan - pearl
necklace - jewel
in hair -
1620's

taffeta with gimp-
lace falling band
and sleeve ruffles -
lace edged fichu -
buttons - rosettes -
beaver hat with
plumes - love lock -
1630's

cloth gown - underskirt
with gimp - double
falling band with
lace and tie -
slashed sleeves -
bow in hair -
mask - muff -
1640's

RTW

English-James I-Charles I

man's slipper-ribbon rosette with jewel-1612

laced stomacher-1644

lawn and lace cap-wired ruff-1614

beaver hat-ostrich and aigrette-1st decade 17th C.

spiral love-lock-lace whisk-ropes of pearls-2nd decade 17th C.

falling band-hair short on right side-love-lock on left-1630's

beaver cavalier hat-pearl earring-hair short on right side-love-lock on left-1630's

felt hat-rolled bands-jewelled brooch-ostrich and aigrette-1st decade 17th C.

man's shoe-black velvet-silver and green ribbon-red sole and heel-1641

tightly curled hair-cap with rolled edge-thread lace collar-1621

falling band-love-lock-1630's

wife of the Lordmayor of London-1646

fringe-ringlets and pearls-1630's

cravat-1630's

formal coiffure-hair curled and banded around face-jewels-ostrich aigrette-1st decade 17th C.

feather fan-1st decade 17th C.

white leather boot-red heel-spur leathers-platform sole-1630's

man's white leather shoe-red heel-shoe-rose-punched design-1633

woman's jacket-velvet and ermine-2nd third-17th C.

folding fan-2nd decade 17th C.

R.J.W.

Chapter Twenty-five

England Under Cromwell
PURITAN—1649–1660

THE REAL mode of this period was the Cavalier fashion, but the Puritans were the ruling power in England at this time. They did not create a style, but simply denuded the Stuart mode of all its fripperies. It should be remembered that the severely plain costume was not worn by all Puritans, as many of the sect wore the prevailing mode with its many colors and ornamentation, while only fanatics seem to have taken on the very sober garb. However, "sadd colours" were the fashion, meaning the grayed tones of any color.

The man's jacket was shorn of all trimming, breeches were moderately full and tight at the knee or sometimes cut straight at the knee, ending with a very simple frill or pleated ruffle. He wore no lace-edged collar or cuffs and his collar was tied with plain strings. The plain collar or band eventually became the two plain tabs of lawn or cambric worn by the professional class. The two tabs were attached to a neckband which fastened in back.

He wore the square-toed shoes or high boots of soft leather, with the broad spur leathers but no lace in the tops. Buckles replaced the spur leathers on the shoes in the next period. The broad-brimmed, high-crowned hat was worn by men and women, usually ornamented with a ribbon or band and buckle. While the Cavalier wore his curled locks flowing to the shoulders, the Puritan, or "Roundhead," as he was called, cut his hair fairly short and, if he wore a mustache, kept it very trim. The heavy oaken stick made familiar in portrayals of the Puritan, was first carried in the 1680's.

The most usual colors were black, dark brown and dull gray, but the jacket sometimes had sleeves of dull red and yellow striped material.

Women discarded the short peplum cut in tabs, leaving only a little tail to the bodice in back. The sheer linen cap which covered the hair, the wide collar and cuffs and the apron had no lace edging.

Comparatively simpler but dressier than the costume of the fanatic was the one with full skirt caught up, showing a petticoat, sometimes quilted of contrasting color, and a low-necked bodice, veiled by the collar or falling band. The cap, collar and cuffs might then be finished with very simple embroidery.

The large felt or beaver hat was worn over the lingerie cap in summer and in the winter over a black hood tied under the chin. Women also wore the voluminous cloaks and carried large muffs. Shoes, like those of the men, were square-toed and had neat shoe roses. Ribbons, in sober colors, were sparingly used, and the materials employed, such as lutestring, heavy silk, cloth and velvet, were in rich subdued tones.

England Under Cromwell·1649-1660

Cromwellian-brown cloth jerkin-red and yellow striped cloth sleeves-white lawn band and cuffs-yellow cloth breeches pleated ruffles-red stripe-dark gray cloth cape-light gray cloth lining and strap-brown felt hat-gray woolen stockings-leather boots with spur leathers

Cromwellian-violet cloth-underskirt and sleeve puff of yellow cloth-embroidered lingerie cap, falling band and cuffs-felt hat-fur muff-small shoe·roses

Puritan-gown of purple, gray or brown cloth-white Holland linen falling band, cuffs and apron-black felt hat-woolen stockings-leather shoes

Puritan-cloth costume black, brown or gray-white Holland linen falling band and cuffs-gray or green woolen stockings-black felt hat-spur leathers on shoes

RTW

Chapter Twenty=six

Louis Fourteenth

FIRST PERIOD—1644–1661

Fashion became taste of etiquette

THE FIRST period in this reign is one of transition in the mode. By this time, with the exception of Spain, all Europe followed France in culture and the mode.

The edicts against the importation of lace, gold and silver trimmings were ignored after Richelieu's death. Mazarin, in 1644, permitted only the employment of silks, to the exclusion of extravagant embroideries, metal and brocaded tissues, thus bringing about a new trimming, that of ribbon. The use of ribbon as ornamentation was carried to such extremes that by the end of this period loops (or *galants,* the French term) of variegated colors were placed all over the costume.

The last sumptuary decrees of Mazarin in 1656 and 1660 were very severe, forbidding the use of lace, passementeries and embroideries in the effort to prevent the outgoing of so much gold. The importation of Venetian and Flemish laces was banned.

After Mazarin's death, Louis XIV, acting upon the advice of his minister Colbert, brought Venetian lacemakers to France. Lacemaking centers were established at Alençon, Quesney, Arras, Reims, Sedan, Château-Thierry, Loudun and elsewhere. Colbert presented to the King the first pieces of lace made; he found them beautiful and encouraged the wearing of lace by the court. Gold and silver trimmings were reserved for the exclusive use of the King and his court.

The masculine jacket shortened to above the waistline, below which the full lingerie shirt bloused all around. The very full shirt sleeves were exposed below the three-quarter-length jacket sleeves.

The wide collar, because of the lengthening full wig, grew smaller and smaller. Neckcloths and cravats had appeared in the 'thirties and the falling band with its rounded corners now fell into two wide pleats over the chest. The jabot appeared, a falling lace ruffle, which filled in the opening of the jacket in front. White lawn, linen, mull and lace were employed for neckwear.

With the man's short jacket, a camisole was worn underneath as protection against the cold. The need for more adequate body covering brought about the wearing of a coat, adopting the style of the soldier's cassock. It reached to the knees, buttoned in front, and usually had short sleeves with turned-back cuffs and no collar. It was worn over the short jacket and is the origin of the classic coat and vest. A short full cape reaching almost to the knees was also in vogue. Large loose cloaks were worn only in bad weather or for travelling.

The tubular-shaped breeches continued to be worn, finished with a frill of ribbon loops. Rhinegrave or petticoat breeches made their appearance in this period. They were brought from Holland by Count Salm, whose title was Count of the Rhine or Rheingraf. Petticoat breeches were in two styles, either in one piece like a kilt, or in divided-skirt fashion and elaborately ornamented with ruches, ruffles, lace and ribbon loops. Often, separate lingerie and lace ruffles, called cannons, were worn just below the knees. A small apron of ribbon loops covered the front closing of the breeches.

Glove-fitting silk stockings with embroidered clocks were worn with shoes reaching to the ankles. The shoes had red heels and stiff wide bows, called butterfly bows or windmill wings. At the end of this period appeared the small jewelled buckle for shoe and garter. Shoes and boots had moderately high heels and square toes. Soft leather boots, called buskins, had wide cuffs, over which fell the lace-edged linen flounces of the boot hose. Sometimes the leather cuffs were lined simply with separate frills.

Buttons became popular—in fact, became a great extravagance—with dozens of jewelled buttons added to a costume.

The sword baldric of fabric or leather was occasionally seen. The hat had a sloping crown and a brim of moderate width and was usually bedecked with ostrich plumes. The hair continued to be worn in flowing curls, shoulder length, with the *perruque,* or wig, gaining in favor. The head was then regularly shaved, the wig taking the place of the man's own hair. At first, the wig was made to look like natural hair, but eventually, an artificial effect was intentionally cultivated. Masses of ringlets fell over the shoulders and down the back. By 1660, wigmaking in France reached such a stage of perfection that the French *perruque* was in demand all over Europe.

In this first period of the reign, the feminine costume remained about the same, but its coming changes were apparent. The bodice was tight and growing tighter, again shaping into the deep point in front and often laced in back. It was worn over a slim corset, which rose high under the armpits and over the breasts. The low neck was ornamented with the deep falling collar of sheer fabric introduced into France by Anne of Austria. The collar and the deep cuffs of the three-quarter-length sleeves were edged with fine lace or embroidery. Another style was the *fichu* of lace which finished the horizontal neckline, baring the shoulders. When the bodice opened over a stomacher of contrasting material, ornamental lacings of narrow ribbon or chenille were sometimes used.

Under the full skirt reaching to the floor was worn the spreading bell-shaped hoop of moderate dimension. Often the skirt opened in front over another of contrasting color bordered with gold and silk embroidery. A favorite style was the overskirt looped up toward the back.

The hair was dressed in the style introduced by Henrietta Maria into England, later called in France "coiffure à la Ninon." The sides were cut short, hanging to the shoulders in ringlets, often wired, short curls running over the forehead and the top drawn to a knot on the back of the head. The wired curls were known as "heartbreakers." Lace scarfs, kerchiefs and hoods served as head covering.

For hunting and horseback, the masculine attire was copied, the hat and often the wig, along with the coat, vest, cravat and sash, even to the light dress sword. Too, like that of the men, bunches of ribbon loops ornamented the costume. Cosmetics and beauty patches were as popular as ever, the mask continued to be worn, riding or walking. Brightly colored boutonnières of silk floss furnished an accent to the costume and were worn on the left shoulder.

In 1660, the King married the Spanish Infanta and there followed a vogue for black lace. This early black lace, resembling Chantilly lace of today, was made at Bayeux, hence the name, Bayeux lace.

Louis XIV - First Period

cloth cape-
short jacket-lingerie
shirt-lace neckpiece-
ribbons on sleeves-
velvet baldric-ribbon
apron-ribbon cannons
on breeches-leather
boots with lace
frills-ribbon
motifs on spur
leathers-wig-
jewels and
plumes on
hat-1646

lingerie shirt with
falling band-band
strings-ribbon apron-
ribbon cannons-wind
mill wings on shoes-
beaver hat with
crushed silk band
and plumes-1650

petticoat breeches-
short jacket-
slashed sleeves-
lingerie shirt
and cannons with
lace-ribbon
loops-lace
falling band-
plumes on
hat-1660

R T W

light blue
taffeta cassock
with gold
galloon, buttons,
lace, crimson
ribbon loops-
gold and crimson
baldric-crimson
petticoat breeches
with loops and
lace-lingerie shirt-
yellow stockings
and shoes-blue ties-
red heels-wig-brown
hat-crimson
plumes-1660

Louis XIV - First Period

velvet and silk with galloon-scalloped lingerie collar, yoke and cuffs-box pleated under sleeves-1645

riding habit-velvet brocade red on gold ground-red cloth skirt-red buttons, loops, bowknots, braid-lingerie shirt with falling band-gray leather gloves gold fringe and embroidery wig-black hat with red plumes-1652

black mourning cloak-wired sheer black cage around back of head-long wing sleeves-2nd third 17th C.

dull yellow silk-embroidered skirt-brocaded pink velvet overskirt-dull red velvet ribbon loops-lace collar and strips-lingerie puffs and ruffles-jewelled buttons-fan-gloves-1661

RTW

Chapter Twenty=seven

Louis Fourteenth

SECOND PERIOD—1661–1670

IN THIS period, Louis reached the height of his reign and France was now, definitely, the arbiter of the mode.

In the masculine jacket, which had become very short, elbow-length, is seen the last stage of the doublet. Below it the full lingerie shirt bloused all around. The short jacket sleeves had either plain edge or turned-back cuffs, often buttoned in place. The full shirt sleeves, tight at the wrists and finished with ribbon loops, ended with ruffles of lawn or lace.

The *rabat,* or lace falling band, with its round corners, became broad and long, and the *jabot,* or frill on the shirt front, frequently appeared with it. By the end of this decade, the ends of the cravat became full lace tabs, tied under the chin with "cravat strings," which were of ribbon or lace.

Rhinegrave or petticoat breeches were the definite feature of this period. They were in various syles, the full gathered skirt, the divided skirt and a shorter skirt which exposed to view the very full knee breeches. They were lavishly ornamented with galloon, lace and ribbon loops, and pockets were inserted in front of the skirt. Ribbon loops now encircled the waist and deep cannons of lingerie material and lace hung from just below the knees. Rhinegrave breeches lasted through the 'seventies, finally surviving in the livery of footmen.

Boots went out of fashion, even in the army, worn only by officers and the cavalry. From 1660 to 1690 buskins were worn. The buskin was a half boot of leather or fabric reaching to the calf of the leg, fitting snugly, fastened in front and having a turned-down cuff. The man's leather shoe of the period had square toes and a broad heel. The up-standing fronts formed little cuffs over the instep and cuffs, heel and sole were often red, the shoe itself being brown or gray. The stiff wide bows lasted until 1680. A bunch of ribbon loops was often placed on the outer sides of the shoes. More important was the jewelled buckle, which appeared about 1660 and, gradually growing larger, entirely replaced the tie fastening in the 'eighties.

Sashes were worn, fringed, lace-edged and tasseled, as was the sword baldric. During the 'sixties, loops and bowknots of ribbon were placed over the entire costume. Handkerchiefs hung from coat pockets, exquisite snuffboxes and elegant combs were carried to be used in public. Handsome, slim walking sticks, ornamented with ribbon bowknots, were in fashion, with gold, silver or carved ivory heads. The muff was a masculine as well as a feminine accessory in those days and hung sus-pended from a ribbon around the neck. It was small and round, either of cloth, velvet brocade or fur, and lined with either fur or silk, trimmed with lace, ribbon and embroidery. Its greatest popularity in this century dated from 1660 to 1680.

Wigs grew in favor, but the King, having a fine head of hair, did not adopt the fashion until 1673, when he was thirty-five. The full curled wig was worn with the low-crowned hat having a brim of mod-erate width and adorned with ostrich plumes. The hat was more often carried than worn on the head, so as not to disarrange the dressing of the wig. The mustache became a very thin line.

Woman's costume also took on extravagant ornamentation in gold and silver passementeries, laces and ribbons. *Galants,* or favors, as the bunches of ribbon loops were called, were of variegated colors. Striped and watered silks and gauzes, hand-painted with flowers in large designs, were popular. The motif in design on fabrics consisted principally of flowers and fruits in realistic form. An interesting note is that, for the first time in weaving, the play of lights and shadows was accomplished. In this flamboyant age of Louis XIV, the flower motif was larger than natural size, just slightly undersize in the reign of Louis XV, becoming diminutive under Louis XVI.

Skirts were long and full with the overskirt, or *manteau,* looped back, held by ribbon bows. The looped-up folds were often bunched in back. Over an underskirt of taffeta, the looped-up outer skirt of brocaded silk ended in a train, the length of which was determined by the lady's social position. The train was carried over the left arm, except in the presence of royalty, when it trailed on the floor.

The long slim-pointed bodice over the tight high corset persisted. Lace was now used principally on the sleeves, which were usually in several puffs and three-quarter or elbow length. The bodice often laced in back, but when fastened in front it had jewelled clasps, buttons or many bowknots. Bowknots of graduated size on the stomacher were called *échelon.* The décolletage was usually bateau-shaped, finished with a scarf or fichu of lawn or lace. The large collar of lace or point coupé, which had been originally introduced into France by Anne of Austria, became passé after her death and by the 'seventies had disappeared.

Transparents, made famous by Madame de Sévigné's description in one of her letters, were gowns of sheer muslin or lawn, painted with bunches of colored flowers and worn over another gown of moiré satin of a bright color. Transparents were also of gold or lace tissue, worn over figured brocades.

Slippers with very pointed toes and very high heels, known as "Louis heels," were of satin, brocade, embroidered fabrics and kid, fastened with jewelled buckles, ribbon and rosettes. Elbow-length gloves were of glacé kid or silk in white or pale colors. The all-lace fan made its appearance in the second half of this century. Women, too, carried the tall, slim cane with head of gold, silver or ivory. Parasols of Chinese shape, edged with fringe, were held over ladies by pages. The necklace of small pearls, which encircled the neck, was worn invariably with the low décolletage. A necklace with a pendant was worn by Louise de la Vallière, first mistress of Louis XIV, the style of which became known as *lavallière*. Rings, earrings, brooches and necklaces of gold were much worn, heavily encrusted with diamonds and colored gems.

There was also a tremendous vogue for artificial or "costume jewelry," as we call it today, fashioned of brilliantly colored stones. This artificial jewelry, which became very fashionable, was made on the Rue de Temple, and from that derived its name of "temple" jewelry. There was also a great fad for extravagant jewelled buttons, dozens of which were used on a costume.

Louis XIV-Second Period

cassock button trimmed-baldric embroidered and fringed-lingerie shirt-lace falling band with bowknot-rhinegrave breeches-inverted pleat front of skirt-ribbon loops-leather shoes-red tongues and heels-sword-cane-wig-hat-1663

rose colored velvet and ribbon-lingerie shirt and panels on breeches-lace falling band, ruffles and cannons-light brown hat and shoes-rose plumes, stockings and wind mill ties-red heels-early 1660's

cloth jacket-rhinegrave breeches of cloth and light satin-galloon and ribbon loops-lingerie shirt-falling band and wrist ruffles-felt hat with plumes and loops-fringed embroidered baldric-sword-red heels-1665

velvet and lace-rhinegrave breeches circular skirt over taffeta-lingerie shirt-falling band-jabot-embroidered baldric with velvet frills-satin shoes with lace and velvet-red heels-velvet hat with ostrich-sword-1670

Louis XIV-Second Period

velvet and satin
with galloon and
lace-lingerie
sleeves-silk hood-
1st half of
the decade

green velvet over
rose taffeta-
rose ribbon rosettes-
gold embroidery
and gimp-white
taffeta band
and sleeves-
lace ruffles-
jewels-fan-
1666

taffeta over fine
cloth-lingerie fichu
and sleeves-lace
ruffles-velvet bow
knots-gimp-painted
silk fan-2nd half
of decade

sky blue velvet over
pale blue taffeta-
gold galloon-lingerie
fichu and sleeves-
lace ruffles-rose
ribbon loops-fan-
2n half of
decade

RTW

Louis XIV-Second Period-1660's

falling band-
bandstring with
pom-pon of
crocheted petals-
natural hair

black silk hood
lined with
rose silk

lady's shoe-
white kid with
silk embroidery

felt hat-
white plumes-
lace falling
band-natural
hair-1665

ringlets
dressed over
wire frames-
ribbon bow knots
tiny cap

corset laced
back and
front

fringed
silk
sash

lawn and lace
cravat tied with
ribbon-natural
hair-1665

fringed
embroidered
sword
baldric

men's shoes-
leather with red
tongue and heel-
buckle fastening

lace wind mill wings-
ribbon loops-red heel-
up to 1680

RTW

Chapter Twenty=eight

Louis Fourteenth

THIRD PERIOD—1670-1715

change in masculine attire

THE BEGINNING of this period was one of great pomp and luxury, which finally settled down to a more conservative style as it neared its end.

A great and lasting change came over men's attire, the doublet becoming a vest and the justaucorps, or jerkin, changing into coat or *habit,* as it was called in French. At first, the length of the waistcoat was just below the waistline, with the coat reaching halfway between thigh and knee. About 1670, the coat lengthened to the knee, with the vest reaching there about 1680. After 1675, the waistline became definitely shaped, even to a flaring skirt, which was later stiffened to stand out from the figure. To the back of either hip the skirt was slit and decorated with a row of buttons. Another style was the insertion of fan-shaped pleats at the side-back, headed by a button, which is the origin of the back buttons on today's tail coat.

From about 1680, buttons and buttonholes were lavishly used on the vest, cuffs and pockets. They were covered with yellow and white silk, simulating gold and silver. When buttons and buttonholes were applied in conjunction with braid, they were termed *brandenburgs,* after the electors of Brandenburg, who invaded France in 1674. Their cassocks were ornamented with like braided loops and buttons.

Embroidery in gold and silk, which was often elaborate, confined itself to the wide cuffs on the coat sleeves and the fronts of the waist-coat. Shoulders and sleeves were ornamented with huge bunches of ribbon loops. French cloth now rivalled that of England and Holland, and after 1677, following the edict of Louis XIV, the justaucorps was made of cloth instead of silk and trimming eliminated, leaving only the ribbon loops on the shoulders. Pockets were placed low in front, and coat and vest were collarless, no doubt due to the full wig. Until 1690, the waistcoat was buttoned with the coat either open or closed. Often the waistcoat had a sleeve which turned back over the cuff of the coat. Gold braid finished seams and edges and was often part of the embroidery design.

Petticoat breeches lasted until about 1678, replaced then by the full knickerbockers, blousing over the knees, where they were finished with ribbon loops or cannons. Plain, close-fitting breeches, knee-length and concealed by the coat, came in the 'nineties, fastened either with buttons or with one, two or three buckles at the side of the knee. These breeches, when not made of the coat fabric, were black, which became standard.

Shirts were full in body and sleeve, gathered at the wrists. The growing size of the wig, with its curls reaching to the shoulders, caused the wide falling band to give way to the cravat of lawn or lace, tied at the neck with the cravat-string of ribbon. The jabot of lace and lawn concealed the front opening of the shirt. The *steinkirk* came in in the 'nineties, a scarf of lace or lawn, loosely tied, with the ends casually twisted into the vest or shirt front or drawn through a buttonhole or ring. Black silk steinkirks were also worn. The name came from the Battle of Steinkerque in 1692, when the victorious French charged the opposing cavalry with their dress in disorder and their cravats untied and flying.

House gowns of Oriental design were worn by men for negligee. They were loose, with flowing sleeves, and were first made of India cottons in bright figured designs, but later developed in velvets, brocades, damasks, striped and figured silks in gay colors with linings of contrasting colored silks.

Mention must be made of the muffs of beautiful furs, carried by men in the winter, attached to a ribbon belt around the waist. The muff was a French fashion and had been carried since the sixteenth century. It now became most luxurious, made of gold and silver tissue, ribbons, feathers and fur, to which embroidery was often added. Fashionable for both men and women was the small plush muff, *couleur de feu,* presumably Chinese red.

Wigs grew in size, becoming more artificial in appearance, being now made of horsehair, which proved more satisfactory in retaining its curl. Louis, who as a young man had a fine head of hair, did not take to wig wearing until 1673, when he was thirty-five years old. In the 'nineties, the "full-bottomed" wigs were parted in the middle, standing high over the brow in double peaks, with curls falling on the shoulders and down the back. The wig was now sometimes powdered, and the hat carried instead of being worn, to avoid disturbing the coiffure. Indoors, for negligee, a nightcap was often worn instead of the wig. By 1685, the thin mustache disappeared and the face was clean-shaven.

From about 1670, the wide-cocked brim was the style in hats with moderate crown and, around 1690, the three-cornered hat became definitely the mode. It was bound or edged with metal braid or lace and trimmed with ribbon and plumes. Later, the tricorne was ornamented with uncurled ostrich plumes or ostrich fringe. The masculine hat was worn indoors until 1685.

Baldrics of leather or embroidered silk or velvet were worn, from which the dress sword hung, the fashion lasting until after 1695. The small dress sword which appeared in the opening of the coat skirt was attached to a braid loop beneath the vest. The sword was often ornamented with a broad ribbon "sword knot" having fringed ends. Even the cane had its ribbon bowknots or tasselled cords. Handkerchiefs were tasselled or edged with lace and were carried hanging from pockets. Paint, patches, handsome snuffboxes, tobacco boxes and combs were all part of the costume.

From the 'seventies, black became the color for men's shoes, brown for hunting. Shoes were square-toed, with red heels and soles, which only nobility and gentlemen at court wore. The tongue over the instep hung down, revealing its red lining. A famous pair of the King's shoes had the heels painted by Van der Meulen, portraying scenes of the victorious Rhenish battles. Until the 'eighties, shoes were fastened with ribbon or lace bows, sometimes very wide, but were then superseded by small oval buckles which grew larger and became square. Eventually, buckles were fashioned with pearls and diamonds, plain bronze being worn for mourning.

Soft fitted boots or buskins without cuffs, from 1675 to about 1690, were fastened at the small of the leg by buckles or buttons. High leather leggings, or *spatterdashes,* came in about 1700. The joining of legging and shoe was covered by spur leathers.

In the 'eighties, cannons and ribbon garters disappeared, giving way to narrow bands with buckles. Stockings were drawn up over the breeches with the garter on the outside, or perhaps hidden in the stocking roll. Stockings were invariably clocked and of different color from the shoe.

Women's costume, at the height of this last period, reached a state of overdecoration, but the King's marriage to Madame de Maintenon, plus critical times for France, had a sobering effect in the latter part of the reign.

Until 1675, only tailors fashioned women's garments, but now there were established couturiers or dressmakers, mantua or cloak makers, modistes or milliners, shoemakers, furriers, glovers, fan makers, jewellers, beauty specialists and coiffeurs or hairdressers, all high-class and very costly. The stage became an influence in launching new fashions. An extravagant use of powder, rouge and patches was the vogue. There were rules of etiquette for the wearing of the mask and definite rules for the length of trains and the wearing of certain fabrics, governed by one's station. The use of perfume declined in this reign, sweet odors being objectionable to the King.

A silkworm which produced pure white silk was cultured in France. Painted and printed linens and cottons became the rage, to last for the next two reigns. Lace ornamented not only clothes but was applied to bedcovers, carriages, horse blankets, even shrouds. There was point de Paris, d'Alençon, de Malines, de Valenciennes, de Bruxelles, also gold and silver lace made at Paris and Lyon.

The waistline of the long, slim, tightly corseted bodice had become very small, with the bust held high. The low neck was finished with a fichu, frills or a falling band. Bows and lace ruffles ended the elbow-length sleeves. There were deep capelike collars of lawn or lace which lay about the shoulders, either cut high to the neck or in bateau line. This style is familiar to us in American colonial dresses. Little capes, first made of fur and known as "palatines," or "pèlerines," were introduced into France by the Palatine Princess Charlotte Elizabeth of Bavaria, who married the King's brother, Duc d'Orléans, in 1671. Women adopted steinkirks in the 'nineties.

In the 'eighties, over a full skirt which hung to the floor, an overskirt with long train was drawn up and bunched toward the back over a bustle. Then the old verdingale, or farthingale, returned by way of England, under the new name of pannier, or hoop. This new hoop was made of cane or reed, rather like a bird cage, thus the French name of *panier,* or basket. But this style did not fully establish itself for years to come.

Gowns were trimmed with heavy embroideries, lace, braid, fringe and tassels. Ribbon bowknots in échelle form adorned the front of the bodice. Cut-out motifs of lace or gold embroidery, called *prentintailles,* were appliquéd or gummed to the skirts, making elaborate ornamentation. The heavy ruffles were called *fabalas,* which, anglicized, became "furbelows." Gowns often had separate sets of false sleeves.

The long trains were carried by pages. The small Negro boy servant or slave, dressed and turbaned in brilliant colors, appeared for the first time in this period. He held the long-handled parasol over the lady.

At home, for negligee, a loose, beltless coatlike robe called a *manteau,* or mantua, came into fashion. It was not unlike the kimono version of modern times and was of a dark color or black. To Madame de Maintenon is accredited its name, the "innocent." The gown worn at home was usually black, accompanied by the lace-trimmed white apron. Aprons were often of silk, edged with gold lace and were called *laisse-tout-faire.* Near the end of the century, there was a fad for *transparents* of black lace worn over colorful brocades. The name transparents was also applied to the sheer fabrics employed in the tall ruffled caps then in vogue.

The wrap of the period was a short, scarflike cape edged with ruffles or lace, called a *mante.* This wrap and the mantua were probably made of a silk imported from Italy in the eighteenth and nineteenth centuries and called mantua silk. No doubt, from that fact, came the name "mantuamaker." Mantes, or broad scarfs of gold and silver tissue, were worn only by women of high rank at court. The scarf of fur loosely tied around the neck was also called a *palatine,* though of different shape from the little cape. Muffs were carried in winter and were often large enough to hold the little pet dogs which were then the fashion.

A coiffure which appeared in 1671 and lasted but a few years was the *hurluberlu,* a madcap, or "windblown bob," the hair cut short and in ringlets. From about 1675, the hair was dressed high off the forehead in clusters of curls, arranged over a silk-covered wire frame, called a *commode.* Occasionally, the hair was powdered. In 1680, the Duchesse de Fontanges, having her hat blown off at a royal hunting party, tied her curls in place with her garter, arranging a bow with ends in front. From that incident, fastened to a cap, grew tier upon tier of upstanding, wired, pleated ruffles of lawn, lace and ribbons. The hair dressed in that fashion was called *coiffure à la Fontanges,* and the cap with its narrow rising front was known as *le bonnet à la Fontanges,* in English, the *fontange.* The cap often had two floating lappets of ribbon or lace in back, and over the whole arrangement was often worn the black silk hood or kerchief. In 1691, the headdress was reduced to two tiers of pleats and became known as the *commode*. About 1710, under ridicule, the cap lost its fantastic front tower and became just a little linen or lace cap. Patches, placed near the mouth and eyes and on the forehead, accompanied this headdress.

The riding habit was founded upon the masculine costume of coat and waistcoat. The skirt was draped for side saddle. At the neck was the lace cravat with huge ribbon bow. The three-cornered hat with plumes and heavy leather gloves were worn with the outfit. The equestrienne held the reins in her left hand, and on sunny days a parasol was carried in her right.

The tall cane continued in fashion; in fact, cane and parasol are shown being carried at the same time. Masks were still worn, hanging from the belt when not in use. Fans of rare beauty were created, miniature paintings mounted on sticks of gold, carved ivory, mother-of-pearl and carved and painted wood. A new accessory was the snuffbox, carried by "ladies of quality" who made use of snuff, a habit which was very displeasing to Madame de Maintenon.

Fine shoes, of exquisite fabrics and beautifully embroidered, were worn with the high "Louis heels." There were also high-heeled slippers with just the front covering, called *pantoffles*. Fastenings were ribbons and jewelled buckles.

The feminine vogue of wearing a small bouqet, or boutonnière, of fresh flowers brought about the invention of the "bosom bottle," to keep the blooms from wilting. It was a small glass or tin bottle about four inches long, covered with green ribbon and holding water, which was tucked into the bosom or the hair. Boutonnières of flowers fashioned of silk floss preceded the fashion of fresh flowers.

The process of manufacturing artificial pearls was perfected by Jaquin of Paris about 1680. Accepted everywhere, the imitation pearl vied with real gem as adornment. The single string around the throat without pendant became classic.

The clothes of children still resembled those of their elders.

Venetian mirrors were now excelled in quality by those of French manufacture. The method of making plate glass was invented in 1691 in Nehou, France, by Louis Lucas, a Frenchman.

cloth coat-braid and buttons-petticoat breeches-ribbon loops-lingerie cravat and shirt-fringed gauntlets-felt hat with ostrich-powdered wig-leather shoes-red tongues, heels-buckles-cane with bowknot-sword-1670's

orange cloth cape-gold and silver embroidery-gray cloth coat-orange embroidery-orange satin vest-orange plush muff attached to ribbon belt-lawn and lace cravat-fringed gauntlets-hat gray beaver-ostrich and ribbon-wig-stockings drawn over breeches-black shoes-red heels-gold buckles-1678

cloth coat with turned back fronts-striped waistcoat with sleeves-lace frills-steinkirk-fur muff on ribbon-beaver hat, uncurled ostrich-stockings gartered over breeches-black leather shoes-red heels-buckles-sword with fringed ribbon-snuff box-1694

cloth coat with braid and buttons-side pleats-lace frills-tricorne hat with braid-wig-cane-1706

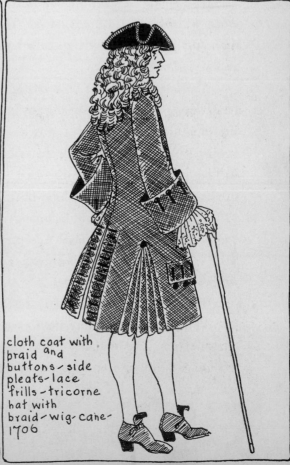

RTW

Louis XIV-Third Period

heavy satin with fringe and pretintailles-lace on bodice and sleeves-velvet paniers and "manteau"-lace vestee-fur "palatine" and muff-fontange of lace and ribbon with lappets-beauty patches-late 17th C.

silk and lace with "manteau" of contrasting color-lingerie sleeves-lace edged silk apron-handkerchief in pocket-ribbon échelle-fontange of lace and ribbon-late 17th C.

brocade with ribbon and tassels-silk "manteau"-velvet mante with lace-lace fontange with lappets-fan-beauty patches-late 17th C.

hunting habit-brocaded green velvet coat-lingerie shirt and cravat-brocaded deep rose cloth skirt-brown beaver hat-rose ostrich-handkerchief in pocket-game bag-gun-negro servant-1690's

RTW

Louis XIV- Third Period

fringed silk parasol

silk parasol

curls dressed over wire frame- 1680

curls dressed over wire frame called "commode" late 17th C.

wig- beaver hat with gold braid-uncurled ostrich-steinkirk- 1690's

fontange- sheer fabric- lace-ribbon- lappets- steinkirk drawn through buttonhole- boutonnière- beauty patches 1680's

powdered wig- tricorne with lace and uncurled ostrich-lace cravat-1695

fontange open in back-lace and ribbon- late 17th C.

the full bottomed wig in high points-lawn and lace steinkirk- late 17th C.

lace fontange- silk kerchief- beauty patch- late 17th C.

man's shoe- black leather- buckle-red tongue and heel-1690's

pantoffle or mule- embroidered fabric- late 17th C.

lady's shoe-lace ruffle-embroidered silk-late 17th C.

the King's white silk sash-gold fringe and embroidery

lady's silk mask- late 17th C.

powdered wig- cravat with lace ends- 1680's

RTW

Chapter Twenty=nine

The English Restoration
CHARLES II—1660–1685
JAMES II—1685–1689

THESE two reigns mark the return of the Stuarts to England. Charles brought back with him the costume worn at the Court of Louis XIV, where he had spent his exile. It was bedecked with ribbons, the very short jacket with short sleeves exposing the full, sheer lace-trimmed shirt with correspondingly full sleeves tied with ribbons.

This was accompanied by full breeches ending in deep lace ruffles or cannons, as they were called, or the petticoat or "rhinegrave breeches." There were two styles of petticoat breeches, one which resembled a kilt, the other like a divided skirt. At the neck appeared the lace or lawn falling band, the cravat or the oblong tabs. The costume was ornamented with glittering buttons, loops or buttonholes, braid, gimp or galloon.

There were the long bushy *peryke,* later called "periwig" (a misconstruction of the French word, perruque), the small mustache, tiny lip beard, silk stockings, squared-toed shoes with high red heels and wide

184

ribbon ties, a cane and the wide-brimmed beaver hat with sweeping plumes. Curls were tied with ribbons.

With the graying of the king's own black hair, he adopted a black wig, which created a fad for that hue. Later, fair and light-brown peri-wigs became popular. For travelling, short bushy wigs replaced those in long ringlets.

With the return of Charles II, the boot again flared out in a wide falling cuff, finished with the ruffle and lace of the boot hose. Cannons, or bunches of ribbon loops, were affixed at the knee from 1660 to 1670. After the 'eighties, breeches were finished with a buckled garter band or the stockings were rolled over the breeches. Black seems to have been the popular color in leather boots after the 'seventies. Buckles appeared for the first time in this age on shoes and garters. Small jewelled buckles were worn, with the butterfly or "windmill wings" gradually growing in size, until, in the 'eighties, they were the only fastening or ornament on shoes.

About 1665 appeared the *jack boot,* a rigid leather boot for hard wear, which had a wide leather cuff, worn either up or down. There were also wide spur leathers, spatterdashes and buttoned or buckled leather leggings. The buskin, a soft fitted boot of leather or fabric, appeared in this period. It sometimes fastened in front with clasps.

Contemporary with the change in men's costume during the early part of the reign of Louis XIV, in fact definitely in October, 1666, came a change in the Englishman's apparel. Giving his court a month's notice, Charles II dressed all his courtiers in a new vest and coat "after ye Persian mode." According to Pepys's description, it was all black and white, the vest reaching the calf of the leg and over the vest, a coat six inches shorter.

The breeches, which were concealed by the vest, were of "Spanish cut," finished with cannons of black ribbon loops. The buskins worn with the outfit were either of cloth or leather, the same color as that of the vest or coat. The lining of the coat and vest was white, which scheme made Charles decide that they all looked too much like magpies, whereupon he ordered a new costume, entirely of black velvet. This somber hue did not survive at that time, but the idea of coat and vest replacing the tunic or doublet, was to last to our day.

From the portrait of Henry Bennet, Earl of Arlington, who was painted in the new coat and vest, the coat appears to be of black velvet, with white taffeta lining and undersleeves. The undersleeves are tied with black velvet ribbons. The vest seems to be of silk brocade in an Oriental design with narrow belt. The sword baldric, coat cuffs and the band on the vest appear to be of contrasting colored silk, ornamented with Italian cutwork. A white lawn and lace falling band tops the costume.

The new coat becoming quite generally worn, the cloak then became of secondary importance.

It was in this period that men adopted robes and turbans for negligee. Though originally worn at home, the use finally spread to the countinghouse or "office." The Oriental turban gave respite from the heat of the wig and the East Indian banyan, or banian, became the lounging robe. The Oriental influence came about through trade intercourse with Persia, India and Arabia. These loose gowns were first made of Indian cottons, but later appeared in silks, damasks and brocades, with contrasting linings and varied in style from the robe with wide sleeves to the flowing coat with turned-down collar and fitted sleeves. The robes were always of brilliantly colored figured or striped fabrics.

The pair of small muffs, or *muffetees,* was still worn in the winter by the men, in the beginning of this reign, but, by 1663, the single larger muff had become the fashion. It hung from a ribbon around the neck or from a button of the coat, and was usually of fabric with fur lining. The sword was suspended from a wide baldric of decorated leather or embroidered velvet.

The feminine gown of the period was quite simple and charming, usually of plain satin or velvet, although brocade, gold and silver tissue are also mentioned. The corset was laced tighter, creating a slimmer figure than that of the previous reign. The waistline was moderately pointed in front, round in back and the neckline either round or bateau-shaped. The center front of the bodice and the short full sleeve were left open at intervals and tied with ribbon bowknots, revealing the chemisette of sheer lawn, linen or muslin worn underneath. The chemisette showed in a tiny edge at the neck, and neck and sleeves were often finished with lace ruffles.

The full skirt was caught up over a petticoat which was of contrasting fabric and color and usually had a train. Petticoats were often elaborately embroidered with gold and silver and sometimes edged with ermine. Skirts of ankle-length were also fashionable.

Muffs, like those of the men, were carried in the winter, and the short cape or palatine, of German origin, called tippet in England, was worn. It later became known as a *pèlèrine*. When travelling, women wore cloaks with enveloping hoods. For horseback and hunting, their hats, decked with plumes, resembled the masculine style. The hair was dressed in ringlets at the sides over wire frames, a fringe of curls on the forehead and a knot at the back. The side bunches of curls were often tied with ribbons.

"Pinners," or aprons of intricate workmanship, were the vogue. A negligee garment for women was the nightgown, worn in the boudoir but not in bed. It hung full from the neck, where it fastened and had full sleeves, gathered at the wrists. It was usually of striped satin or damask, padded and lined with taffeta to match.

A special "habit" for horseback was designed in this period, which had a long-skirted, buttoned-up coat worn over a sidesaddle skirt. See Page 166. With it were worn a doublet, the peruke and a tall crowned hat. In bad weather, a "safeguard," or "riding petticoat," of heavy linen protected the habit. Masks were worn in winter to protect the face from the cold, even on horseback. Masks were much used in our colonies for the same reason.

In accessories, added to the mask, there were the fan, patches, powder, rouge, the muff and long gloves of soft chamois or doeskin delicately scented. A new note for women was the garter of ribbon and lace fastened with a beautiful jewelled buckle. The English Court took up Bayeux lace, a black lace introduced at the French Court upon the marriage of the Spanish Infanta to Louis XIV. A novelty was the bouquet or nosegay of flowers worn on the left shoulder.

In the reign of James II, the coat and vest of the preceding regime became the accepted costume of men, taking on more of the French cut with shaped waist and flaring skirt. The coat was worn half-buttoned and the skirt was slit up center-back and at the sides. A wide turned-back cuff finished the sleeve, with the puffs and frills of the full lingerie shirt showing below. The coat front, cuffs, slits and low-placed pockets were trimmed with buttons and braid loops and galloon or all three. The cravat of fine lawn and lace finished the neck.

Breeches were moderately full, bagging at the knees, and shoes were now fastened with buckles on straps instead of strings. The cotton stockings made in England appeared in the 'eighties and, though the silk stocking remained the smart thing, knitted stockings of cotton or wool were generally worn.

Hats had brims of medium width and low crowns, with the newer trimming of ribbon loops. Although always removed in the presence of royalty, hats were worn indoors until 1685. There does not seem to be any definite record of when it became bad manners for a man to keep his hat on the head in house or at church. Broad sashes and the baldric were worn outside the coat.

The changes in the feminine gown were slight. The neck of the bodice was higher, and the wide, flat collar, whisk or falling band continued in fashion. The stomacher or front of the bodice was ornamented with ribbon bowknots in graduated size, a style called *échelle,* or ladder. Another decoration of the stomacher was the cross-lacing of narrow ribbon. Sleeves had wide turned-back cuffs, with the white lingerie puffs of the chemisette showing below. The popularity of sheer aprons, or pinners, continued.

The hair was now waved and parted in the middle, the hanging ringlets were retained, placed lower, also coming over the shoulders from the back. Black hoods, with or without capes, were fashionable, also the large hat finished simply with a ribbon band. While sunshades and umbrellas, coming by way of Spain, appeared in France about the middle of this century, they did not reach England until the end of the seventeenth century.

The first of the great "dandies" who exercised an influence over fashion lived in these two periods. His name was Robert Feilding. "Beau Feilding" was known at the Court of Charles II as "Handsome Feilding." He died in 1712.

The second dandy, of later date, was Richard Nash, called "Beau Nash," a leader of English society and fashion. The King appointed him master of ceremonies at Bath, where he ruled in matters of deportment and dress. He was born in 1674 and died in 1761.

The English Restoration

short doublet
open front and back-
slashed sleeves-
lace edged pleated-
falling band-
lawn shirt-petti-
coat breeches-ribbon
loops-leather boots-
lace edged boot
hose-beaver hat
with ostrich-cloth
cloak-before 1666

coat and petti-
coat breeches-
cloth with velvet
loops-taffeta lining
and cuffs-low pockets-
handkerchief with
jewelled button-white
lawn shirt-pleated
lace falling band-
black wig-beaver
hat-leather shoes-
red heels-
after 1666

velvet with
taffeta lining-
satin vest-velvet
baldric-lawn
cravat and shirt-
lace ruffles-satin
bows-wig-felt
hat-cane and
sword-1670

cloth with
silk vest-cloth
cloak-fur lined
cloth muff with
velvet loops-
leather shoes-
red heels-wig-
felt hat with
ribbon loops-
1688

RTW

The English Restoration

heavy silk with
gimp – ermine
tippet or pelerine-
lace edged low
neck of gown-
white lawn puffs-
silk shoes with
ribbon ties
1666

rose velvet over
gray satin-white
lawn under bodice-
yellow bowknots-
bowknot in hair-
ringlets over
wire frame-
Charles II period

figured dull red
brocade-white satin
skirt and stomacher-
lace ruffles-blue
velvet bowknots
in "échelle" form
shoulder puffs edged
red fringe-white
lawn puffs-
1685

cloth over dull
silk – lacings
over stomacher-
white lawn
band or whisk
and sleeves-
black hood-
James II
period

RTW

The English Restoration

lady's shoe-white kid-black velvet-punched design-attached clog

beaver hat-ostrich plumes-ribbon loops-hair late in the period

black wig-bowknots-beaver hat-ostrich-lawn and lace cravat

wig and falling band

man's shoe-red heel and buckle-1682

corset to lace in back-false lacing in front

wig-falling band and bandstrings

pearls-knot in back-wired ringlets

man's shoe-"wind mill wing" ties-red heel

fitted buskin-boot hose frill

jack boot

slit in coat back-manner of wearing sword

coat-vest and breeches "after ye Persian mode" October 1666-for description see text

sword baldric

two styles of petticoat breeches

RTW

Chapter Thirty

Louis Fifteenth

1715–1774

I N THE eighteenth century, from 1750 to 1770, French costume is considered to have reached its perfection. There are definitely two periods: that from 1724 to 1750, known as "Rococo," with its basic motif, the shell combined with flowers, feathers, ribbon bowknots and all manner of curves and curls, often all in one design; the second, from 1750 to 1770, was less fantastic, more dignified. The manners and fashions of the French Court influenced social life throughout the civilized world.

The *habit à la française,* while adhering to the three fundamentals of coat, vest and breeches settled in the reign of Louis XIV, became perfected in design during the Regency, from then becoming the formal attire of the gentleman of Europe, lasting a century. The coat retained its name, *habit à la française,* to the end of the eighteenth century, with very little change in cut. Up the center back to the waist has always appeared the slash, originally necessary on horseback.

The sleeves, usually slit part way up in back, were straight with

wide cuffs. The skirt of the coat, reaching to the knees, was reinforced
with linen, buckram or whalebone and cut to flare when buttoned at
the waist. The hilt of the sword protruded from these pleats, attached
to a baldric or belt worn under the coat or vest. The full, rich-looking
undersleeves were often part of the vest, in which case the back, sometimes laced, the fronts and the lower section of the sleeves were all of
one material. The vest was buttoned or simulated thus, by three or
four buttons at the waist. Under the vest was worn the lingerie *chemise,*
with cravat or jabot attached.

In the 'fifties, the fronts of the coat began to slope away from the
waist and the side pleats with buttons moved toward the back. The skirt
of the vest gradually shortened, by the middle of the century, reaching
just over the hips and cut away in front at the waist. The neck was cut
away in front, leaving an opening filled in with cravat or jabot. The
small, flat, turned-back collar developed along with pointed lapels, and
the sleeve became tight with a small cuff. From the 'fifties, the large
pocket flaps disappeared.

The tight breeches were either buttoned or buckled above the knee,
with the silk stockings rolled over the breeches. The garters were concealed in the roll. Breeches were furnished with pockets, sometimes as
many as eight, made of white kid. Later, the breeches, still fastened
with buttons or buckles, came below the knees. Although *gallowses*
appeared at the beginning of the century, breeches were still held by
their cut and fit over the hips.

Fabrics employed for the *habit* were silks, velvets or woolens. Vests
were brocaded or embroidered, as embroidery had returned to favor for
both men's and women's garments. Designs were more delicate, executed
in silk, gold and silver thread, which was finer than that of the preceding
century. The most popular ornamentation consisted of loops and buttons
in metal, jewels or silk.

Greatcoats, or overcoats, were full with a flat collar and wide cuffs.
The redingote, or riding coat, came from England in 1725 and was worn
throughout the century. It often had two or three small shoulder capes.

The heels of men's shoes were lower, but still red for the noble and the gentleman at court, worn with blue or red silk stockings, clocked in gold or silver. Leggings or spatterdashes, buttoned or buckled at the side, became fashionable for riding. In the 'seventies appeared the large square buckles.

Also in the 'seventies, men took to wearing the boutonnière of artificial flowers.

At the beginning of the century, the full-bottomed wig was drawn to the back and tied at the nape of the neck with a black silk ribbon, which style was known as the "tie." The wig was now dressed up off the forehead, with a soft roll or bunches of curls at either side of the face. The bunches of curls were called "pigeon's wings." Pigeon's wings were replaced by set rolls over the ears about 1755, when the *cadogan, catogan* or "club style" began to appear.

In the cadogan wig, the back hair was looped under and tied with a concealed string or the *solitaire* of black taffeta, satin or velvet. The solitaire, which no doubt is the origin of the black tie, was the black ribbon tied to the wig in a bow at the back, with the ends—brought around over the white cravat and tied in a bow under the chin. Sometimes the solitaire was held in front by a diamond pin or a barette. The "Macaronies," or "exquisites," of England were the first to adopt the cadogan wig. The name of the wig is attributed to the first Earl of Cadogan, of earlier period.

Another popular style was the bagwig, in which the black silk bag, with draw string at the back of the neck, encased the ends of the wig. This idea is supposed to have originated with the French servant, who thus kept his hair covered when at work. The solitaire was attached under the bag and the ends carried around the neck and fastened in front.

Among the many styles, there was the *ramillie* wig, of English origin, named in honor of the victorious battle of Ramillies in 1706, of Duke of Marlborough fame. The wig had one or two hanging braids tied top and bottom with black ribbon. Later, the end of the braid was often looped under and tied. Another was the knotted or full-bottomed wig, with several of its hanging curls tied in knots. The pigtail wig had its tail bound spirally by black ribbon and tied top and bottom.

White wigs were most popular in the first quarter of the century, changing to gray in the next quarter. From 1760, many wore their own hair dressed and powdered in wig fashion, but the use of powder declined. Under the wig, the head was shaved or close-cropped.

The hat of the period was the *tricorne,* three-cornered or cocked hat, edged with braid and trimmed with ostrich fringe or a ribbon band. It was fairly small, often being carried under the arm to avoid disturbing the wig.

The vogue of the cane continued, in various woods, including bamboo and ivory.

In women's costume, the gown designed by and named after the painter Watteau is the principal style of the Regency. The original Watteau gown was a loose sack or dress worn over a tight bodice and very full underskirt. The loose folds, falling from the shoulders in back, became part of the skirt. The front of the gown varied in design, either hanging loose or fitting at the waist, worn closed or open, and if open revealing a bodice and underskirt. The elbow-length sleeves had vertical pleats and soft wide cuffs, but from the 'forties the pagoda sleeve took hold, tight from shoulder to elbow, where it spread into flaring ruffles, headed by ribbon bows. The neck in front was low and the stomacher was ornamented with ribbon loops in graduated size or lacings of narrow ribbon finished with gauze or lace known as the *modestie*—in English the "modesty bit."

In the 'thirties, the Watteau gown became the *robe à la française,* and, by 1770, this loose gown was the formal dress for court functions, developing six box pleats, stitched flat to the back and ending in a train. Under the upper part of the gown, attached to the bodice, was a fitted lining which was laced in back.

The *robe volant,* or flying gown, was a variation of the gown with the Watteau pleats. The soft pleats flowed from shoulder to hem, both back and front. The dress was usually ankle-length, worn over a wide hoop which created an undulating movement as the wearer walked. The style lasted to the end of the reign.

Panniers returned in 1718 by way of England, where they had already been in fashion for six or seven years under the name of hoop skirt, but did not really take hold in France until 1730. The hoops were of reed or whalebone, held together by ribbons, basket-like, thus the French name *panier* meaning basket. The frame work was covered with taffeta or brocade, and was called accordingly a taffeta or brocade hoop. The hoop was first funnel-shaped, but from the 'thirties to the 'forties grew very broad at the sides and flat front and back. The circumference is said to have reached, later, eighteen feet. A Mademoiselle Margot, a coutourière, invented an inexpensive pannier, which made the fashion accessible to women of all classes.

About 1750, the hoop was divided into two sections with pocket openings in the sides, from which, on the inside, hung pockets in the form of bags. The wearer reached the pockets through openings in both the outer and under skirts.

In a popular style, called "pocket panniers," the panniers were formed by pulling the drapery through the pocket holes. This dress, which was usually ankle-length, also had the box pleats attached to the shoulders in back. This fashion, by the next reign, had spread to the bourgeoisie, finally becoming the habitual costume of servants. See Page 216.

The extremely broad panniers on which the elbows could be rested were named "elbow panniers," and the very small ones, worn for morning or negligee, *considérations*.

The feminine riding habit continued along masculine lines in coat and waistcoat with cravat. Its full skirt was worn over panniers, and the three-cornered hat topped the costume. By the 'forties, women were changing their costume three or four times a day. There were special toilettes for morning or negligee, walking, theatre, supper, and formal for night.

The "pair of bodies," bodice or corset was long and slim, laced in back, made of heavy linen or brocade, reinforced by whalebone, still a confining garment but of lighter weight than its predecessor. It had eyelets on tabs below the waist, to which the underskirt was held by lacing.

Fabrics changed from heaviness to daintiness in crisp taffetas, flowered, striped or plain, lustrous satins and damasks, lutestring, or lustring, flowered lawns and dimities, in pastel shades and all trimmed with lace, ribbons and artificial flowers. A fine soft lace in natural silk, known as *blonde lace,* appeared in 1757 and became very fashionable. Flower and fruit motifs on fabrics were just under natural size.

Aprons continued in fashion, now short and of silk, satin or gauze, edged with fringe or bobbin lace either in gold or silver.

Petticoats of silk or satin with wadding between the outer fabric and a lining, were quilted in attractive designs. These underskirts were especially popular in England and the American Colonies.

There were all styles of scarflike wraps and mantillas, edged with ruffles and ruches; in fact, the vogue of the shawl is supposed to have had its beginning in the 'seventies of this reign. These wraps were short for summer and long for winter, some had armholes and some had loose hoods attached. The long winter *mante,* or mantle, was fur-lined throughout and buttoned down the length of the front. The summer mantilla was draped over the head, loosely tied in front or crossed over the bosom and tied in back.

From 1730, collarettes of ribbon and lace were worn around the throat. Gloves were of light-colored kid or silk, and silk and lace mittens were of the period.

The hair was dressed simply, close to the head, off the forehead and up in back, until past the middle of the century. From about 1750, the front hair, cut short, was dressed off the forehead with the ends set in curls, going over the head from ear to ear. A dressing of pomatum and flour held the ringlets in place, and a tiny black taffeta cushion stuffed with straw or cotton supported the curls. False hair, flowers and aigrettes were also attached to the cushion. Powder was used on the hair for full dress. From 1760, the coiffure gradually increased in height. An interesting note is that, by 1769, there were twelve hundred hairdressers in Paris.

For everyday wear until the 'fifties, small dainty caps of lawn and lace were worn, but, from 1760, they grew in all dimensions with the coiffure, frills and ruchings framing the face and lappets hanging in back. About the 'seventies, hats became fashionable. They were of straw, felt and fabric, in all styles, worn at all angles, trimmed with lace, ribbons, feathers, artificial flowers and fruits and jewelled buckles. A great favorite was the leghorn hat encircled with a wreath of flowers.

Make-up, though still applied too freely, was done with more artistic technique than in the preceding reign. Paint and powder were a court requirement and patches of all shapes and sizes were worn. Madame de Pompadour and Madame du Barry both made extravagant use of perfume, a fashion which the whole court followed. All personal articles and clothes were scented. There were exquisite perfume cases and rings with tiny compartments for holding scent. Parasols did away with the necessity of wearing the mask. The parasol became smaller and could now be carried by the lady herself. Parasols or sunshades did not close. The invention of a folding frame was employed only for the *parapluie,* or rain umbrella.

Slippers of satin and brocade, with the high Louis XV heel, slim and curving, were worn; they were also made of kid in all colors, embroidered in gold and silver, and ornamented with buckles in gold and cut steel. Silk stockings had gold or silver clocks, and white cotton stockings, which were popular, had colored clocks.

Less jewelry was worn but there were such gadgets as patch boxes, vanity boxes and rouge pots. Watches were beautiful works of art. Women carried the lorgnette, and men the single glass, or *perspective.* Tall, gold-headed canes for feminine use were made of scented wood, tortoise shell and ivory, and were held halfway down the stick. Very small handkerchiefs embroidered in colored silks and edged with costly lace were used as ornaments, while the most beautiful fans were created in the eighteenth century.

The folding fan had sticks of ivory, tortoise shell, mother-of-pearl, gold or silver. Satin, kid or vellum leaf, stretched over the sticks, was decorated with miniature scenes, painted by the great artists of the day. Women, like the men, wore the small bouquets of artificial flowers. Small bags and purses were carried throughout the century, made of the costliest fabrics, beautifully embroidered in silk, steel, gilt or colored beads. Of that period is the beaded bag of heavy silk thread done with crochet hook or knitting needle. Muffs grew larger for both sexes, fashioned of rich furs and finished with frills of lace and ribbon.

A novelty in jewelry of the eighteenth century was paste, or *strass,* invented by a German jeweller named Strasser. Buckles, buttons, court and military orders glittered with the clear, brilliant sparkling stones. Paste seems to have been considered more as a substitute than an imitation, and was worn by the aristocracy. The French employment of paste surpassed that of the other countries in delicacy of design, and the periods of Louis XV and Louis XVI have been noted as the "golden age of paste."

Louis·XV

cloth coat-silk vest
and breeches-buttons
and buttonholes-white
lawn shirt, cravat
and jabot-powdered
bag-wig with pigeon's
wings- cocked hat-
gold braid-black
leather shoes with
buckles-sword-cane-
1st half 18th C.

habit of silk-
coat-vest-breeches-
buttons and
buttonholes-white
lawn shirt, cravat
and jabot-cocked
hat with braid-
powdered bag-
wig-pigeon's
wings-leather
shoes with
buckles-
1st half 18th C.

heavy cloth redingote-
buttons and buttonholes-
leather belt-habit
cuffs showing-Ramillies
hat with braid-
powdered bag-wig-
pigeon's wings-
buckled leather
shoes-sword-
muffler-1740

habit with
shortened vest-
lawn shirt, cravat,
jabot-handkerchief
in coat pocket-
watch fobs-clocked
stockings-leather
shoes-large buckles-
sword-powdered
cadogan wig-
hat under arm-
3rd quarter 18th C.

RTW

Louis-XV

"flying gown" of pink
taffeta-underskirt
same edged with
gimp-lingerie
neck and sleeve
ruffles-lingerie
cap with lappets-
powdered hair-
embroidered
yellow slippers-
green stockings-
1st quarter 18th C.

changeable pink and
green striped satin-
gray satin stomacher-
tiny peplum-lingerie
ruffles and cap-
twisted lace scarf-
black silk mantilla
with self ruche-
gray kid gloves-
1st quarter
18th C.

"Watteau pleats" and
train-taffeta gown
and underskirt-bowknot-
lace frills-lace
edged lingerie cap
with lappets-
2nd quarter
18th C.

"flying gown" of
satin- underskirt
same-tightly
laced underbodice-
velvet bows-
pagoda sleeves-
lingerie cap and frills-
powdered hair-
1730

soft pleats flowing
from shoulders
when ... them
backs front

RTW

Louis · XV

taffeta with self
ruchings-double
panniers-satin bows-
jewelled buttons-
pagoda sleeves with
lace ruffles-collarette
of bowknots and pearls-
satin slippers-
powdered hair
with velvet and
satin ribbon, and
pearls-earrings-
1762

"robe à la française"
with pleats in back-
old blue taffeta-
scalloped edged
ruffles-rose ribbon
bows, stomacher and
collarette-pagoda
sleeves-lace ruffles-
pink roses, green
foliage-rose in
powdered hair-
fresh flowers
on shoulder-
embroidered
gold slippers-
pearl
bracelets-
1760's

satin gown
with lace
frills-powdered
hair with
velvet ribbon-
middle 18th C.

same as Watteau

"robe à la française"-
satin with contrasting
colored underskirt-
pleats stitched to
fitted bodice-pagoda
sleeves-lingerie frills-
self ruching on skirt-
powdered hair-cap
with bowknot-
3rd quarter 18th C.

formal dress
for court

6 box pleats
stitched flat
to back
ending in
a train

RTW

Louis XV

silk hood with shoulder cape- mantilla of flowered silk presumably held to the figure by a cord or ribbon belt-1730's

riding habit with double panniers- coat and waistcoat resembling masculine cut-lingerie blouse- powdered hair with bowknot- tricorne-boots- 1st half 18th C.

fur-lined mantle of cloth-silk hood with shoulder cape- 1755

taffeta cloak with wide self ruching at waist- elbow sleeves with deep cuffs-silk hood with ribbon lappets-lorgnette- 1720's

RTW

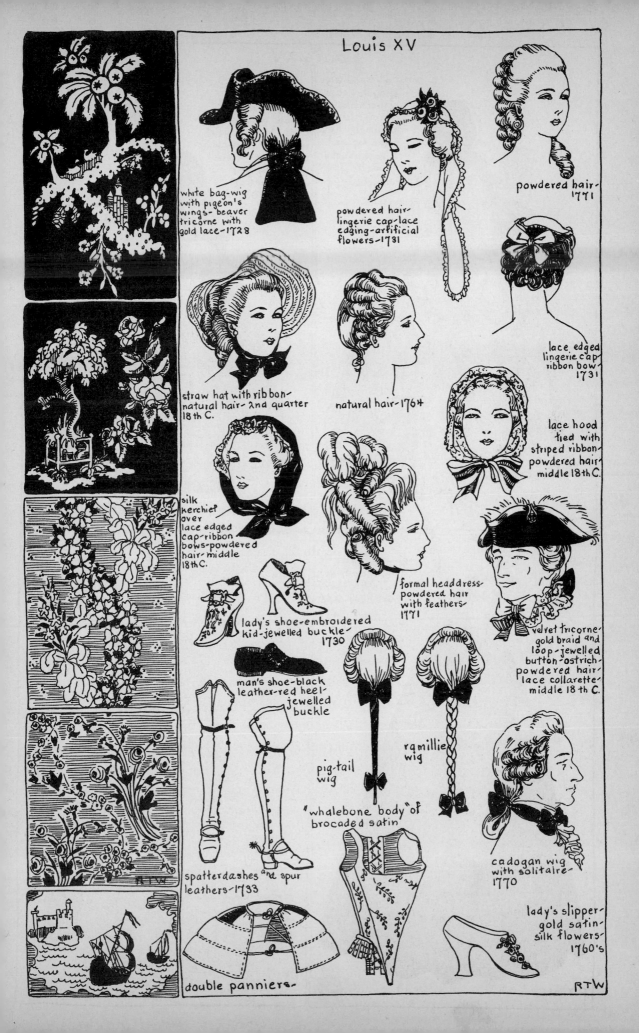

Louis XV

white bag-wig with pigeon's wings - beaver tricorne with gold lace - 1728

powdered hair - lingerie cap - lace edging - artificial flowers - 1731

powdered hair - 1771

lace edged lingerie cap - ribbon bow 1731

straw hat with ribbon - natural hair - 2nd quarter 18th C.

natural hair - 1764

lace hood tied with striped ribbon - powdered hair middle 18th C.

silk kerchief over lace edged cap - ribbon bows - powdered hair - middle 18th C.

formal headdress - powdered hair with feathers - 1771

velvet tricorne - gold braid and loop - jewelled button - ostrich - powdered hair - lace collarette - middle 18th C.

lady's shoe - embroidered kid - jewelled buckle - 1730

man's shoe - black leather - red heel - jewelled buckle

pig-tail wig

ramillie wig

cadogan wig with solitaire - 1770

"whalebone body" of brocaded satin

spatterdashes and spur leathers - 1733

double panniers -

lady's slipper - gold satin - silk flowers - 1760's

RTW

Chapter Thirty-one

Louis Sixteenth—
Marie Antoinette

To the French Revolution—1774-1789

THE BEGINNING of this reign was a period of great extravagance, artificialty and daintiness. The mode had spread to all classes and was worn by all who could afford to spend. By 1780, came a complete change toward simplicity, with a dominant English influence in both men's and women's costume. The English have held, up to the present day, the leadership they now acquired for the first time, as arbiters in designing men's apparel.

There was slight difference between the masculine mode of Louis XV and that of Louis XVI. The *habit à la française* still existed but was worn only at court. The coat opened wide in front over the vest. Color was more important, with a distinct preference for apple green and light yellow. Waistcoats were usually white, with colored silk embroideries in bouquets and garlands of flowers. There was a tremendous vogue for spotted and ribbed silks. Dress suits were often white with handsomely embroidered waistcoats.

The *frac,* or frock coat, origin of the cutaway, had a turndown

206

collar, no visible pockets, the coat itself usually plain green or striped yellow. Near the end of the reign, striped fabrics dominated in frock coats. About 1780 appeared the English frock coat, usually buttoned in front, the waistcoat showing below and the frilled jabot of soft batiste at the neck. It, to, had the collar of contrasting fabric. Woolen fabrics were usurping the place of silk in the masculine coat.

Also of English derivation was the *redingote à la lévite,* a double-breasted long coat with turndown collar and two or three shoulder capes. The English also called the garment the carrick.

From under the vest, on either side of the breeches, hung tassels or fobs attached to key, locket or a pair of watches, the second watch often being false. The wearing of two fobs or charms originated with the idea of concealing the closing of the breeches to either side of the center front. However, watches were often made in pairs, probably so that, one failing, the other would still give service. Buttons were enameled, painted or of cut steel.

Breeches were very tight, fitting the thighs and ending below the knees, where they fastened with buckles, buttons and occasionally bunches of ribbon. The stocking was often rolled over the breeches, with the garter concealed therein. Both silk and cotton stockings were usually white, and silk stockings for dress wear were clocked with gold or silver.

Men's shoes retained their square toes and, for dress, red heels. Large square buckles were still worn, but their vogue began to decline in the 'seventies, giving way to string ties. Escarpins, or pumps, low-cut slippers with a thin flexible sole, were fashionable, also walking boots of soft black leather. *Guêtres,* or gaiters, known in England as leggings, or spatterdashes, were worn as protection in bad weather. They were of leather and buttoned at the sides.

Black was worn more and more as an economy by gentle people of small means, because it saved the expense of a mourning costume. Upon the death of a royal person, custom required every one to observe such an event occurring among crowned heads. The period of mourning, lasting a year, was reduced to a period of three months just before the Revolution.

The wigs of the preceding period and hair arranged in a postiche were worn for the greater part of this reign, but by 1779 wigs had begun to disappear, to be retained only by men in certain professions. The principal styles were the bagwig and the cadogan. The wig or hair was dressed high off the forehead, often with a single large roll over the top from ear to ear or with two smaller rolls over each ear. The Brutus, or "hedgehog," cut was popular in the 'eighties, its name describing very well the style.

The tricorne, or cocked hat, of Louis XV continued to be worn. From the 'eighties, a very small version was especially favored by the Macaronies of England, where it was known as the Nivernois hat, so named after the French diplomatist and writer.

The Macaronies were a group of idle young Englishmen, who, upon returning from a tour of Italy, formed the Macaroni Club in London, and thereafter everything extreme in dress was attributed to them.

The most popular hat of the period was a variation of the Swiss military hat. It was really a bicorne, having a front and back flap, with the highest point or corner in center front, caused by a pinching of the front flap, thereby resembling a tricorne. The French called their version the *Androsmane,* and the English named theirs the *Khevenhüller,* or *Kevenhuller,* after the famous Austrian field-marshal of that name. It set comfortably down on the head.

A forerunner of the top hat made its appearance in the 'eighties, a high crown with rolling brim. Other styles were the Holland, or Pennsylvania hat with flat crown and rolling brim, the Quaker hat with low crown and rolling brim and the jockey hat. The jockey hat also had a low crown, but its brim of moderate width was bent down in front to shade the eyes. This hat came from England, where it was first worn by grooms, then adopted by their masters. It was ornamented with a band and a cockade at the side or a buckle in the front.

The lingerie shirt was of fine material, with jabot and wrist ruffles of plain or embroidered lawn and lace. With the decline of the vogue of the wig in the 'seventies, the neckcloth appeared, lasting well into the nineteenth century. It was wrapped around the neck and tied in front in a soft bow.

Malacca canes were of all heights, with various styles of heads and tasselled cords and muffs were still used by the masculine sex in winter. Lace-trimmed handkerchiefs and exquisite snuffboxes were other accessories.

In feminine costume, all Europe now followed the French fashions, of which Marie Antoinette and her modiste, Mlle. Rose Bertin, were the dictators. Large dolls dressed in the latest creations, called "fashion dolls" or "fashion babies," were sent periodically from Paris to the capitals of the other countries, to be exhibited to the eagerly waiting fashionable world. There were many changes of style in this period, but from 1784 to 1789 the changes were constant.

Still worn was the whalebone corset, with eyelets in the tabs around the waist, to which the underskirt was laced. The garment was softer and more normal in shape, curving in decidedly to accentuate the small waist and curving out above to accent the line of the bosom. It gave a long, slim look to the body and was laced in back. Very wide side panniers were fashioned of metal bands connected by tapes, by means of which the hoops could be drawn up under the arms. In the 'eighties, panniers, though still retained for formal court wear, were supplanted by the *tournure,* or bustle.

The most extravagant use of ornamentation, pearls and jewels by the court marked the years 1776 to 1778, even slippers being encrusted with diamonds.

Gowns were made of plain, striped and painted satins, plain and striped taffetas, soft lustrous velvets and brocades. The motifs used on figured fabrics were small and dainty, festoons of flowers, bowknots, flower baskets and the like. Trimmings consisted of lace, tulle, ribbon and fur. Over the shoulders were draped scarfs of lace, tulle and ribbon. Hoop and pannier gowns were lavishly ornamented, knots of ribbon, puffs, loops, garlands of flowers, fluted flounces or quilting, all on one dress. Straw-colored satin was a great favorite; other colors were apple green, lemon yellow, canary yellow and pink.

The black silk laces of Chantilly were introduced in the last quarter of this century and were popular for scarfs and headdresses. Blonde lace, that soft fine lace of natural silk, was a great favorite of the Queen's. All parts of the costume were given curious names, an amusing example being *puce,* or flea color. The bowknot of ribbon which hid the fastening of the décolletage on the bosom was called "perfect contentment."

The sacque, or *robe à la française,* of the preceding reign, with its very broad panniers and stitched back pleats, became full dress for court, theatre and balls. It was most elaborate, ornamented with garlands of artificial flowers, furbelows, pearls and other gems.

The pocket panniers of the last period were taken up by the bourgeoisie, eventually becoming the costume of servants. The principal styles of gowns of this period were the *polonaise,* the *circassienne,* the *anglaise,* the *lévite,* the *caraco,* the English and the Queen's gown.

The *polonaise* lasted from 1776 to 1787, and its special feature consisted of three panniers, one back and two side sections, which rounded away in front. The panniers of the polonaise were drawn up on cords and could also be let down to form a flying gown. The cords were run through slots and were finished with tassels or rosettes, although later the panniers were sewn in position, with the cords simply ornamental.

The *circassienne* was a variation of the polonaise. It too had three panniers run on cords, but very short and of even length. The gown had double sleeves, that is, the outer bodice had short cap sleeves worn over the longer sleeves of the underbodice.

The *caraco* was a gown with long basque, finished with a peplum ruffle, and often a train, called a *figaro,* was attached under the peplum.

The *lévite* gown was really a type of redingote with train. Its creation was inspired by the Englishman's redingote of the same period. There was a definite redingote gown, which had a jacket, double breasted and with wide lapels. This costume was considered "very mannish."

The masculine wig and cravat, the redingote with its capes, were adopted for horseback, while from under the waistcoat hung the two watches or charms, such as the men wore. Shoes with low heels and a "switch stick" completed the attire of the "Amazons."

The Queen's playing at farming brought about a vogue for cotton prints, sheer aprons and fichus, large simple leghorn hats combined with feathers and jewels.

A very popular style, from 1781, was the *chemise à la reine,* worn by Marie Antoinette. Comparatively speaking, it was a simple frock made of sheer cotton or light silk. The neck was low in front, finished with a full standing ruffle. The skirt was edged with a deep-fluted flounce and a soft, wide sash was tied around the waist. It is noteworthy, as being the introduction of the lingerie frock into Europe. It was nevertheless a luxury, as cottons and prints were still imported from India.

In 1783, fashion suddenly changed from utter extravagance to extreme simplicity, and, by 1786, panniers, trains and trimming had all disappeared. There were several reasons for the change, the loss of immense fortunes, the writings of Jean-Jacques Rousseau, the country clothes of the Queen at the Petit-Trianon and the influence of English simplicity in dress.

About the middle of the century, at Jouy, France, had been established a shop for the hand-block printing of linen, cambric and cotton, which now came into its own with the vogue for *indiennes,* as they were called. *Tulle* made its first appearance in this period, named after the town of its fabrication, Tulle, France.

The *robe à l'anglaise* was simple, rich-looking and artistic, a great delight to the portrait painters of the period. It was usually of satin in plain colors, with tight bodice and long full skirt, a soft full fichu finishing the neck. The sleeves varied from the long, slim shape to the soft, full elbow-length puff.

The fichu was a feature of the period, worn with the different styles of gowns. It was bunched above the small, tight waist, giving a pouter-pigeon look to the figure.

Sheer cottons, fine linens and cambrics were embroidered with white cotton, the finest embroidery being done in Saxony. Such fabrics were employed for scarfs, collars and cuffs. The apron was now all white, of soft cotton ornamented with needlework and drawn work.

In the beginning of the period, the hair rose high off the forehead, dressed over pads at the sides and back of the neck. For full dress, strings of pearls and flowers were added. Later, the hair was kneaded with pomatum and flour, twisted into rolls and curls and dressed over a cushion or pad of wool. False hair was added to build up the coiffure, from then growing to unbelievable heights, with every conceivable decoration placed on top. To rows of curls were added ribbons, flowers, laces, feathers, blown glass or straw, models of ships, coaches and windmills. The back hair was dressed in loose curls, in chignon or cadogan fashion.

There were many styles of headdress, but two unusual ones in the 'eighties were the coiffure *à la l'enfant* and *à la hérisson. L'enfant,* or "baby headdress," was cut short like a bob, due to the Queen's illness necessitating the cutting of the hair. The *coiffure à la hérisson,* or hedgehog fashion, appeared in 1778, resembling that of the men, cut fairly short in front, frizzed to the ends and brushed up high off the face, with long loose curls or the cadogan in back.

Toward the end of the period, powder, always used for full dress, was but lightly employed for ordinary wear. After her hair was dressed, the lady covered her face with a paper bag and powder was thickly applied. Pertaining to the elaborate headdress, contemporary advice was that the head should be "opened up" at least once a week.

The face was literally painted red and white, accented with various shapes of black taffeta patches. The use of heavily scented perfume declined, the Queen preferring delicate rose and violet odors.

As the size of the coiffure increased, so did the lingerie caps, or *bonnets,* as they were now called, the name bonnet having been applied to men's toques heretofore. The *dormeuse,* or sleeping bonnet, so named because it was also worn at night, hugged the head tightly, covering the cheeks, and was threaded with a ribbon tied into a bow on top of the head. The dormeuse of daytime wear was worn higher on the head, revealing the ears and back of the head.

Then came the *demi-bonnets* and bonnet-hats imported from England. They were very large, with soft full crowns, wide brims which almost hid the face, and they were usually trimmed with ribbon bands and loops. The large cap was known in England as the *mob-cap,* or Ranelagh mob, because much worn in the Ranelagh Gardens, a place of entertainment founded by Lord Ranelagh upon his estate and frequented by the fashionables. The English name for the small cap was *close Joan.*

The bonnets called *thérèse* and *caliche* or calash were, according to a French description, cages. They covered the huge coiffures and were therefore very large. The thérèse was of gauze or tulle, sometimes of black taffeta edged with tulle and made over wires or whalebone. The calash had reed or whalebone hoops which could be raised or lowered by a ribbon like the hood of a carriage.

About 1783, with the lowered style of hairdressing, bonnets became smaller and hats appeared. Hats were of felt or beaver, in all sizes and shapes, worn at all angles, trimmed with plumes, ribbons, fruits and flowers. Very wide brims originated in England, as did the most elegant hat of all time, known today as the Marlborough or Gainsborough hat, perpetuating in the mode not only the name of the British painter, Gainsborough, but also that of his sitter, the Duchess of Marlborough.

Straw hats, with very wide brims and a simple ribbon band around the low crown, became popular during the Queen's "milkmaid period." That style, considered a "rustic fashion," also came from England, where people were very fond of country life. Straw was new for fashionable hats, and enjoyed quite a vogue, great quantities being imported from Italy, leghorn, horsehair and chip being the most fashionable.

The pelisse, a fur-trimmed wrap, capelike with armholes and broad collar, continued to be worn. In the winter, large fur muffs protected the arms and hands against the cold. Muffs were occasionally tiny, of silk and satin with ribbon bows and embroidery. They were carried in the summer and to balls. Long gloves of soft light-colored kid were worn during the whole century.

Slippers of satin, brocade and kid were the fashion, with moderately high heels, sometimes covered with white kid. The back seam was occasionally encrusted with gems. Women of quality wore fabric slippers of reddish brown or pigeon gray. Leather slippers were worn only by the demimonde and the lower class. Stockings were white in both silk and cotton.

Jewels were many and exquisite in necklaces, lockets, beautiful crosses, ivory writing tablets, with tassels, needlecases, handsome watches and eyeglasses mounted in gold and enamel. The use of paste or strass in jewelry reached its height in this period. Cut steel was employed for buttons and buckles. Necklaces were finally supplanted by a simple velvet ribbon tied around the neck. Later, a pendant or miniature was suspended from the ribbon. Exquisite and costly fans remained in vogue. The boutonnière of fresh or artificial flowers was worn by both sexes.

Dress for children had begun to change from the tightly fitted clothes of their elders. A portrait of Marie Antoinette with her two children, painted in 1785 by Wertmüller, portrays the Dauphin in long trousers and a short buttoned jacket with a frill at the open neck. The little girl wears a simple frock of English style, also with a frill at the low round neck and a sash about the waist.

Louis XVI - Marie Antoinette

habit à la française-
silk embroidery-
boutonnière-felt
cocked hat-ostrich
fringe-powdered
hair-lingerie
shirt-cravat-
jabot-two
watch fobs-
sword-
1770's and 1780's

frockcoat-buttons
and embroidery
on waistcoat-
cravat-jabot-
two watches with
fobs-Swiss or
Androsmane hat,
beaver with braid-
cane with tassels-
1778

lévite redingote or
carrick-Holland
or Pennsylvania
hat with ribbon
band-lingerie
cravat-velvet
breeches-black
leather shoes-
strass buckles-
powdered hair
in cadogan-
cane with
tassels-1780's

frockcoat with
tassels-jockey
hat with ribbon
band and buckle-
powdered hair
in cadogan-
two watch
fobs-fur
muff with
bowknot-
leather
jockey boots-
1779

RTW

Louis XVI - Marie Antoinette

pocket panniers-
heavy silk with
lingerie fichu
and pleated ruffles-
powdered hair-
lingerie cap-
1775

polonaise gown-
striped and plain
silk-cords, tassels
and ruches-hat
with turned-up
back-ribbon, ostrich
and aigrettes-neck
ribbon-satin
slippers with
buckles-
1776

circassienne gown-
silk in two colors-
medici collar-
boutonnière-
tassels-hat with
flowers, ribbon,
ostrich, pleated
frill-powdered
hair-fan-satin
shoes-buckles
handkerchief-
1780

caraco gown of
hunter's green
silk-white lawn
frills, fichu and
apron- black hat
with dotted rose
ribbon-white
ostrich-blond hair
in cadogan-
fan-
1785

RTW

Louis XVI - Marie Antoinette

"queen's gown" of gauze or thin silk-Medici collar-satin sash and bow-straw hat-striped ribbon and flowers-natural hair in hedgehog style-cane with tassels-1783

X

redingote with train

lévite gown, silk with satin trimming-lingerie underskirt-knotted ribbon tassels-straw hat with ostrich and ribbon-powdered hair in cadogan style-cane with tassels-neck ribbon-1780's

green   white

redingote gown-velvet jacket and sash with tassels-satin revers, cuffs and train-lingerie tie and jabot-gauze with scalloped edge and checked embroidery-gold buttons-powdered hair-hat of dotted gauze, ostrich, embroidery and flowers-cane with carved bird and ribbon-1787

English gown-velvet bodice with lingerie fichu and sleeves-satin skirt-Gainsborough hat with pearls and ostrich-neck ribbon-powdered hair-1780's

RTW

Louis XVI - Marie Antoinette

riding habit-
cloth jacket-silk
waistcoat and
skirt-fringed
silk sash-knotted
neckcloth-natural
hair in braid-felt
hat with ostrich-
1780's

silk pelisse, fur
trimmed-fur
muff-gown of
flowered silk-
bonnet tied under
chin-silk puffings
and ruchings-
powdered hair-
satin slippers-
1778

pale blue satin
pelisse with mink-
mink muff with
violet bow-lingerie
gown with violet
silk train-
lingerie bonnet,
violet and cerise
ribbon-natural
hair in hedgehog
style-1787

transparent summer
coat-stripes and
embroidered dots-
satin collar, bow
and fronts-gauze
thérèse over
powdered hair-
silk gown with
galloon, ruches and
tassels-fringed
sash-jewelled
buttons-kid
slippers-
1770's

RTW

Louis XVI - Marie Antoinette

dormeuse bonnet-
sheer muslin-
satin ribbon-
1770's

man's coiffure-
natural hair-
1780's

dormeuse bonnet-
sheer muslin-
taffeta ribbon-
1770's

hedgehog and
pigtail-
1780's

powdered hair-
thérèse of sheer
black-satin
band-colored
bow-1784

hedgehog-
1788

back view
of calash

calash of
black silk
shirred on
wire hoops-
1780's

Quaker
beaver hat-ribbon
and buckle-1780's

beaver hat-
natural hair
in cadogan-
late 1780's

Pennsylvania hat-
beaver with ribbon-
powdered hair in cadogan-1780's

lady's
riding
boot-
1780's

formal headdress-
powdered-cadogan-
pearls, flowers and
feathers-1780's

silk kerchief-powdered
hair-ribbon-back in
cadogan-1780's

folding metal panniers with tapes

RTW

Chapter Thirty=two

The French Revolution
1789-1795

[handwritten marginalia: king wicked ruled by maria ... rapid middle class ... very inefficient govt. ... group of philosophers helped ... middle class ... people swapped away class distinction ... cosmetics sparsely used ... very little elegance]

I N THE years before the Revolution, the mode had begun to change. A desire for simpler design in dress, less splendor and less class distinction was indicated. The English, with their love of country life, had already eliminated formality from their everyday clothes, and thus it came about that they became a distinct influence in the modish world.

With the crash of the upheaval, hoops, paint, powder, beauty patches, artificial flowers and fruit and magnificence in costume disappeared. A very few dared display elegance in public. Social life ceased with the ending of court, and fashion journals were no more. Information of the mode in Paris must be had from contemporary English and German sources. Evidence of social distinction by means of dress was abolished by the National Assembly. The privilege of wearing brocades, feathers, red heels and embroideries, now extended to the citizens, was scorned, surviving only in servants' costume.

The standard simplicity of masculine costume worn today dates

220

[handwritten marginalia: London took hold of fashion leadership → now labeled their costumes]

in millinery Charlotte Corda hat

from the French Revolution. The principal change was the substitution of trousers for breeches or culottes. The wearing of trousers created a new trade, the manufacturing of suspenders, and caused stockings to shorten into socks.

The trousers opened in front by means of a panel buttoned to the vest by three buttons and were called *pantalons à pont,* bridge trousers, the panel operating like drawbridge. These trousers, hitherto worn only by British sailors, were accompanied by either a vest or jacket, named a *carmagnole.* The carmagnole was originally worn by Piedmont workers who came from "Carmagnola," and the deputies of Marseilles took the garment to Paris, where it was adopted by the Revolutionaries.

Those who wore trousers were called *sans-culottes,* meaning "without breeches," differentiating them from the aristocrat, but eventually the term came to signify the patriot. The red bonnet or cap, symbol of liberty with its cockade, completed the costume of the patriot or democrat.

The red liberty bonnet or cap varied in shape, being of Phrygian origin, or with hanging pointed crown, or just a skullcap with the pointed crown, but always ornamented with the tricolor cockade. The large felt hat with brim held up in front by the cockade was also seen. The red was always placed between the blue and the white.

The patriot of 1789-1790 wore the frock coat, with high turndown collar and lapels, cut away in front with tail in back. His breeches were tight, descending below the knees, sometimes finished with ribbon loops.

Heels, buckles and rosettes disappeared with the Revolution, leaving a soft, heelless slipper fastened with plain strings, worn with white or striped silk stockings. The indecision as to the length of the trousers was settled by wearing boots. They were of soft, highly polished black leather, with light-brown leather turndown cuffs and bootstraps hanging at the sides. This was the English jockey boot, commonly known as the top boot. The white or striped stockings showed between boot top and stocking. Well-fitting gaiters were also the fashion.

Wigs continued to be worn but powder was sparingly applied, a fashion note of 1790 being the use of mouse-colored powder. The back hair was generally worn in a very short pigtail wound with narrow ribbon. In the army, the short pigtail or cue was often false, fashioned of chamois or black leather, with a tuff of hair at the end.

The tricorne, or three-cornered hat, disappeared, supplanted by the bicorne and a round shape with brim of even width, tall tapering crown encircled by a silk cord and the red, white and blue cockade at one side.

The anti-revolutionist wore a black turndown collar, as a sign of mourning, on a light-colored coat. He changed, in 1791, to a coat of green with rose collar. About 1792, elegants or muscadins, in protest against the negligee appearance of the sans-culottes, returned to the frock coat with lapels, its collar of brilliant contrasting color and the frilled shirt front. The fronts of the coat, ornamented with two rows of steel buttons, did not close. The frock-redingote fastened by means of tabs or frogs.

A *muscadine* is a pastille scented with musk, and the name was applied to effeminate men who overdressed and used quantities of this scent. The muscadine carried a short or long stick weighted with lead.

A costume called the "true patriot" became official in 1794. It consisted of the pantalons à pont, the carmagnole, a brown redingote with collar and lapels faced with red, sabots and a bonnet or low bicorne. However, it did not meet with success, and the Convention commissioned the painter David to create a national costume. David's design consisted of tight trousers with boots, a tunic and short coat, in an attempt to fill the requirements of an outfit suitable to the new social order and work.

As with that of the men, women's costume took on a simplicity, while retaining the basic lines of the style of the last years of the Louis XVI period. The only noticeable change was in the raised waistline. This fashion, which is wrongly referred to as English, was created by Rose Bertin in London, whither she and her assistants had fled.

The bodice was tightly laced from waist to breasts, emphasizing the bosom. Still more emphasis was given by a full fichu of sheer white fabric, usually tulle or gauze, tucked into the neck of the bodice. Full folds of satin were often added, causing the whole to reach the chin in pouter-pigeon effect. Sleeves were long and tight, skirts were full, shirred at the waist and worn over many petticoats.

A ban against silks and velvets caused the increase of simple figured cottons and linens. The soft full lingerie gown, called the *chemise à l'anglaise* with its crushed satin sash, was worn both summer and winter. Satin, sparingly used, was brownish green or dull blue, while mat-surfaced silks such as *crépon de chine* were in plain color or simple stripes of one color.

There were high-crowned hats trimmed with flowers and ribbons, and bonnet-shaped hats with ribbon loops and streamers which tied under the chin. Ostrich plumes reappeared by the end of the period. Added to these were toques and caps of various shapes with puffed crowns, ribbon-trimmed. The peasant or milkmaid cap, called today the "Charlotte Corday cap" and termed by the English the mobcap, had a full crown, shirred frills, ornamented with the tricolor cockade. The national colors were used throughout the whole costume.

The prevailing coiffure was dressed low on top, sometimes parted in the middle, with soft puffs placed low at the sides, the back hair hanging in cadogan or ringlets.

Along with other aristocratic frivolities, heels of slippers disappeared. Instead was worn a soft, flat slipper of fabric or kid, cut low, sandallike in appearance, occasionally laced across the instep and round the ankle with ribbon. A tiny bow or edging finished the slipper.

By the end of this period, the feminine English redingote of the previous period had taken on a full shirred skirt in place of the broad silk train, and was made of cloth. While occasionally seen, the enveloping buttoned coat with its turndown collar and lapels did not really become the fashion until after 1800.

The embroidered handkerchief and the fan continued to be carried, but, in place of the exquisite and costly works of art of the preceding period, fans were smaller, made of tulle and gauze, spangled and scented.

Because of royal patronage, the lace factories were demolished, especially those of Chantilly, while some of the lacemakers were put to death and their patterns destroyed.

With the ending of this period, we find the democratic mode turning toward Ancient Greece and Rome for its inspiration.

It is recorded that shops carrying ready-made clothes, which filled the needs of the citizen and his wife, have existed in Paris since 1791.

The French Revolution

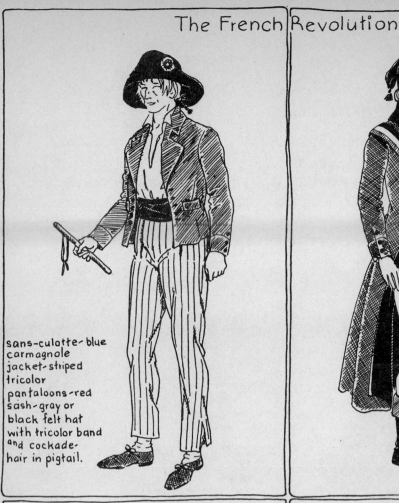

patriot-redingote of
brown cloth-red
cloth collar and
lapels-vest with
striped band-
pantaloons-black
jockey boots, straps,
brown cuffs-red
woolen cap-tassel-
tricolor baldric-
1793

sans-culotte-blue
carmagnole
jacket-striped
tricolor
pantaloons-red
sash-gray or
black felt hat
with tricolor band
and cockade-
hair in pigtail.

an elegant or
muscadine-frockcoat-
claw hammer tail-
fancy vest-folded
lace edged cravat
fastened with jewel-
knee breeches with
ribbon loops-striped
silk stockings-
black jockey boots,
straps, brown cuffs-
felt hat, silk cord-
tricolor rosette
1790

muscadine-
redingote frockcoat-
claw hammer tail-
tabs, buttons-satin
collar-knee breeches
with ribbon loops-
black jockey boots,
straps, brown cuffs-
hair in cadogan-
felt hat
watch charm
1792

RTW

The French Revolution

gown of fine cloth-double collars-satin loops on jacket tail-tulle and satin fichus-straw hat with satin rosettes

cloth redingote-felt hat with ribbon and buckle-hair in cadogan-dotted cotton gown-gauze fichu

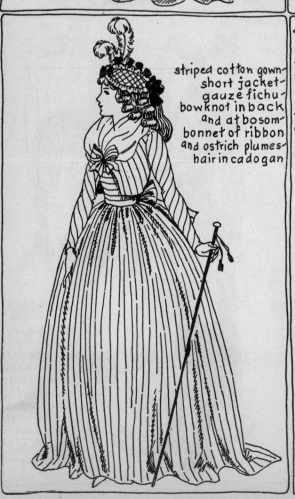

striped cotton gown-short jacket-gauze fichu-bowknot in back and at bosom-bonnet of ribbon and ostrich plumes-hair in cadogan

"chemise à l'anglaise" or the English frock-forerunner of the classic style to come-fewer petticoats-larger waist-lingerie fabric-satin sash-draped gauze turban-ostrich plume-hair in flowing curls-satin slippers

RTW

The French Revolution

felt bicorne-
tricolor cockade-
hair in pigtail

the Phrygian
bonnet-red
wool with
tricolor
cockade-
earrings

soldier's bonnet-
red cuff, piping
and tassel-blue
crown -cockade
on left
side

bonnet of the
populace-
tricolor band
and rosette

bonnet of gauze
and taffeta-
tricolor
cockade-hair
in cadogan-
earrings

straw hat-
taffeta in
several colors-
flowers-hair
in cadogan

bonnet of tulle
and taffeta

felt hat with
satin ribbon

gauze bonnet-
ribbon loops
and ruching-
ostrich plume

straw bonnet
with
ribbon band

hair dressed
with flowered
ribbon

lady's hair
in cadogan

RTW

new costumes, new democratic society public social
ball for anyone who could afford it
great vogue for white & cottons Classic

Directoire
1795-1799

English simplicity slim silhouette high
waist line emphasis on bust

ITH the Directoire came the trend toward the classic style of Ancient Greece and Rome. Gradually the luxuries of living returned to daily life, even fashion journals making their reappearance.

The muscadines of the preceding period were to be seen in a group of young dandies, who went to extremes in their dress and were known as the *incroyables,* or *impossibles.* Their coats, which sloped away in front from the waist, when buttoned, had a high turndown collar, very wide lapels and were usually worn open. Sometimes the coat had bulky pleats across the back, giving the ugly effect of a hump; in fact, the incroyable strove for a careless, wrinkled appearance.

With this coat was worn a waistcoat of contrasting colored satin and a very full, sheer white cambric cravat. The cravat, or neckcloth, was loosely wound round the neck several times, often over padded cushions, so that it rose up over the chin, its ends tied in front.

The culottes, or breeches, ended below the knees, where they

dresses higher with turndown collar

fastened with buttons and finished with ribbon loops. A strange idea was a button at the knee which came through a buttonhole in the breeches, presumably holding the stocking underneath. If the coat were of solid color, the waistcoat was striped, but, as often, the coat was of striped fabric and the waistcoat plain. Blue and white and green and white were favorite striped combinations.

When the refugee aristocrat returned to France, he wore, with his blond wig, the black collar as a sign of mourning on his light-colored coat. His green cravat or neckcloth was symbolic of royalty. The blond wig of the anti-revolutionist of the preceding period had now become the fashionable coiffure for both sexes.

The revolutionist finally gave up the sans-culottes, adopting the dress of the rest of the world, but wore a red collar on his coat, which gave rise to many bloody street quarrels between the "blacks" and the "reds."

The incroyable cut his hair raggedly in "dog's ears." His hat was extreme in size, either bicorne or with tall crown and hoop earrings hanging from his ears. Later, he changed to simple ringlets, lightly powdered, or the shaggy "Brutus" cut.

A more elegant costume was in vogue in this same period, consisting of frock coat and "hussar" breeches of dull blue cloth with black satin waistcoat, sometimes the breeches of satin. Hussar breeches were different only in that they were very tight. Favorite colors for breeches were canary yellow and bottle green, with the coat usually brown. The lapels of the coat were generally small and there was a small standing collar of black or violet velvet. The cravat, of fine white muslin or silk, in green, black or scarlet, was worn in the fashion of the incroyable. The hair was cut short in "Brutus" style.

There were boots of various heights and pumps, or *escarpins,* all of soft leather with pointed toes, worn with silk stockings, either plain white or striped on white.

The two watches were worn with the charms or fob seals hanging below the vest. The single eyeglass was fashionable, attached either to

chemise gown

a long slim stick or a short one. Canes and short sticks of knotty and twisted wood, weighted with lead, were part of the ensemble.

The Directoire Period in the feminine mode is interesting in the fact of its being the first time that the creators of fashion turned back to another period for inspiration, this time to Greece and Rome of antiquity. Lacking the knowledge that we now possess of the ancient colors employed, it was thought, because of the aged and bleached-out ruins unearthed, that everything had been originally white. So white in interiors, fabrics, even complexions became the predominant color of the Directoire, the Consulate and the Empire Periods to follow.

Sheath or chemise gowns were the fashion, slightly fulled over the breasts with a sash tied directly under. The skirt hung soft and full, usually with a train which was carried over the arm or pulled through the girdle, often leaving the leg exposed to the knee. There were tunics, knee-length with a skirt below, and long slim gowns, slit up at the side, revealing a bare limb or flesh-colored tights. Sleeves were either long and tight or very short with long gloves covering the bare arm. For conservative ladies, there was the Roman style of gown with underslip.

Sheer white materials, in mull, linen, lawn and silk, were employed for these gowns, regardless of the season in which they were worn and this was instrumental in bringing on an epidemic of tuberculosis.

These "Athenians" and "Romans" wore very long narrow scarfs, and in winter carried very large muffs of fur or silk. Scarfs were of cashmere, cloth, serge, knitted silk and very often of gray rabbit wool, in such colors as flame, orange, apricot and black and white. Bonnet and scarf generally matched in color.

The white cashmere shawl was making its first appearance. The English and French armies, in the Egyptian campaign, took note of the Oriental shawl, thus bringing about the great vogue for the lovely Egyptian, Persian, Turkish and Indian shawls.

Although the Spencer jacket appeared in 1799, it did not become a fashion until the Consulate and Empire Periods, the same being true of the feminine redingote of English origin.

Since the lines of the figure were entirely revealed, no pockets were possible, necessitating the use of a small bag or reticule, which name was humorously changed to "ridicule." A larger receptacle for toilet articles was the *sabretache*. It hung from the belt or balantine and was rather like a cavalry bag, elaborately embroidered, fringed and tasselled.

The *merveilleuse* was the feminine counterpart of the incroyable. The neck of the short tight bodice of her diaphanous gown was very low. The sheer lingerie muffler, resembling the masculine neckcloth, was often added and worn in the same fashion. The merveilleuse went bareheaded or wore an extreme style of hat. It frequently was a bonnet with a very large brim rising high off the forehead, an exaggerated version of the English jockey hat.

Wigs came in again after 1794, with blond the favorite color. Madame Tallien wore a black wig, but is known to have had thirty wigs of various colors. She was a great beauty of royal Spanish birth, wife of Jean-Lambert Tallien, later Princess Chimay, and is credited with introducing the Greek gown to the mode under the Directoire.

The classic coiffure with the psyche knot and net was adopted, in which the hair was plaited or curled and waved like the ancients' and made glossy with "antique oil." The wide, jewelled band was also seen. In the hairdressing establishments were exhibited busts of goddesses and empresses of antiquity.

Then followed various bobs, particularly the Titus style, in which the hair was cut short and brushed in all directions from the crown of the head, with uneven ends hanging over the forehead and ears. There was also the feminine "dog's ears," long, straggling ends hanging at the sides of the face.

Much jewelry was worn, bracelets, necklaces, rings, cameos and, in the hair, bands or strings of pearls. Jewelled "corset belts" about two inches wide were placed just under the breasts.

The styles in headgear were many, in caps, turbans and bonnets of all sizes, fashioned principally of crêpe and tulle, trimmed with ribbons, feathers, aigrettes and flowers. It is interesting to note that the

jockey cap worn

receptical for toilet articles was the

hosta especius were worn
stockings of white silk

word bonnet, from this time, designates a woman's hat tied under the chin. In the Middle Ages, the name was used in connection with men's head covering; then, to the latter part of the eighteenth century, was applied generally to all feminine headgear.

Shoes followed the classic design in sandals or cothurns and buskins laced with narrow red bands, inset with gold and precious stones. More generally worn was the very soft, pointed, heelless slipper of kid in red or the favored color of apple green. Stockings, when worn, were of white silk with inserted pointed clocks of pink or lilac satin. The "Grecian lady," with her bare feet encased in sandals or buskins, wore jewelled rings on her toes and bracelets around her ankles.

Artificial flowers became an important accessory in feminine costume, and a gruesome fad of a moment was a neck ribbon of red velvet, recalling the victims of the guillotine.

It is to be noted that from this period, with the elimination of tradition or social background, especially in women's costume, there has been constant change and, in her desire for distinction in dress, woman discards the mode as soon as it reaches the masses.

Directoire

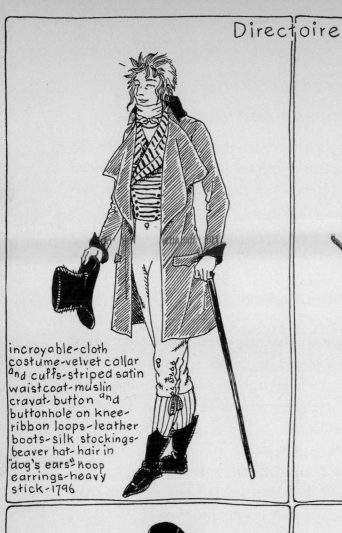

incroyable-cloth
costume-velvet collar
and cuffs-striped satin
waistcoat-muslin
cravat-button and
buttonhole on knee-
ribbon loops-leather
boots-silk stockings-
beaver hat-hair in
"dog's ears"-hoop
earrings-heavy
stick-1796

incroyable-cloth
costume-embroidered
satin revers-velvet
collar and cuffs-braid
and buttons-figured
silk waistcoat and
cravat-ribbon loops on
breeches-leather
pumps-silk stockings-
felt bicorne-cockade-
hair in "dog's ears"-
short heavy stick

incroyable-
cloth costume-
velvet collar and
cuffs-figured silk
cravat-crescent
brooch-ribbon
loops on breeches-
silk stockings-
leather pumps-
felt bicorne with
cockade-heavy
stick

a conservative
costume-cloth
with velvet
collar-muslin
cravat-light
silk waistcoat-
leather boots-
hair Brutus style-
beaver hat-short
light stick

RTW

Directoire

a "merveilleuse" in white lingerie gown - silk bodice - cashmere scarf with fringe - muslin cravat - velvet bonnet - hair cut in "dog's ears" - clocked silk stockings - red kid slipper with jewel - long gloves - 1796

sky blue jacket edged black velvet - white silk bodice - jewelled brooch - pink lingerie skirt - red silk bonnet edged black velvet - red ribbon loops - lingerie frills - embroidered yellow slippers - clocked silk stockings - fan - hair in cadogan - 1799

Roman style in embroidered linen - balantine of heavy cord, tassels, fringe and embroidery - earrings, chain necklace and brooch - sandals - hair in Titus cut

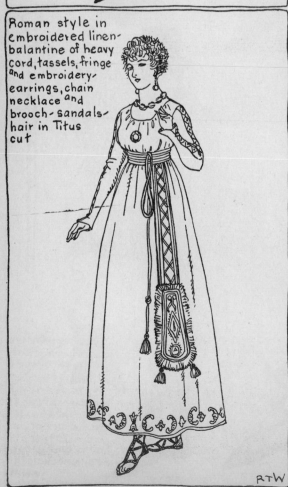

riding habit of cloth - velvet collar - striped silk waistcoat - muslin cravat - felt bonnet with cord and tassels - hair in Titus cut - clocked silk stockings - kid slippers - riding crop

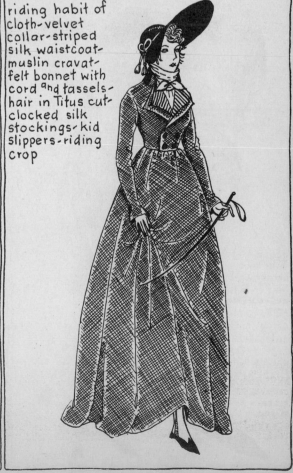

RTW

Directoire

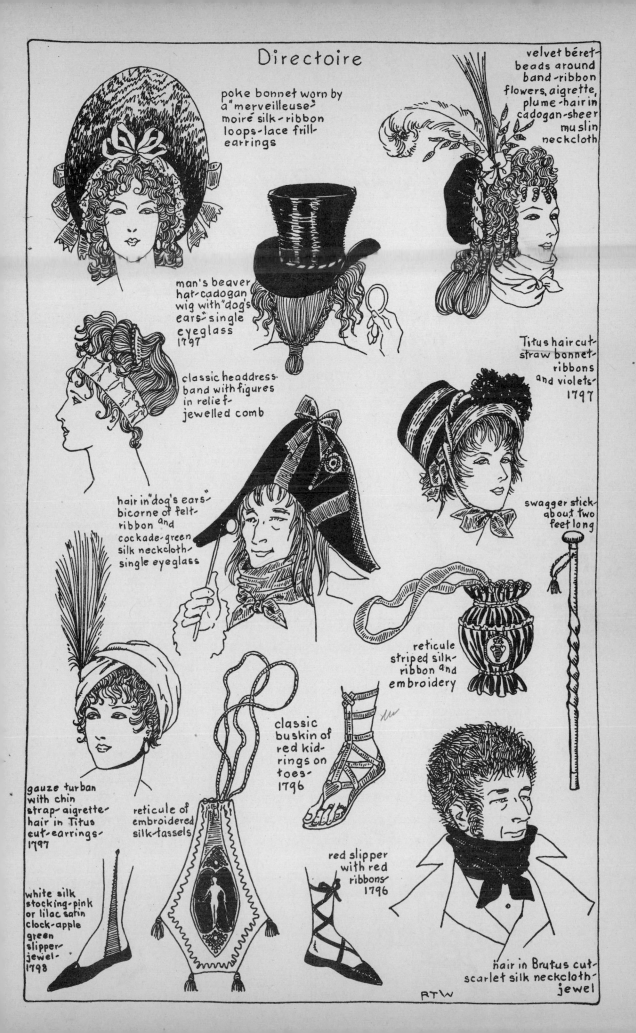

poke bonnet worn by a "merveilleuse" moiré silk-ribbon loops-lace frill-earrings

velvet béret-beads around band-ribbon flowers, aigrette, plume-hair in cadogan-sheer muslin neckcloth

man's beaver hat-cadogan wig with "dog's ears" single eyeglass 1797

classic headdress-band with figures in relief-jewelled comb

Titus haircut-straw bonnet-ribbons and violets 1797

hair in "dog's ears"-bicorne of felt-ribbon and cockade-green silk neckcloth-single eyeglass

swagger stick-about two feet long

reticule striped silk-ribbon and embroidery

gauze turban with chin strap-aigrette-hair in Titus cut-earrings-1797

reticule of embroidered silk-tassels

classic buskin of red kid-rings on toes-1796

red slipper with red ribbons-1796

white silk stocking-pink or lilac satin clock-apple green slipper-jewel-1798

hair in Brutus cut-scarlet silk neckcloth-jewel

RTW

The French Consulate and First Empire

1799–1815

more trade between countries, male fashions changed — more fashion journal, more people interested in fashion

[handwritten note in margin: monarchies are not a dictator / courtiers, actors decided fashion / wealth more widely distributed / social life wouldn't wear copies]

HE MODE was no longer dictated by Versailles but was launched at summer gardens and at public winter balls.

With the nineteenth century, pantaloons or trousers became definitely a feature of the masculine mode. In the opening years, under the Consulate, breeches still ended below the knees, the full-length trousers not making a more general appearance until the Empire. Breeches and trousers were tight-fitting, of elastic fabrics such as stockinet, buckskin or finely striped cotton, but the most popular material of the period for formal and informal wear, for young and old, in summer and in winter, was buff or yellow nankeen, imported from Nanking, China. Between 1810 and 1815, trousers and gaiters, made in one, appeared.

The coat of the incroyable of the Directoire left its mark in the bulky effect around the neck, also retaining its casual look of wrinkles around the armscye and through the body. Habits or suits were of cloth in dark blue, green and brown, with tobacco brown and pea green favorite

Consulate so struckeng costume - more stabelize
Cameos became popular
napolwn liked display - built own tomt + even encouraged women of court to be a little more extrava especially Josephine

colors. Waistcoats were usually of colored piqué or percale, with a border of contrasting color and a row of ball buttons down the front. Quilted piqué waistcoats appeared about 1811. The starched points of the shirt collar showed above the cravat or neckcloth. Two cravats were often worn, to give the desired thick look around the neck, a black satin over one of white linen.

Full dress consisted of velvet coat in color, black satin breeches, an elaborately embroidered silk waistcoat and a shirt having frilled wrist ruffles, a jabot and neckcloth. The powdered tie wig, bicorne and sword accompanied this habit, which was worn for evening and all ceremonial occasions.

For winter wear, there were two styles of greatcoats, both double-breasted: the redingote, a fitted coat and the carrick with its several capes. Both had a rather wide square collar which in winter was often of astrakhan. The single-breasted did not appear until the end of the Empire Period.

Only hats with narrow brims and tall crowns were worn, but brims and crowns varied in shape. They were fashioned of felt, made from beaver, shaved or long-haired angora, in the summer, of straw; and the colors were gray, beige and black. A silk cord or galloon encircled the crown, fastened by a steel buckle. The polished tall hat invented in Florence, Italy, in 1760, appeared in 1803, but was not adopted until 1823. The process of polishing was not perfected until the 'thirties.

The string or ribbon, laced through the béret of the Renaissance to hold the hat to the head, reappeared in the tall hat for hunting. An inner band was drawn tight by a narrow ribbon, the leather sweatband with the tiny bow in the modern hat being the remains of that idea.

Boots were worn with breeches and under trousers. They were elegant, well-fitted, usually of British make, of soft black leather, the white stocking often showing between boot and breeches. Short gaiters appeared about 1804. Low-cut escarpins, or pumps having very flat heels or none at all, were worn with striped or plain white silk or wool stockings. Trousers brought in the short stocking or sock for men.

napoleons army was reponsibles for full hats braid trim

The English jockey boot continued in favor, with cuffs of buff or chamois leather, or gray or beige cloth. The hussar, or Souvaroff boot, named after the Russian general, appeared around 1800. It was cut lower in back than in front, the front often ornamented with a swinging tassel. It varied in height, and was known in England as the Hessian boot. Another boot of military style was popular, high over the knee in front and cut out below the knee in back. Though known as the Wellington boot, it is seen worn by Napoléon in many of his portraits.

The Brutus haircut was the vogue, wigs and powder having disappeared in the masculine world. Slim, small bamboo sticks or riding whips were carried.

In the feminine costume, the mode of the Directoire Period continued in the semi-transparent lingerie chemise gown, belted under the breasts and worn over a sheer slip, sometimes of thin taffeta. The continued wearing of sheer cottons in winter brought on an epidemic of influenza in Paris in 1803, which was called "muslin disease."

A variation of the classic style was the wearing of a tunic of colored silk, satin or velvet over the white sheath gown. In materials, there were fine muslin, batiste, lawn, mull, also tulle, gauze, taffeta and moiré, and in cloth, rep and cashmere. Embroidery in delicate classic designs was popular, even muslin dresses being ornamented with gold or silver thread or tinsel and spangles in gold, silver, copper or steel.

Long sleeves, divided into several puffs by narrow bands or ribbons, were called "mameluke sleeves." "Betsies," small neck ruffs, came from England. They were introduced in Paris by the famous tailor Leroy, who named them *cherusses*.

Due to the sheer frocks, petticoats edged with lace frills became an important feature, often showing 'neath the hem of the dress. Sheer gowns also brought in the singular fashion of pantalets of flesh-colored satin instead of a petticoat. About 1805, muslin pantaloons edged with lace frills were shown in fashion publications, and there is a note of their being worn in 1807, but they do not seem to have become popular in France. The wearing of pantalets, or drawers, did not become an established custom until the 'thirties; until this time, woman's body linen never consisted of other than a chemise or smock, under-petticoats and stockings.

A bandeau which held the breasts firm was now worn over the slip or chemise and, about 1811, stays returned in the form of a corset waist fitted to the normal figure and but slightly boned.

Definitely of this period was the spencer, which originated in England. It was a very short jacket, or bolero, open in front and with long, tight sleeves. It was usually in velvet of a dark color, which contrasted with the gown, had a standing collar, the whole often edged with fringe or a narrow band of fur or swansdown. A variation of the spencer was the *canezou,* or little "hussar" vest, its difference being that it was pulled on over the head, did not open in front and was tight at the lower edge.

Women also wore the redingote, a long coat with several short capes, the coat built on the same lines as the gown, fastened down center-front and belted under the breasts. It had a standing collar, and in winter was often edged with bands of fur such as astrakhan, martin or sable. Around 1808 appeared the same coat of fur, silk-lined, or of cloth, fur-lined, called by the Russian name *witzschoura,* fur coats having come originally from Russia. The same style of coat was made of percale for summer wear.

Such colors as Egyptian earth, pea green and tobacco brown were used for the long coat and the tiny jacket, with the dress invariably white.

An outstanding style of the Empire Period was the court dress established by Josephine. She wore two costumes, one the "little costume," the other the "grand costume." The "little gown" was of embroidered blue satin with short puffed sleeves and the train falling from the belt. The "grand gown" was of brocaded silver with long, tight sleeves, the gorgeous train falling from the left shoulder. The neckline of both was square in front, with a standing lace collar, rather like the Medici collar, but ending at the corners of the décolletage. Both gowns were embroidered in silk, pearls and spangles, the most elaborate ornamentation being confined to the grand costume.

An accessory of importance which took hold in this period and continued to be worn for a century was the shawl, of fine cashmere with embroidered border, an article of great luxury. Shawls, though not unknown in Europe, had never before become a vogue. This fashion dates from the return of Napoléon's armies from Egypt. Shawls were large and small, hand-woven and embroidered, of silk, wool, chiffon, lace or cotton. Although originally made on hand looms in the Orient, beautiful ones were now made in France. From Paisley, Scotland, came shawls woven on power looms, following the intricate East Indian patterns, in which "Paisleys" achieved a high artistic value. While the design layout required four months, the actual weaving on the British power looms was accomplished in a week.

Josephine is said to have owned three to four hundred of them, costing fifteen to twenty thousand francs each. Ladies took lessons in the art of posing in and draping the shawl.

In the beginning of this period, wigs were still worn, and the simple classic coiffure was fashionable, but the Titus cut seems to have been the favored style. Another coiffure was *à la Chinoise,* with the hair drawn tightly back. From 1809, the headdress rose in height and all through the period the ears were uncovered.

The Egyptian campaign was responsible for luxurious turbans of brocade, satin, striped sheer gauze and velvet trimmed with aigrettes and feathers. Bonnets were of all shapes and sizes, the pokebonnet, or cabriolet hood, predominating, made of plush, velvet or satin for winter, of gauze or straw for summer. Headgear was ornamented with plumes, ribbons and flowers and invariably tied under the chin. With the return of lace to favor, due to Napoléon's interest in the industries, lovely lace veils hung over the front edges of bonnets. Fur bonnets were worn with the long fur coats.

The feminine riding habit resembled that of the Directoire Period, the short-waisted, double-breasted jacket with lapels over a waistcoat and lingerie shirt with full cravat, but the masculine top hat was now adopted.

Lace was used to edge caps, aprons, gowns and handkerchiefs.

In the early part of the period, crocheted bags, enriched with embroidery, colored beads, tassels and fringe were in fashion, but later waned in popularity. The handkerchief was carried in the hand and a small purse for money was concealed in the bosom of the dress.

Very small fans, about five or six inches long, came back into the mode. They were made of fine silk and decorated with designs using spangles of gold, silver, copper and steel. The costly, exquisitely painted fan and the jewelled fan reappeared.

The slippers of the period were cut very low and were heelless; they were made of kid or fabric, laced across the instep and tied around the ankle.

In jewelry, there were rings, long earrings, jewelled hairpins and hatpins, lockets and watches worn on chains. Cameos were very popular and beaded and gold chains were twisted six or seven times around the neck.

Artificial flowers were worn in the hair, on bonnets and as corsages, the workmanship having reached a high artistic standard.

Bathing and lingerie became very important. Men and women began their day with a bath, perhaps perfumed, and now changed their undergarments once a day. Both Napoléon and Josephine used perfume and toilet water lavishly. Rouge was discarded by the feminine sex and left to the men, women adopting a white or pale complexion.

In 1801, Joseph Marie Jacquard, son of a weaver, revolutionized the textile industry by inventing a mechanical loom to weave patterns or brocaded fabrics. The French government bought his loom in 1806, granting him a royalty and a yearly pension.

A Frenchman named Camus, Jr., in 1808, patented the first known invention for the production of hooks and eyes by power.

Consulate·First Empire

single breasted-
claw hammer
tails-cloth
coat-velvet
collar-striped
waistcoat-collar
tabs-cravat-tricot
breeches with
loops-black leather
boots-brown cuffs-
beaver hat-
1809

single breasted-
claw hammer tails-
cloth coat-satin
collar-checked
waistcoat-collar
tabs-cravat-frill-
striped nankeen
trousers-pockets-
pumps with ribbons-
beaver hat-
bamboo stick-
1811

cloth coat-claw
hammer tails-
pockets-inverted
pleats-buckskin
breeches-hussar
boots-tassels-
beaver hat with
laced inner
band-riding
whip-1811

formal dress-
claw hammer
tails-colored
velvet coat-velvet
buttons-embroidered
satin waistcoat-lace
frills-cravat-black
satin breeches-white
silk stockings-black
pumps with leather
buckles-sword with
ribbon rosette-
powdered bag-wig-
bicorne with white
ostrich-1814

FTW

Consulate·First Empire

carrick or greatcoat with deep capes-long wide sleeves-beaver hat-black leather boots

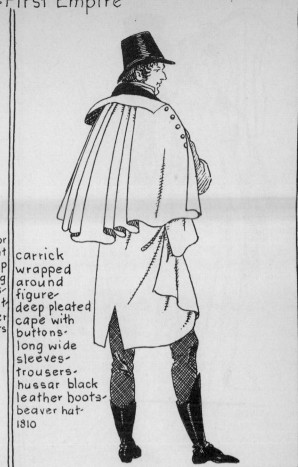

carrick wrapped around figure-deep pleated cape with buttons-long wide sleeves-trousers-hussar black leather boots-beaver hat 1810

double breasted redingote-satin collar-pockets with flaps-buttoned bands on sleeves-neckcloth-collar points-beaver hat-leather boots-1814

carrick or greatcoat over formal habit-tabs and buttons-slashed pockets-neckcloth-collar points-black satin breeches-white silk stockings-black pumps-beaver hat-1814

RTW

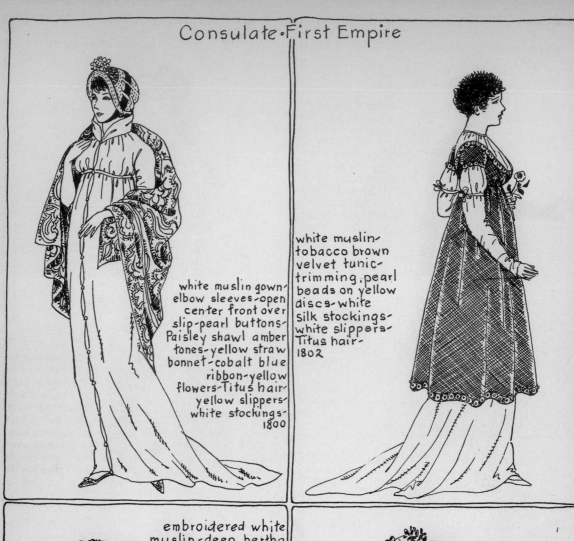

white muslin gown-
elbow sleeves-open
center front over
slip-pearl buttons-
Paisley shawl amber
tones-yellow straw
bonnet-cobalt blue
ribbon-yellow
flowers-Titus hair-
yellow slippers-
white stockings-
1800

white muslin-
tobacco brown
velvet tunic-
trimming,pearl
beads on yellow
discs-white
silk stockings-
white slippers-
Titus hair-
1802

embroidered white
muslin-deep bertha
edged with lace-
short puffed sleeves-
"cherusse"or"Betsie"
of pleated muslin-
green velvet sash-
green slippers-
white silk stockings-
Titus hair-
long gloves-
fan-1803

white percale
dress with pleats-
mameluke sleeves-
triple shoulder
ruffles-straw
hat with white
cotton embroidery-
velvet ribbon-
foliage-colored
slippers-white
silk stockings-
1811

RTW

velvet spencer-
white muslin
gown-cord
with tassels-
embroidered bag
with tassels-
tucked silk
bonnet with
lace frills-
ribbon bowknot-
Titus hair-
1800

cloth redingote-
satin collar and
and lapels-tabs
and buttons-
bonnet with
bead trimming-
frilled lace
neck ruche-
handkerchief-
Titus hair-
1806

velvet canezou-
self ruffles-silk
gown-embroidered
band and pleated
frill-lace "Betsie"
around neck-
velvet bonnet-
pleated taffeta
pompons-
handkerchief
in hand-
1810

dark green cloth
coat-yellow
collar-black
felt bonnet-
velvet and white
ruches-black
satin ribbon-
black ostrich-
handkerchief-
Titus hair-
black slippers-
white stockings-
1814

RTW

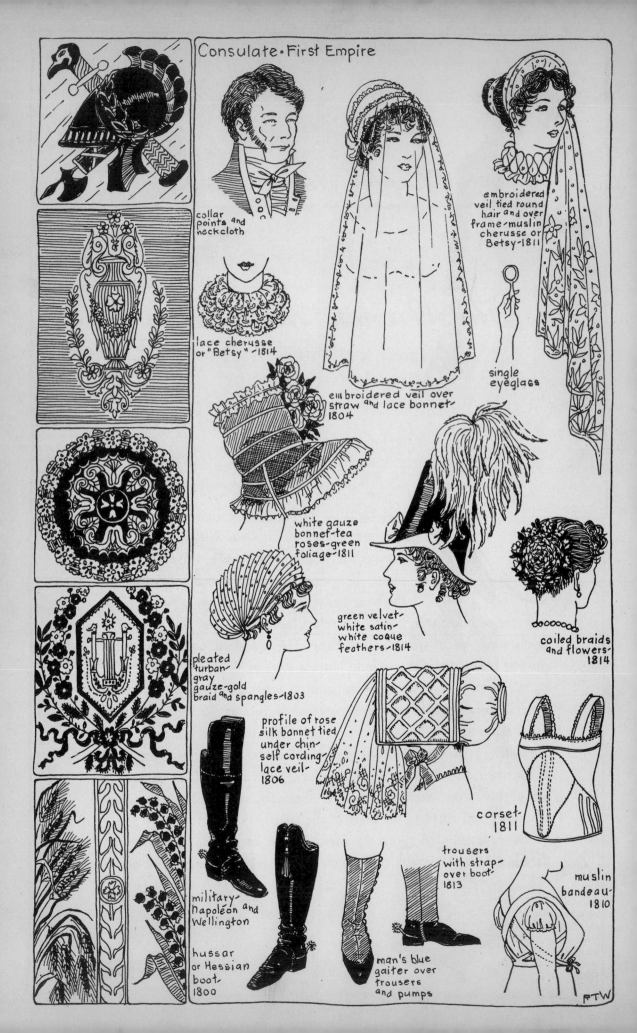

Consulate · First Empire

collar points and neckcloth

embroidered veil tied round hair and over frame-muslin cherusse or Betsy-1811

lace cherusse or "Betsy" -1814

single eyeglass

embroidered veil over straw and lace bonnet- 1804

white gauze bonnet-tea roses-green foliage-1811

green velvet-white satin-white coque feathers-1814

coiled braids and flowers 1814

pleated turban-gray gauze-gold braid and spangles-1803

profile of rose silk bonnet tied under chin-self cording-lace veil-1806

corset- 1811

trousers with strap-over boot-1813

muslin bandeau 1810

military- Napoléon and Wellington

hussar or Hessian boot 1800

man's blue gaiter over trousers and pumps

R.T.W.

Chapter Thirty=five

The French Restoration

Louis XVIII—1815–1824
Charles X—1824–1830

MEN'S COSTUME varied little, except in the style of the waistcoat, which was single or double breasted, of bright color in silk, velvet or striped piqué. For some years, an evening fashion was the wearing of two waistcoats, one of white piqué over one of black velvet, with the velvet lapel rolled over the white. The lapels were cut in shawl collar shape. The waistcoat points sometimes showed below the coat and gold buttons were popular.

Coinciding with the smaller-growing waist of the women and the general wearing of stays, men's coats and waistcoats also became tightly fitted at the waist. This style necessitated some sort of lacing, which was secured by a basque belt worn next to the body. Padding was employed at the chest and the hips to give the exaggerated fitted look. Instead of being cut in one with the body as formerly, coattails were now cut separately and fitted to the body of the coat.

Knee-length redingotes appeared, single or double breasted with flaring skirt and a shawl collar buttoned up high. Redingotes of alpaca

247

became the fashion about 1824, becoming very popular. Greatcoats, often worn thrown about the shoulders and held in front, were generally double-breasted.

Trousers continued tight, often ankle-length, but the popular style seems to have been that with the strap under the boot. They were made of nankeen, drill, white piqué or of fine white corduroy.

Coat colors were blue, claret, buff, with velvet collars and buttons of pearl, steel or gilt. Topcoat colors were gray, buff, with blue and bronze green most popular.

Habits or suits were topped off by handsome cravats or neckcloths of fine white linen, black satin or figured silk. Heavy silk mufflers were also in fashion pinned at the neck with a single jewel. A watch fob hung from under the vest.

A book published in the 1820's by H. Le Blanc, supposedly none other than Honoré de Balzac, described thirty-two styles of tying a cravat. The manual was republished in English in London and again in Philadelphia in 1828.

The hair was moderately short, and, if straight, curled by tongs into ringlets, with a thin line of whiskers on the cheeks. The mustache and a very small Vandyck reappeared.

Hats of beaver felt, in fawn, gray or white, were high with varying-shaped crowns, the most popular being that widest at the top. The silk hat, or polished beaver, invented in Florence, Italy, in 1760, began to be taken up about 1823 but was not generally worn until the 'thirties. Later, plush was employed in its fabrication. A Frenchman named Gibus, in 1823, invented the collapsible top hat.

Boots were short, only about fifteen inches high, the vogue being for the hussar, or Hessian, and the military guard boot, called the Wellington in England. Spatterdashes and gaiters regained popularity. In the late 'twenties appeared the first high shoe, worn by both men and women. It rose about three inches above the ankle, had a leather vamp and a cloth top, usually nankeen, laced on the inner side. The toe was long, narrow and square and, for street wear, the masculine version often had a low, flat heel.

With the Restoration, a complete change in style occurred in women's dress. From 1819, the corset, with a steel busk front fastening, became a definite part of the costume, the waist becoming very small in the 'twenties and placed normally. The slim, straight skirt changed to a bell shape, clearing the ground and revealing the tiny heelless slippers, laced with ribbons. The lower edge of the skirt was stiffened with buckram and ornamented with rows of trimming, which consisted of ruffles, puffs, scalloped flounces, lace, ribbon, bowknots, flowers and, later, rows of braid.

The shoulders were broadened by the cut of the garment, epaulettes and berthas, while sleeves were stuffed and wired. Sleeves were long and short, of various shapes, the leg-of-mutton shape appearing in 1820. Large full transparent sleeves of gauze were a feature, also the "pagoda sleeve," a long sleeve in a series of puffs, large at the top and diminishing in size to the wrist.

Chemise and petticoats were lavishly ornamented with lace and embroidery. Ribbon sashes were favored on dresses.

Colors were light, the favorite being white, and the materials used were principally sheer muslins, unbleached batiste and cambric. There were striped gowns and fine pink or blue checked ones. Gauzes, silks and tulles were employed in evening gowns. Woolen cloth for dresses appeared in 1828, and was indeed a novelty after so many years of the use of cotton. Every new color, fabric or article of dress was given a fanciful name, such as "water of the Nile," "frightened mouse," "amorous toad" and many others. Upon the occasion of a gift of a giraffe from Egypt to Charles X, various accessories of dress of both sexes were called *à la giraffe*. English, Russian and Polish ornaments came into fashion with the presence of the Allied troops in France.

The modern wedding gown of white seems to have originated in this period, a result of the prevailing mode for that color. Another new idea was a bodice of contrasting colored material from that of the skirt, a dark one with a light skirt or the other way around.

The canezou spencer was now made of embroidered cotton or lace; in fact, it became a transparent overbodice. See Page 280.

The redingote, or full-length coat, was made of cloth or velvet, and when fur-trimmed was known as a pelisse.

The tippet of fur and the boa of ostrich originated in this period. Huge muffs of fox and chinchilla were carried. Scarfs were of tulle, lace and silk, and shawls were of crêpe, silk and fine cashmere, in brilliant colors, red being much used. They were also in plaids and stripes, the East Indian scarf being known as the *bayadère*. Cashmere shawls were the "rage" and very costly. Shawls of French cashmere and the British Paisley were beautiful and desirable substitutes, inspired by the East Indian originals.

Long gloves, which were most expensive, were worn with the short sleeves and were often chamois-colored.

Bonnets and hats varied in shape and fabric, fashioned of straw, leghorn, silk plush, velvet and felt lined with taffeta. Long ribbon streamers floated from bonnet or hat and the ends of ribbon were cut into many points. Caps were military in style, such as Polish, Austrian or simple morning ones of white muslin or black velvet edged with tulle. There were turbans and bérets in tam-o'-shanter style, turbans later being worn only by older women. All this headgear was ornamented with feathers, ribbons, flowers, cockades, puffs and ruches, several different articles of trimming being applied to one hat. A flattering note was the lace cap worn under the bonnet.

The hair was dressed up off the ears and high in back, with curled puffs at each temple. Sections of the hair were tightly braided and the coiffure *à la Chinoise* remained in fashion. The latter was tightly drawn up into a knot with a high tortoise-shell comb to hold it in place. The ferronière was revived, a very fine chain around the head, with a jewel, either a pearl or ruby, hanging in the middle of the forehead. The band was also fashioned of tiny artificial flowers, strings of beads or a narrow velvet ribbon. For evening wear, large flaring fans of lace, sheer lawn, gauze, or silk were worn in the hair, to which flowers or a jewelled ornament was added.

Little jewelry was worn in the early part of the period, but later on its use became general. Cameos were popular and the favorite stones were pearls and garnets, set in bracelets, rings, long earrings, necklaces, brooches and the large ornate belt buckle. Nearly all these articles were often worn at the same time. When in mourning, hand-wrought silver jewelry was substituted for gold.

The soft slipper, with narrow ribbons tied around the ankle, had long, rounded pointed toes at first, changing to long, slim square toes later. Women also wore the soft high shoe, which appeared late in the 1820's, described earlier in this chapter.

Toward the end of the period, horseback riding became general, brought about by the returning émigrés from England. The feminine habit was of cloth, with satin collar and full skirt and a tightly fitted jacket with leg-of-mutton sleeves. A military cap or the masculine top hat of silk or beaver was worn, from which hung a floating green veil. Under the full skirt, fitted tricot drawers were worn, which were tight over the instep and held in place by a strap passing under the shoe.

Parasols gained in popularity, often the tilting parasol used when walking. The handkerchief was carried in the hand and in the evening the tiny bouquet and a small fan were added accessories. Fans, as formerly, were decorated by famous artists of the day.

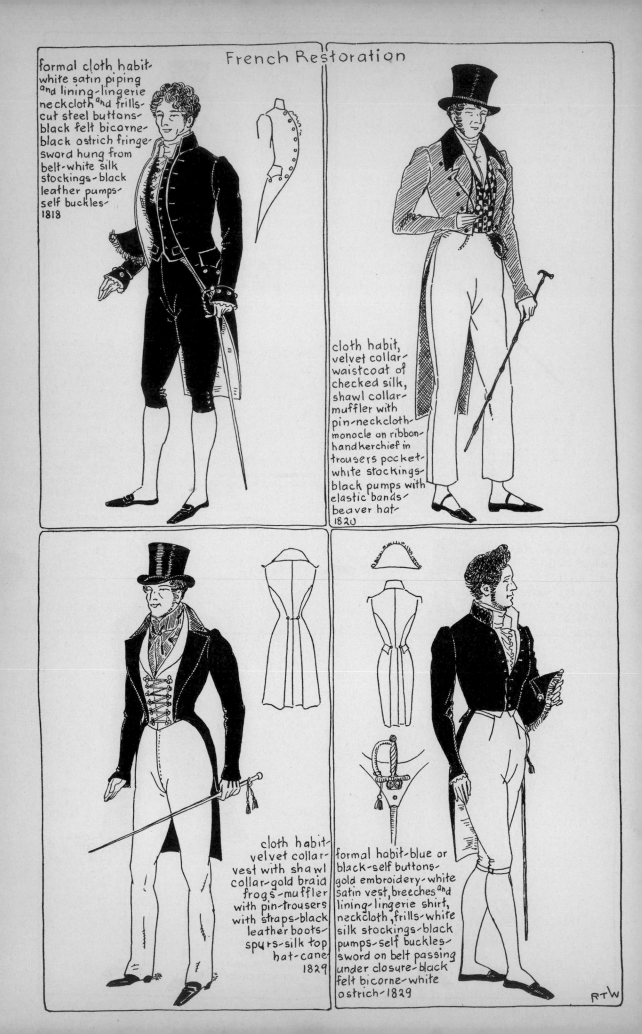

French Restoration

formal cloth habit-
white satin piping
and lining-lingerie
neckcloth and frills-
cut steel buttons-
black felt bicorne-
black ostrich fringe-
sword hung from
belt-white silk
stockings-black
leather pumps-
self buckles-
1818

cloth habit,
velvet collar-
waistcoat of
checked silk,
shawl collar-
muffler with
pin-neckcloth-
monocle on ribbon-
handkerchief in
trousers pocket-
white stockings-
black pumps with
elastic bands-
beaver hat-
1820

cloth habit-
velvet collar-
vest with shawl
collar-gold braid
frogs-muffler
with pin-trousers
with straps-black
leather boots-
spurs-silk top
hat-cane-
1829

formal habit-blue or
black-self buttons-
gold embroidery-white
satin vest, breeches and
lining-lingerie shirt,
neckcloth, frills-white
silk stockings-black
pumps-self buckles-
sword on belt passing
under closure-black
felt bicorne-white
ostrich-1829

RTW

French Restoration

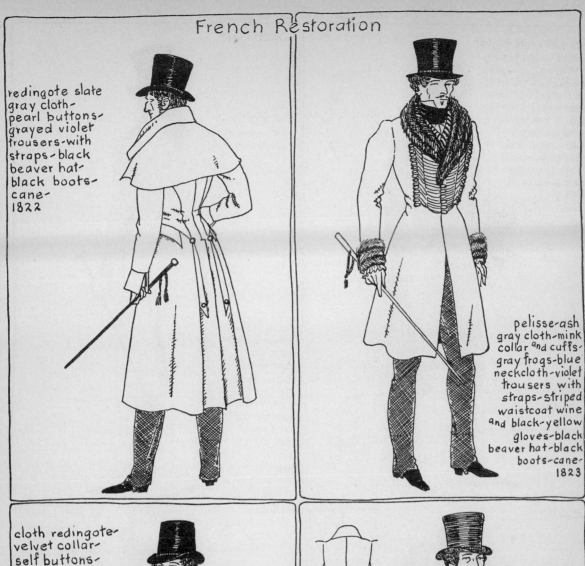

redingote slate
gray cloth-
pearl buttons-
grayed violet
trousers-with
straps-black
beaver hat-
black boots-
cane-
1822

pelisse-ash
gray cloth-mink
collar and cuffs-
gray frogs-blue
neckcloth-violet
trousers with
straps-striped
waistcoat wine
and black-yellow
gloves-black
beaver hat-black
boots-cane-
1823

cloth redingote-
velvet collar-
self buttons-
trousers with
straps-beaver
hat-black
boots-cane-
1820's

cloth redingote-
velvet collar-ribbed
silk waistcoat-
pleated shirt-
jewelled buttons-
cravat-collar tabs-
white piqué trousers
with straps-white
stockings-black
pumps-self bows-
beaver hat-cane-
1828

ATW

embroidered colored
silk bodice-white
muslin skirt with
cotton embroidery-
sleeves, interlaced
silk strips-lingerie
neck frill-straw
hat-ostrich plumes-
embroidered
cashmere shawl-
white silk
stockings-colored
slippers-
1822

pink taffeta-
pleated surplice-
sleeve tabs edged
white lace-taffeta
petals, tabs, buttons
on skirt-white
gloves, stockings,
slippers-pink roses
in hair-fan-
earrings-gloves
handkerchief-
1825

yellow cotton printed
in black-white
lingerie ruche,
bertha and sleeves-
cut-out work on
bertha-embroidered
white cravat-
ruffle and tabs
edged narrow
black velvet
ribbon-black
straw hat-
yellow flowers-
yellow flowered
ribbon-white
frills-white
silk stockings-
black slippers-
1828

pink cotton, green
embroidery-white
muslin bodice
and frills-pink
and green tie-
white straw hat-
pink flowers and
ribbon-pink and
green bag-white
silk stockings-
black
slippers-
1829

RTW

French Restoration

pelisse of peacock blue velvet-chinchilla fur-gray silk belt-embroidered white cotton dress-black and white velvet bonnet over lace cap-black plume-lingerie neck frill-white stockings-blue fabric slippers-ribbon bows-1818

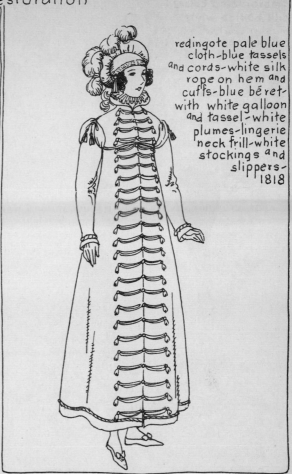

redingote pale blue cloth-blue tassels and cords-white silk rope on hem and cuffs-blue béret with white galloon and tassel-white plumes-lingerie neck frill-white stockings and slippers-1818

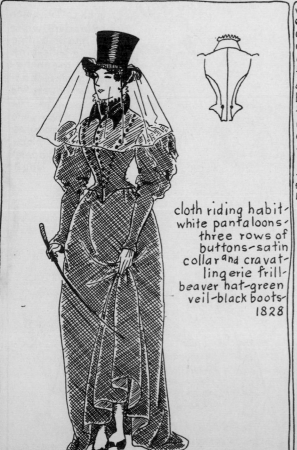

cloth riding habit-white pantaloons-three rows of buttons-satin collar and cravat-lingerie frill-beaver hat-green veil-black boots-1828

woolen cloak embroidered in cashmere shawl motifs-velvet collar-jewelled fastening-taffeta dress-lingerie frill-belt with buckle-felt hat-striped ribbon-silk ruched edge-cloth top shoes-leather toecap-side lacing-1829

RTW

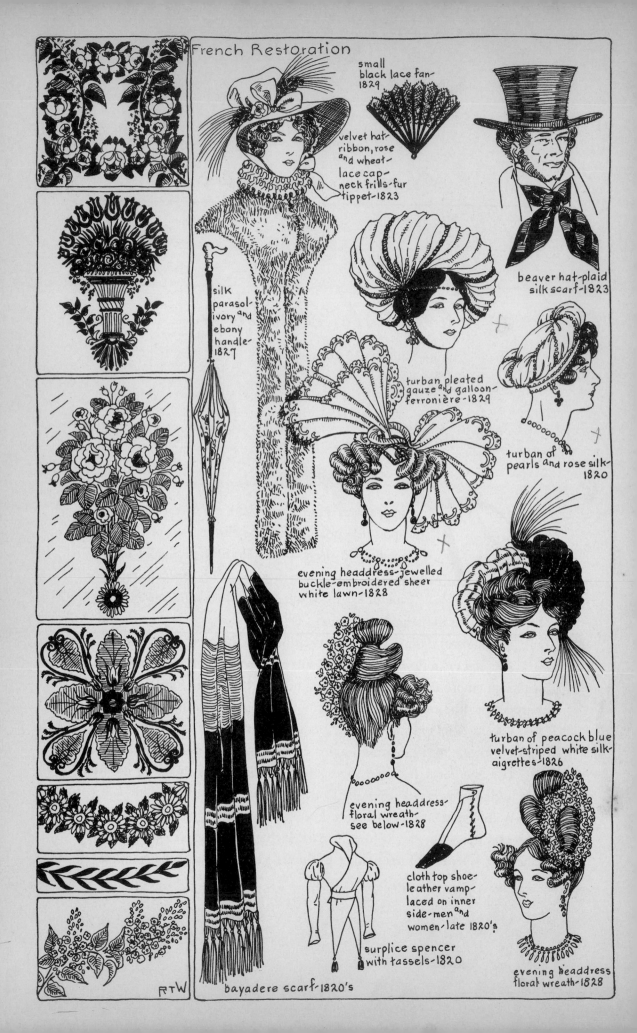

French Restoration

small black lace fan- 1829

velvet hat- ribbon, rose and wheat- lace cap- neck frills- fur tippet-1823

beaver hat-plaid silk scarf-1823

silk parasol- ivory and ebony handle- 1827

turban pleated gauze and galloon- ferronière-1829

turban of pearls and rose silk- 1820

evening headdress-jewelled buckle-embroidered sheer white lawn-1828

turban of peacock blue velvet-striped white silk- aigrettes-1826

evening headdress- floral wreath- see below-1828

cloth top shoe- leather vamp- laced on inner side-men and women-late 1820's

surplice spencer with tassels-1820

bayadere scarf-1820's

evening headdress floral wreath-1828

RTW

Chapter Thirty=six

English Fashions
1790–1830

THE FRENCH REVOLUTION had a far-reaching effect upon society and, with the elimination of class distinction in dress, men's costume gradually settled into a more conventional style. French refugee couturiers in London continued to create fashions for women, but in the masculine mode, English tailors, seizing the ascendency in taste and design, continued their hold to the present day.

The *habit à la Française* of the Court of Louis XV, of velvet and satin with rich embroidery and sword, remained the masculine formal dress of Europe into the nineteenth century, but the English riding coat, which first appeared in 1725, developed, from 1780, into the frock coat or cutaway, which is today the morning or evening coat of formal dress.

The fine boots, hats and shoe polish of British make were in use by the "well-dressed man" over the Continent.

With the wearing of somber hues, the cut of a garment was concentrated upon, as never before. A marked change in men's clothes was in fabric, dark tones of brown, blue and green cloth and leather being used instead of light-colored silks and velvets. There was an ease or air·of studied carelessness about the whole costume.

The trousers of the sans-culotte became the fashion, knee breeches, or "smallclothes," gradually lengthening, until the original short ones for informal wear, were seen only on elderly gentlemen. After the Battle of Waterloo in 1815, when George IV, as Regent, decreed the wearing of trousers, knee breeches disappeared, to be seen thereafter only upon ceremonial occasions. Trousers with the strap under the boot appeared, also those of ankle length. They were made of cloth, nankeen, drill, piqué, corduroy and stockinet in light colors, especially white and chamois yellow.

Evening breeches were very close-fitting, reaching just below the knee or above the ankle, where an opening at the side was buttoned part way up. This latter style was invented by Beau Brummel. It is said that the smartness of his black pantaloons made trousers popular. A great departure was his evening coat of dark blue, worn with a white waistcoat.

The frock coat was double-breasted with lapels, and a high turned-down collar and claw-hammer tails. In the 1820's, a closer fit was secured by cutting the tails separately and sewing them to the body of the coat. Padding was resorted to on the chest and hips to make the waist appear smaller. The black frock coat and evening coat appeared in 1828. Colors were gray, buff, green, blue and claret and a fine cord edged the coat.

The overcoats of the period were the carrick with its several capes and the long-skirted redingote.

The already muffling cravat grew in dimensions. In the first decade of the nineteenth century, two cravats were often worn, one of white lingerie material, the other of black silk. The white one was put on first, then covered by the black, thus giving the desired bulky look of the period. Eventually, the white cravat was replaced by the standing collar of white linen with pointed corners. The cravat then began to decrease in bulk, while the collar points rose higher, finally touching the cheeks. Black or white was favored for the neck dressing, tied into a bow in front.

Late in the 'twenties, mufflers fastened with a stud or tie pin, became fashionable.

Beau Brummel was famed for his skill in tying a cravat. His muslin scarf, which he changed three times daily, was only slightly starched. Gentlemen took lessons in the art of tying the cravat, which were given by experts.

Of the "Beau," it is said that he raised good dressing to cleanliness, conservatism and therefore to elegance. He introduced daily bathing and daily clean linen into English society, a luxurious supply of underlinen becoming one of the requisites of a well-dressed man.

As in France, the cocked hat gave way to the tall round hat of felt or beaver. Beaver hats, from 1818 to 1830, were in light colors, usually fawn, gray or white. The "silk hat," invented in 1760 in Florence, Italy, was seen in the early 1820's, but did not reach perfection until the 'thirties, when it was generally adopted. It was first made of polished beaver, called silk beaver, but later was fashioned of plush.

Wigs were demoded by 1800. The hair was worn short in the ragged Brutus style, brushed down over the forehead. From about 1809, short loose curled locks and side whiskers prevailed, with curling resorted to, if the hair was straight. The short cut, with slight variations, has lasted from that time. Powder was occasionally seen in dull pink, violet, gray or blue, but, by 1820, powder and the wig had completely disappeared, retained only by the English judiciary as part of the professional uniform.

Elegant footgear in high and low boots of black leather were part of the costume, with silk or wool stockings, white or striped. Pumps were popular, low-cut slippers with a flexible sole, always worn with the dress habit. Shoe roses were no more, shoes now being fastened with plain strings or latchets.

In the first decade of the century, the Hessian boot with swinging tassel and the English jockey boot with turndown leather cuff were seen. The turndown cuff was usually yellow, but, about 1818, cuffs of gray or beige cloth appeared. The Hessian and Wellington boots (see Page 246) were the fashion from 1820 to 1830. Boots grew quite short and were worn under trousers. Gaiters and spatterdashes appeared intermittently throughout the period.

Due to the increased popularity of horseback riding, the riding habit was often seen indoors, even in the drawing room. Morning or "office" coats, made of flowered chintz, appeared in the late 'twenties, the style lasting into the 'forties.

Muffs, which men had carried since the sixteenth century, were still modish; in fact, the muff was also a mark of dignity, and was in use even by judges of the court. From 1790 to 1820, the muff was very large, reaching to the elbows, attaining its largest size around 1810. It was first made of fabric filled with feathers, later, of single large fur pelts. This masculine fashion was also popular in our American Colonies.

Before 1800, sword sticks and heavy club sticks were carried, the short bamboo stick and riding whip becoming more popular later.

In this period, men's handkerchiefs settled into an accepted size of about eighteen inches square, of white linen with perhaps a hemstitched border and a monogram in one corner.

A watch with a dangling fob seal was often carried in each of the two front pockets of the trousers, but a single timepiece occupied the right-hand pocket.

Perfection and a low cost in gilding brass buttons was reached about 1818, making gilt buttons accessible to those dressy young men who could not afford hand-wrought gold.

In accessories, men carried the indispensable snuffbox and the small bag purse. Purses were of leather set in gilt mounts or of knitted silk worked with steel beads and tasselled ends.

The single lens, or monocle, came into fashion in the early years of the eighteenth century. It was carried in England and on the Continent. The use of the monocle has been and continues to be more favored in England than elsewhere. Pince-nez, worn on a heavy black cord, appeared in the 1820's.

Both the English and the French claim credit for the feminine classic mode, but the truth is that all Europe, influenced by the writings of Rousseau and Voltaire, was considering a reform in dress. The English, with their well-known love of country life, were the first to adopt simpler clothes.

Dresses were made of cottons, such as lawn, percale, batiste and calico, with ribbon sashes. The chemise gown, fuller than the French model, had a belt just under the breasts and had usually high neck and long sleeves. It also had the long train and there were knee-length tunics of colored cloth, silk or velvet, worn over the invariably cotton sheath gown.

Corsets were discarded, but the Englishwoman, being more conservative, wore more underclothing under the sheath gown than did her French neighbor, usually several petticoats of fine muslin edged with embroidery and lace.

The low-necked gown brought in a small neck ruff of several rows of fluted or ruffled Brabant lace. (See Page 246.) This fashion originated in England and was called a "Betsie" after Queen Elizabeth, which style was taken up in Paris by the tailor Leroy and renamed *cherusse*. By 1807, the collarettes were of six or seven falls of lace.

About 1808, the train disappeared, the feet were revealed and, by 1809, the skirt was ankle-length. During the winter of 1809, stays returned in the English mode.

The very short waist remained through the next decade, but skirts became fuller, bands of trimming ornamenting the lower edge. Sleeves developed puffs, and both neck and wrists were finished with frills. There were satin and velvet evening gowns, swansdown being used as a border, and color was making its appearance. Morning dresses of chintz were worn, and bombazine, a mixture of silk and cotton, was considered very smart, both in England and the American Colonies. Transparent fabrics were worn over colored satins.

Between 1820 and 1830, the waistline gradually dropped back to normal, shoulder lines lowered and sleeves grew very full, especially at the top. By 1830, the fullness was puffed out with the aid of tiny feather cushions or wicker frames. The skirts of both day and evening gowns cleared the ground or were ankle-length. Delicate colors were the vogue, white still retaining favor, but Indian red became very popular. Late in the 'twenties, chintzes and printed muslins were reserved for morning dresses and the very young. From 1820, ribbon became a featured trimming on both dress and hat.

From 1796, a demand for English flannels for scarfs developed with the wearing of muslin dresses in all seasons. Cloaks were not popular, because they concealed the figure, and thus came about the great vogue of the shawl, which was to last a century or more.

The shawl of English cashmere first appeared in London about 1786 and immediately took hold. It was a piece of fabric six yards long and two wide, making it quite understandable why the ladies of that day took instructions in the draping of such a garment. While the original hailed from India, beautiful imitations woven on power looms were made at Paisley, Scotland. At the height of the fashion, shawls were of all sizes and fabrics, fine wool, silk, lace, chiffon or cotton, often hand-woven and embroidered. At the end of the first quarter of the century, shawls of bright red cashmere were fashionable, also plaids and stripes.

In the first two decades of the nineteenth century, the mantelet, a capelike garment, was worn. It was fastened at the neck, was cut away in front and hung to the knees at different points. It was usually of silk, lined or not, and often edged with a lace ruffle.

The spencer, a very short-waisted jacket, was worn with the Empire dress. It was invented by Lord Spencer, who claimed that fashion was so absurd that he himself could concoct a ridiculous, impractical style and it would become the "rage." He cut the tails off his own coat and went for a stroll. In two weeks, all London was wearing the "spencer," and soon fashionable men, women and children of the Continent and the colonies were wearing the same little jacket. The masculine spencer has come down to date in the mess jacket of the officers of the British Army. It certainly filled a serious need in women's costume. Spencer jackets were in black, purple, mulberry or bottle green, of satin or velvet, lined and sometimes padded. Occasionally, a narrow peplum was added and very elegant jackets were bordered with swansdown. The short spencer type of overjacket, of sheer muslin or lace, was called a canezou spencer or a cannezout. See Page 280.

Muffs of silk and lace were carried in the summer, but added warmth was furnished in the winter by the large muffs in vogue from 1790 to 1830. They covered the arms to the elbows and were made of various fabrics, gathered cloth and strips of fur or large single skins.

About 1812, the long cloth or velvet coat, called the *redingote* by the French, became the fashion. It was high-waisted, was at first knee-length, later reaching to nine or ten inches above the hem of the dress. By the end of the decade, the coat was full-length and edged with wide bands of fur. The pelisse, or fur coat of Russian origin, was first worn in Vienna in 1808. *Pelisse,* a word whose root means pelt, signified a fur-lined or fur-trimmed cloth coat, and was so used in France, but it seems that the English applied the name to any long outer coat.

An entirely new garment for women came into existence in this period, namely drawers, later called pantalets. Until 1800, only two or three known references to them exist, but the sheath gown made some leg covering necessary. Even so, drawers, as then conceived, were a decorative part of the costume. From about 1805, English and French fashion journals occasionally displayed evening gowns of shoe-top length, with fancy frilled satin pantalets showing below. Frequent references to them occur until about 1820, and from then they were worn only by little girls. Such drawers were of merino for winter and of lace-edged white dimity or colored calico for summer. Pantalets were often false, being ruffles held at the knees with tapes. Drawers were not generally worn by the feminine sex until the 1830's.

The classic style of headdress prevailed in the latter part of the eighteenth century, dressed close to the head with plaits, curls, the psyche knot finished with antique oil. The Queen and the court ceased powdering in 1793, but wigs were still worn and not always in the wearer's natural color. Later, the hair was formed in short ringlets, very few, however, adopting the shaggy Titus cut worn in Paris. In the 'twenties, it was parted in the center, with bunches of curls at the sides over the ears and a topknot on the crown of the head. The evening coiffure was bedecked with striped tinsel ribbon, flowers and high tortoise-shell combs. Upon the death of George IV, black-and-white crêpe flowers were worn in the hair for full dress.

The standing ostrich plumes in the coiffure of English court dress is a survival of the feathers worn in the Paris of Marie Antoinette.

In the first decade of the nineteenth century, draped turbans with feathers were inspired by the Egyptian campaigns. In the next ten years appeared bonnets of all shapes and dimensions, of straw, tulle, silk and light felt trimmed with ribbons, ruches, flowers and feathers. Lace caps edged with frills were often worn under hat or bonnet. Hats grew very large in the 'twenties, were faced with silk or velvet and ornamented with plumes, flowers and wide ribbon, looped, fringed and pinked. The plumed hat was worn at the opera and at dinner parties.

The use of jewelry in these unsettled times waned, although on formal occasions pearls and garnets were seen. Women also wore the monocle on a black ribbon. Handbags were of silk on gilt frames or of silk knitted with beads, and were called reticules. They were embroidered, appliquéd and painted.

Late in the eighteenth century and early in the nineteenth century, machines were invented in England making the mechanical manufacture of net and lace in large pieces possible for shawls and bridal veils. Lace or net veils were attached to the brims of bonnets or hats, either a short frill to the eyes or one hanging to the knees.

Early in the nineteenth century, shoes were soft heelless slippers tied with ribbon across the instep. These fabric shoes grew higher in the 'twenties, sometimes had leather toecaps and were laced in the back or at the inner side. (See Page 256.) Various fabrics were employed but satin and morocco were the principal ones. Slippers were often made at home by English and American women.

Long gloves were of kid in delicate colors and there were also long knitted ones and mittens.

The umbrella, or parasol, which had been in use in France from the middle of the eighteenth century, became popular in England from the beginning of this period. The year 1787 is the first date of their manufacture in that country, and many styles are to be noted in the fashion illustrations thereafter. The small tilting parasol was often carried when walking.

The first patent for making rubberized cloth was taken out in 1801 in London by Rudolph Ackerman, but another note says that E. Mackintosh, of England, patented the first practical process for waterproofing in 1823. In 1820, we find that T. Hancock, of Middlesex, England, invented the first elastic fabric with rubber in it. Elastic cloth or *webbing,* as it was called, replaced ribbon garters and the ribbons which secured the low slippers.

In Birmingham, England, in 1807, B. Sanders invented the metal button formed of two disks locked together by turning the edges, and the shell button with metal shank; and in the United States, in 1827, Samuel Williston of East Hampton, Massachusetts, patented the invention of a machine to produce cloth-covered buttons.

In 1831, also in the United States, the first successful machine for making solid-headed pins was invented by John Ireland Howe, of New York.

cloth frock coat-white linen cravat-buckskin trousers-fob seals covering the two front pockets-Hessian boots with tassels-beaver hat-1797

formal habit-chocolate brown cloth frockcoat-self buttons-beige drill breeches buttoned and tied-white waistcoat, shirt and cravat-black bicorne-white silk stockings-black pumps-watch fob seal-1810

Court habit-violet satin frockcoat-white satin lining, waistcoat and breeches-gold and green embroidery-jewelled buttons-lingerie shirt, jabot, cravat and collar points-lace wrist frills-white silk stockings-black pumps, gold buckles-black felt hat-white frill and lining-sword on violet ribbon-1810

green cloth frockcoat-flowered embroidered white waistcoat-light brown muffler-white collar tabs-white stockinet breeches-white stockings-black pumps with small spurs-brown beaver hat-riding whip-1830

RTW

heavy cloth
greatcoat-green
frockcoat-white
trousers-front
pockets-fob
seal-white cravat,
collar tabs-
black felt hat-
black Hessian
boots, tassels-
leaded
oak stick-
1803

redingote chamois
colored cloth-self
buttons-gray green
trousers and
coat-black
satin neckcloth-
collar tabs-
frilled shirt-
brown beaver
hat-black
boots-
1820

cloth redingote-
self buttons-
trousers over
black boots-
white linen
cravat-collar
tabs-beaver
hat-late
1820's

fur-lined redingote
with frogs-pockets-
braid trimmed-
high-necked waist-
coat-satin collar-
black silk
neckcloth-collar
tabs-white
stockings-black
pumps-silk hat-
1830

RTW

English - 1790 to 1830

velvet gown with galloon-lingerie yoke and sleeves-embroidered shawl-bead necklace-natural hair in ringlets-satin slippers with ribbon lacings-1795

silk tunic over lingerie skirt-lace edging-bowknots on tunic-lace veil on bonnet-single lens on black ribbon-parasol-1809

lingerie gown, cap and Betsie-self ruching-eyelet embroidery-green velvet spencer and hat-self ruching-white ostrich edged with tan-plum silk parasol-black slippers-1819

cotton dress in light color-braid trimmed-lingerie Betsie-straw hat with pleated lingerie frills-green foliage-rolled ribbon under brim-silk purse-black slippers-1830

RTW

English - 1790 to 1830

embroidered white
lingerie gown-lace
edged petticoat-blue
velvet spencer-lapels
edged red-lingerie
Betsie-black velvet
hat-dotted yellow
lawn-yellow and
black ribbon-
powdered hair-
white slippers-
brown fur muff-
brown kid gloves-
1795

swansdown edged
velvet stole-brown
and black fur
muff-striped
cotton gown-
striped silk
bonnet, ribbon
and slippers-
powdered hair
in cadogan
and curls-
1796

cloth redingote-
velvet bands and
tassels-pleated
dotted lingerie
dress with self
frill-lingerie
neck and wrist
frills-cloth
béret-velvet
band with
ruche-ostrich
plume-fabric
slippers-
1812

wine colored
velvet pelisse
with ermine-
ermine "shako"
with orange beads
and tassels-
ermine muff-
white silk
dress and
slippers-
1817

RTW

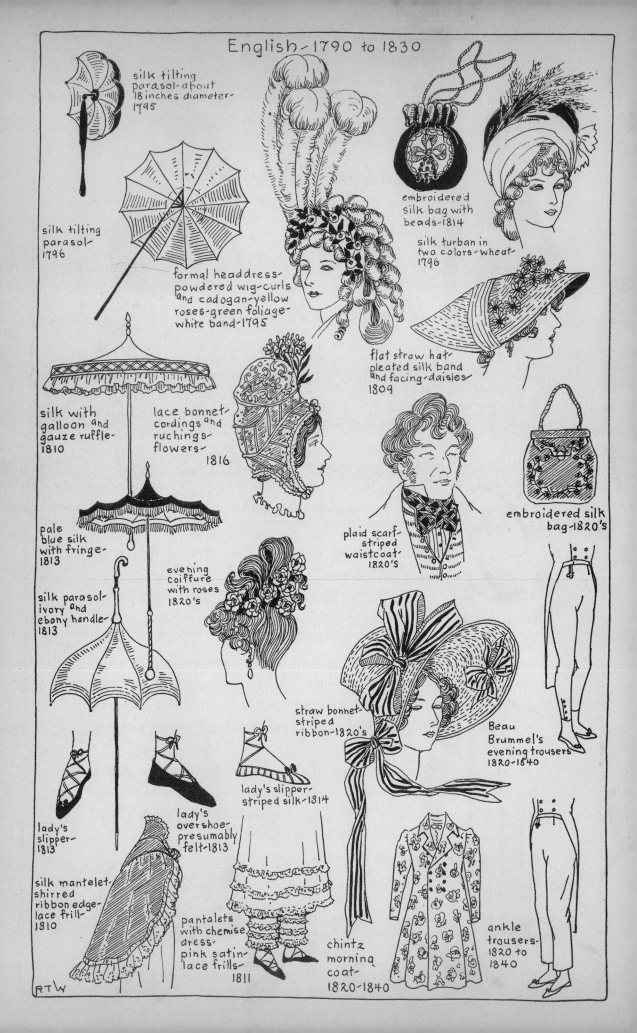

English - 1790 to 1830

silk tilting parasol-about 18 inches diameter-1795

silk tilting parasol-1796

formal headdress-powdered wig-curls and cadogan-yellow roses-green foliage-white band-1795

embroidered silk bag with beads-1814

silk turban in two colors-wheat-1796

flat straw hat-pleated silk band and facing-daisies-1809

silk with galloon and gauze ruffle-1810

lace bonnet-cordings and ruchings-flowers-1816

pale blue silk with fringe-1813

evening coiffure with roses 1820's

plaid scarf-striped waistcoat-1820's

embroidered silk bag-1820's

silk parasol-ivory and ebony handle-1813

lady's slipper-1813

lady's overshoe-presumably felt-1813

lady's slipper-striped silk-1814

straw bonnet-striped ribbon-1820's

Beau Brummel's evening trousers 1820-1840

silk mantelet-shirred ribbon edge-lace frill-1810

pantalets with chemise dress-pink satin-lace frills-1811

chintz morning coat-1820-1840

ankle trousers-1820 to 1840

RTW

Chapter Thirty-seven

Louis=Philippe
1830-1848

[handwritten marginalia: Period of romantic impulse, slight revolution, trade expanded, public education, publication of newspapers, trade unions, women did very little beyond housework, clothes simpler, main characteristic of period was flat top sleeves, skirt expanded short, redingote with flounce, skirt, velvet color trimmed with braid, slight English influence]

DEFINITELY ESTABLISHED by now were trousers, the frock coat, top hat and the greatcoat, change or variation being furnished only by details. English influence held in the masculine mode. *Skirt*

The fitted waist or corseted look continued, smallness being acquired by the wearing of a basque belt or corset. Comparatively speaking, colors were somber, albeit greens, blues and violets were worn, but in grayed tones. Waistcoats were in bright colors, even to the use of crimson velvet with gold embroidery, and sometimes fastened with jewelled buckles. Blue and black became the accepted colors for evening wear, with embroidered waistcoats of velvet, satin, brocade, piqué or cashmere.

The shirt for informal dress was generally finished with a pleated frill at the opening, the goffered shirt it was called, because the pleats were set with the aid of a goffering iron. The evening shirt was of embroidered linen, finely pleated and fastened with a diamond stud. A bow-tied white neckcloth or cravat dressed the neck.

[handwritten marginalia: Louis was known as a citizen king, Lieurendt General 1830, Louis broke transactions concerning Spanish marriages]

[handwritten marginalia at bottom: Seeking to reestablish his families influence in Spain, extension of franchise was demanded by people, followed by revolution when Louis had to abdicate & flee to England]

271

For informal wear, cravats, neckcloths and mufflers varied in fabric and color, black satin usually worn while white was *de rigueur* for dress. Mufflers filled in the space above the waistcoat to the chin and were tied in back. Long scarfs began to be worn in the 'forties, passing twice around the neck, loosely tied in front and held in place by a stickpin, the ends left hanging.

In the short redingote, with its flaring skirt, can be seen the "Prince Albert" of the next period. The collar was generally of velvet, changing to silk about 1845. In the 'forties, overcoats had flaring collars and were often trimmed with braid and frogs or brandenburgs. Coats and capes were lined with colored silks, usually white for dress.

In the 'thirties, or about 1837, appeared a short topcoat, entirely new in shape, the box coat. It was made of fawn-colored cloth, single or double breasted, and had a shawl collar of either velvet or satin.

Early in this period, the breeches of the formal habit were tight and ended above the ankles, below which showed silk socks in white or brown and the heelless pumps. For day wear, yellow, fawn or gray striped trousers were popular, with a dark coat, finished with canary-yellow gloves.

The black boot, especially the Wellington, soft, high and fitted, continued to be the fashion. It was covered by the long trouser with a strap under the shank of the boot, this style lasting to 1848.

Top hats of beaver or silk, in gray, fawn and white, remained in style, although the black silk hat appears to have been the favorite. The hair was brushed over the forehead in short ringlets, accompanied by short side whiskers. The "imperial" and the mustache were also worn.

At home, for negligee, men wore "lounging clothes" or smoking suits, with a velvet cap. The *robe d'intérieur* was of brilliantly figured silk or velvet.

In the feminine world, the leg-of-mutton sleeve, by 1830, had reached its largest size, stiffened with horsehair and whalebone. From then, the stiffening gradually diminished; by 1835, the large full sleeve falling softly over the tight cuff. Sleeves then grew smaller, the fullness disappeared, evolving into the fitted top or cap in the 'forties, eventually flaring at the forearm over a puff of contrasting fabric. The plain tight sleeve was also in fashion. To about 1835, the sleeves of evening gowns, while short, were full and stiffened, and called the béret or pancake sleeve.

Berthas, fichus and frills always accentuated the dropped shoulder line and the high necks of day dresses were always finished with a lingerie collar or frill.

Skirts became longer, ankle-length or just clearing the ground, with ornamentation sparingly used. Worn over five or six petticoats, the coming of the crinoline is apparent in the silhouette of extreme fullness.

Crinoline made its appearance in the early 'forties and was a band or braid of horsehair, *crin* being the French word for horsehair. The *crinoline* was a petticoat, corded and lined with horsehair and finished with braid straw at the hem. A flannel petticoat, in winter, was put on first, then the crinoline, then another corded calico skirt, over that a wheel of plaited horsehair and finally the starched white muslin petticoat.

The tightly laced waist of the fitted bodice remained in normal position but gradually dipped to a point in front.

The feminine greatcoat of the period was dresslike in design, full-length with small fitted waist, leg-of-mutton sleeves and a broad collar, lined for winter and of sheer material for summer. There were also mantles, shawls, scarfs, fur tippets and boas.

Shawls were of fine cashmere; lace-edged ones came from Spain, and from China those of silk crêpe, fringed and embroidered. The canezou spencer was a separate short transparent jacket with sleeves, its two scarflike ends held in place by the dress belt. It was usually of sheer muslin, with embroidery, and was worn over the bodice. The false canezou was a deep ruffle, or bretelle, falling over the short puffed sleeve.

After the conquest of Algeria, there appeared the burnous (see Pages 289–292), a wrap for both sexes, but the feminine side did not take up the style until the next period.

For evening wear, much pink and white gauze and white organdie were worn, other favored colors being yellow, blue, lilac and violet de Parme. By the 'forties, heavy fabrics were in fashion, such as brocade, poplin, damask, moiré and velvet. Black tulle and net were extensively used, often embroidered in color and spangles. Black Chantilly lace was revived and, between 1830 and 1840, was especially seen in scarfs, shawls, flounces and frills, covering almost the entire foundation gown of satin or taffeta. Challis was a new material and stripes, checks and plaids were revived late in the period. Striped ribbons were very popular.

The bonnet, which appeared in the 'twenties, continued in high favor, to be worn for fifty years. It was made of all fabrics, often draped with a lace veil either white or black, and there were such shapes as the coal-scuttle bonnet, the poke bonnet and the calash.

Important, too, were caps of sheer lingerie fabric, lace-edged and trimmed with ribbons, worn principally at home. The bonnet was often worn over the cap, the exposed ruche framing the face. An evolution of the cap was a wire band with an outstanding lace frill, flowers and ribbon, this arrangement also framing the face. The English named the latter an *arcade*.

The coiffure of the period was sleek in silhouette, despite its braids and prim curls. In the 'thirties, the hair was elaborately dressed and, in the evening, ornamented with flowers, ribbons, feathers and the ferronière around the forehead. Late in the 'thirties, the "English ringlets" at the sides of the face began to descend, reaching the shoulders by 1840. In the 'forties, for evening dress, Oriental scarfs were tied around the head in turban fashion.

Silk mittens, especially black ones, became more and more popular, and the fine lace handkerchief was again brought into view as an important accessory.

The vogue for jewelry grew, specially in gold and elaborate settings in brooches, rings, long earrings and bracelets. Favorite gems were the diamond, pearl, ruby, emerald and topaz. Fine gold-chain fringe, onyx jet and cameos were characteristic of the time, as were "sets," which consisted of a brooch, a pair of bracelets and earrings. Very small, carefully arranged bouquets of fresh flowers were often carried in jewelled holders, attached by a chain to a finger ring.

A low broad heel appeared in the late 'thirties, but the low slipper with crossed elastic bands and the ankle shoe, both of fabric, were still worn. White slippers and light-colored silk boots were popular, while black satin slippers, with a fine white silk stocking, seem to have been the thing for evening. A novelty was the black net stocking worn over one of flesh color.

From 1836, when Charles Goodyear made his important discovery of a method of treating the surface of gum, the use of elastic in dress became more practicable.

Horseback riding was very popular for both sexes. A particular feminine riding habit is noted, of "London" smoke-colored cloth, with white cambric jacket, really a blouse, with full sleeves, a full skirt over petticoats, riding trousers, boots with silver spurs and yellow gauntlets. These particular riding trousers of white muslin were finished with a two-inch frill over the boot. In the cambric bodice can be seen the origin of the shirtwaist. As noted, it was of cambric, finely tucked and lace-trimmed.

Only young girls wore pantalets in France, but in England and America, both women and children adopted the fashion.

The small hinged or tilting parasol was used when riding in a carriage.

A machine for making flowered net, resembling the handmade lace, was invented in 1837, by Joseph Marie Jacquard, the inventor of the history-making mechanical loom for weaving patterned fabrics.

Louis-Philippe 1830-1848

dark blue or black cloth evening habit-velvet collar-self buttons-white waistcoat-pleated shirt-diamond studs-cravat-collar tabs-front trouser pockets-fob seal-white silk socks-black pumps-silk hat-1830

frockcoat in redingote style-velvet collar-self buttons-white waistcoat-black silk neckcloth-strap trousers over black boots-handkerchief in right trouser pocket-beaver hat-1830

"habit" or "suit" frock coat-waistcoat with satin collar-checked strap trousers over black boots-black silk cravat-turned down collar tabs-silk hat-1842

suit with black frockcoat-self buttons-lilac plaid trousers over boots-fullness at waist-white waistcoat-black silk cravat-turned down collar tabs-silk hat-yellow gloves-1844

RTW

Louis-Philippe 1830-1848

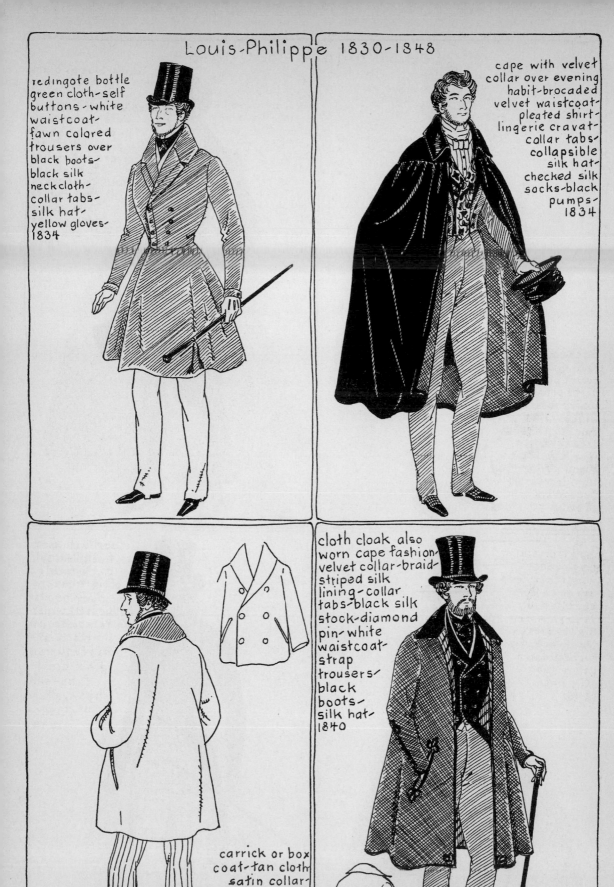

redingote bottle green cloth-self buttons-white waistcoat-fawn colored trousers over black boots-black silk neckcloth-collar tabs-silk hat-yellow gloves-1834

cape with velvet collar over evening habit-brocaded velvet waistcoat-pleated shirt-lingerie cravat-collar tabs-collapsible silk hat-checked silk socks-black pumps-1834

cloth cloak also worn cape fashion-velvet collar-braid-striped silk lining-collar tabs-black silk stock-diamond pin-white waistcoat-strap trousers-black boots-silk hat-1840

carrick or box coat-tan cloth satin collar-self covered buttons-black striped gray trousers-black boots-silk hat-1837

Louis-Philippe 1830-1848

rose taffeta skirt
and sleeves-fluted
white organdie
ruffles-double
organdie hem-
embroidered neck
and belt-straw hat-
drooping plume-
striped ribbon-
shirred frills
at cheeks-
black
satin
slippers-white
silk stockings-
embroidered
handkerchief-
fan-
1832

black taffeta and
black lace net-
braid ornaments
on cord-tassels-
black taffeta rose
on bosom-white
lace bonnet-pink
roses and ribbon-
fur boa-
white silk
stockings-
black
satin
slippers-
necklace-
buckles
on cuffs-
1834

velvet gown-lace
bertha and collar-
three jewelled
buttons-bonnet
of shirred and
corded silk-
lace veil-
1842

"London smoke"
gray cloth
riding habit-
velvet collar-
black satin
stock-white
ruche and
shirt-black
silk hat-
gray veil-
white
muslin strap
trousers-black
boots-
1844

RTW

Louis-Philippe 1830-1848

cloak-figured cloth-
silk lined-neck
ruche-felt bonnet
with ruching, ribbon
and flowers-fur
muff-cloth shoes-
leather toecap-
1834

pelisse-brown
cashmere-lined
mauve silk and
wadding-
white fur-gray
felt bonnet-
paradise gray
and magenta-
gray ribbon-
black silk
shoes-
1833

taffeta cape-self
rope trimming-
gown with lingerie
collar and cuffs-
embroidered
handkerchief-
fabric bonnet-
ostrich plumes-
1841

ermine stole
and muff-white
bowknot on muff-
black silk gown-
green velvet
shirred and corded
bonnet-green
ribbons-green
and gray
ostrich-
1844

FTW

Louis-Philippe 1830-1848

evening coiffure-
wired black velvet
ribbon bands-
earrings-flowers-
1838

evening
coiffure-
looped
braids-
wired black
velvet ribbon-
flowers-
1838

striped cravat-
collar tabs-
flowered
waistcoat-
1831

black net over
flesh color-
black satin
slipper-
crossed
elastic-
1830's

black
velvet cap
worn with
lounging robe or
smoking suit-
1839

corset-
back lacing-
1837

evening
coiffure-
braids-
pearls-roses-
lily of the
valley-earrings-
1830

negliee
headdress-
shirred
lace on
ribbon
band-
lace
rosettes-1839

lady's
boot-fur
top-
tied with
ribbons-
1830

waves and
curls-collar
tabs-satin
stock-pearl
stud-
1848

curls and
braid-
1844

man's shoe-
cloth top-leather
toecap-laced
on inner side-
1832

white lace
and taffeta-
appliqued
green leaves-
1838

black
organdie-
self ruched
edge-
yellow
tie-red
roses-
green
foliage-
1835

white
organdie
canezou-
1832

black silk mitten

RTW

Chapter Thirty=eight

French

Second Republic, 1848–1852
Second Empire, 1852–1870

T HE MASCULINE MODE had now settled into its severely tailored state of somber colors, plain, striped, or checked, colored waistcoats and black for formal wear, with but slight variations in accessories. It should be borne in mind that the basic style element in male attire had its origin in London; nevertheless, certain Latin preferences have always been apparent in the clothes of Frenchmen.

After 1850, the jacket or sack coat became definitely the costume for informal occasions, with the frock and tail coat reserved for dress. The sack coat was the outcome of the lounging or smoking habit, and since has signified any jacket with body and skirt cut in one or without waist seam. The double-breasted frock coat was named the "Prince Albert," after the consort of Queen Victoria of England.

The fold of white piqué edged the neck of the cloth vest or waistcoat.

The tight trousers, with straps under the boots, disappeared in the 'fifties; from then, the leg gradually widened. Stripes, checks and plaids were used and fancy braid appeared at the sides.

281

About the same time, the boot worn under the trousers gave way to the laced-up shoe which was followed in the 'sixties by the side-buttoned shoe. Pumps were revived at the Court of Napoleon III. Patent leather for shoes became very popular. It was japanned or lacquered leather which came into existence in the first quarter of the nineteenth century and was used for harness. A harness maker, Seth Boyden of Newark, New Jersey, in America, seeing harness blinders which came from Paris, experimented on his own and is known to have made the first patent leather in this country in 1822.

There were many styles in topcoats: among them, the short box coat of fawn-colored cloth with shawl collar; a short capelike coat; the Mac-Farlan, with its separate sleeve capes (see Page 304); the burnous, a variation of the Arab's cloak; and the *paletot*. The paletot, pall coat in English, worn past the middle of the century, was a heavy overcoat, three-quarter length, with the waist slightly repressed. An important coat which appeared in the 'fifties was the raglan topcoat, named after Lord Henry Raglan, hero of the Crimean War. The wide armhole was, no doubt, the result of his having lost an arm. Linings of winter coats were often of brilliant colored silks, padded and quilted. Overcoats were also fur-trimmed and fur-lined and fastened with heavy braided loops.

The steam locomotive brought about travelling to the seaside and inland watering places, with "casual clothes" for such visits. Sport clothes, although not so called, first appeared in the 'fifties and were made of alpaca, nankeen and foulard in white and light colors.

With these sport clothes were worn the long loosely tied scarf and the wide laydown soft collar of the shirt. Neck dressing became more trim, with soft collar rising above the cravat. In the 'fifties, the cravat was stiffened by an inner lining. It was often fastened in back by means of a strap and buckle with a sewn-on, made-up bow in front. A flat scarf, the forerunner of the later puff or Ascot tie, made its debut in the early 'fifties, the two ends crossed in front and held by a stickpin. In the 'sixties, starched detachable cuffs and collars replaced the soft attached shirt collars.

Wide woolen scarfs or folded shawls of dark colors and plaids were often worn around the shoulders when travelling.

In hats, the vogue of the gray, fawn and white beavers continued, with the black silk top hat becoming more and more the headgear for dress. Hats worn with sport clothes were of felt or straw, low-crowned with wide rolling brim, a ribbon tied round the crown, the ends often hanging to the neck in back. The melon-shaped hat appeared. The hard felt hat, known in France as the melon, in England as the bowler and to us as the derby, was designed in 1850 by William Bowler, the hatter.

Men still curled their hair, but wore it trimmed up higher on the back of the neck. The mustache, side whiskers, or "cutlets," the French name, and "Dundreary" in English, and the "imperial," the tuff of hair on the chin and lower lip, were worn even by very young men.

The use of the walking stick had become general. The monocle, in either round or square frame, was worn round the neck on a fine chain, cord or ribbon, also the pince-nez in like frame and fashion.

In feminine costume, the tight steel corset persisted and the full skirt widened, until it measured ten yards around by 1860, in this period of flounces.

Underclothing, in the early 'fifties, consisted of long lace-trimmed white muslin drawers, a flannel petticoat in winter, the crinoline or petticoat of calico, quilted and reinforced with whalebone, and several starched, checked, striped or white muslin petticoats with flounces. The outer petticoat was invariably tucked and embroidered.

These many petticoats were replaced by a cagelike frame of steel hoops, still called a crinoline. An improvement in crinolines was the *cage américaine,* in which the crinoline could be raised, making it possible to wear the garment in the street with short dresses. The decline of the crinoline began in 1860.

The bell-shaped skirt took on the shape of a cone, with steel hoops only from the knees down. The skirt still flared into a wide circumference on the ground, but was smooth and flat over the hips. In the early 'sixties, both trains and ankle-length skirts appeared. The short skirt brought into vogue petticoats of colored taffeta.

In 1869, the bustle replaced the crinoline. The bustle was really a crinoline, but with the rows of whalebone running only from the sides round the back. The wide flare at the bottom of the skirt disappeared, but the bunched-up polonaise or tunic in back created the bustle silhouette. Women returned to the stiffly starched muslin petticoats.

The fitted, boned bodice was finished high at the neck with a frill or small collar, while the décolletage was low for evening wear, its off-the-shoulder line finished with fichu or bertha. The *péplum Impératrice* of the late 'sixties was a basque bodice with draped-up tunic or panniers. From 1850, for about ten years, the pagoda sleeve prevailed with its full white lace-trimmed and tucked undersleeve, puffed out by light steel hoops. Then came the long tight sleeve.

The princess dress, called the "Gabriel," appeared in the 'sixties. It was in one piece from neck to hem, ornamented with buttons or bow-knots the length of the center front. Women also had clothes for the country and the seashore in pilot coats, boating jackets and rowing blouses worn with the short skirt.

Shawls, mantles, capes and flaring coats, hip-length and three-quarter, accompanied the full flaring skirt. A short coat which was fashionable in the 'sixties gave rise to the name of "turkey back silhouette." It hung fairly straight in the front, flaring out abruptly in the back from the neck.

In shawls there were black silk ones, the Indian cashmeres and those of fine wool, the striped Tunisian and those of crêpe de chine with embroidery and deep fringe. Mantles were made of woolen cloth, velvet, lace and changeable taffeta, finished with ruffles of all widths, fringes, cords and tassels.

Fashions in cloaks changed constantly with the Swedish cape, the Moldavian mantle, the Algerian burnous, the Talma and others. Then there were the Greek, Turkish and Zouave jackets. All these were made of rep, heavy silks and damasks.

The feminine jacket and skirt costume appeared for the first time in

Gauche long mantle + trimmed in
fur   dalman was cut same as polonase dress
except for + sleeve   which was wide + tigwat
waist

this period and, comparatively speaking, was a tailored mannish costume with its jacket shorn of lace and frills. The separate shirt or blouse often had a masculine collar, with a narrow bow tie and the tightly buttoned waistcoat also was adopted.

Ornamentation on gowns and wraps was lavish in embroidery, galloon, silk or woolen lace, braid, frogs, tassels, fringe and passementerie. Gowns for formal wear were of such fabrics as gold and silver brocades, handsome patterned materials, heavy satins, silks and moirés. Taffeta became the most popular of all fabrics. Ribbon continued in high favor, plaids and tartans especially so. Day dresses were made of fine wool, alpaca, mohair, English velveteen and foulards. Ball gowns were of gauze, tulle and tarlatan, and lace and summer dresses were of linen, cambric, muslin and batiste. Fashionable laces were Brussels net, Mechlin, point laces, with the black Spanish and Chantilly laces most popular.

Colors typical of the period were tender browns, olive, amber and vanilla. A color scheme introduced by Empress Eugénie was the combination of various shades of brown silk, combined with black velvet. Stripes of all widths were popular, and dyed astrakhan was much used.

Every lady had her dressing gown of thin silk or lingerie material for summer and for winter, of satin or brocade, often lined with quilted silk and trimmed with lace, velvet, ribbon or galloon. Relief from tight lacing was afforded in the boudoir when the stays were taken off and the dressing gown worn.

By 1860, bonnets and caps were replaced by the hat, fastened to the hair by hatpins. The little round hat with low crown was known in England as the "pork pie." The crown was encircled with flowers and a ribbon. The two long streamers hanging in back were named *suivez-moi jeune homme,* or "follow me, young man," in English. An important hat known in France as the "Empress hat" was revived in 1931 as the "Empress Eugénie." Other styles were the Windsor cap, with its peak, and the tiny shepherdess hat, which tilted down over the eyes. Paradise and aigrettes were added to millinery ornamentation.

Suff sleeves + sleeveless dresses for evening where brought
about kid gloves and soft shoes
Polonaise became elaborate with Trim
evening where + neckline was high - sleeves
long + close fitting

The "nose veil," a short veil reaching only to the nose, came in in 1860, and the "face veil," longer and covering the face, in 1863.

The hair was parted in Madonna style, drawn into a cadogan or large bun at the back of the neck and often held in place by a coarse net. Nets were very popular and were made of silk or velvet ribbon, followed by nets of chenille and, in the 'sixties, by nets of human hair. From 1860 to 1865, the chignon was placed higher and grew very large, finally reaching the crown of the head, with cascading curls. Evening coiffures were ornamented with lace, flowers, ribbon, gold and silver nets and jewelled combs. The hair was waved by means of hot irons or tongs, and many women resorted to coloring and bleaching to effect the desired blond type.

Caps finally retired to the boudoir and eventually were worn only by elderly women.

High shoes, of very soft black leather, appeared in the 'sixties, in black or gray, of black patent leather, satin or kid or a combination of satin and leather. They had very high heels and very thin soles and were either buttoned at the side or laced up center front. The trim Hessian boot worn with the short skirt often flaunted a tassel at the top. Carriage shoes were made of brocade. Day shoes were usually black and the stocking generally white.

Colored stockings came in with colored silk petticoats in the 'sixties, although the first to appear were gray with red clocks. For evening wear, stockings matched the gown. Later, bright-colored stripes running round the leg and even red stockings were worn.

Accessories carried in the hand were the handkerchief, the fan, gloves and a parasol, while, in the evening, the conventionally arranged small bouquet of fresh flowers was an added note to the costume. Gloves were always worn and were of various lengths, of beautiful kid in white and delicate colors. Silk and lace parasols were trimmed with ruffles and fringe, and the small tilting carriage parasol continued very much in fashion.

There was a tremendous vogue for artificial flowers, which were sewn on evening gowns. Very elegant ladies employed fresh flowers, however.

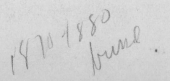

The gold locket and shell cameo were favorite ornaments, worn on a black velvet ribbon round the neck, also the cross. Black velvet ribbon was tied round the wrists. There were jewelled hatpins, long and short earrings, rings, bracelets, brooches, necklaces, bandeaux and tiaras. A combination in design, characteristic of the period, was several colors of gold employed in one piece with small pearls and black enamel. Tiny scent boxes of gold and silver were carried, containing a small sponge saturated with perfume. Beads, pearls, coral, amber, marcasite and the newcomer crystal were more often worn in the daytime.

The frame of the feminine lorgnette, like that of the masculine monocle, had also taken on a square shape.

An event of great importance was the introduction into Europe, in the 'fifties, of the American sewing machine.

The Empress Eugénie was dressed by the famous couturier, Worth, whose clientele comprised most of the European royalty. Monsieur Charles Frederick Worth, an English lad of Lincolnshire, England, came to Paris before twenty years of age and, in 1858, founded the House of Worth. He was the first to exhibit his new creations on living mannequins.

French prussian war which destroyed paris considerably. The recovery was very much in spirit in the 3rd republic

Travelers were coming from everywhere to see paris. In '70 panniers & dresses were popular

French 1848-1870

striped cloth
suit-satin
cravat-collar
tabs-beaver
hat-black
boots-
1849

evening dress-
black cloth-self
buttons-white
silk waistcoat-
pearl studs-white
linen shirt and
cravat-tucked
front with pearl
studs-black
silk hat-
black patent
leather shoes-
chamois
gloves-
monocle on
fine chain-
1858

striped sack coat
with plaid
trousers-hard
felt melon
hat-black
patent leather
shoes-
1862

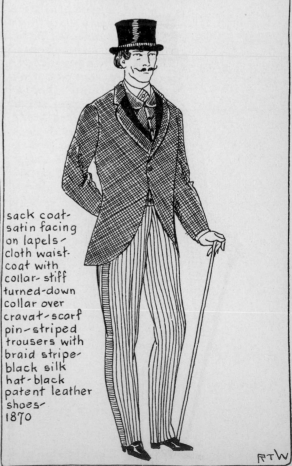

sack coat-
satin facing
on lapels-
cloth waist-
coat with
collar-stiff
turned-down
collar over
cravat-scarf
pin-striped
trousers with
braid stripe-
black silk
hat-black
patent leather
shoes-
1870

RTW

French 1848-1870

cloth burnous-
hood with tassel-
silk cravat-
trousers with
braid-silk hat-
black leather
shoes-
1851

dark green cloth
box coat-satin
binding-collar and
cuffs green self
striped silk-gray
and red striped
cravat-black
silk hat-tan
trousers with
black braid-
black leather
shoes-
1853

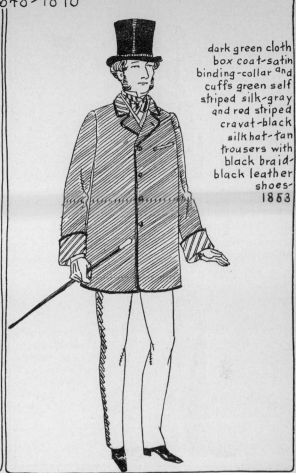

raglan coat stone
gray cloth-lined
gray checked cloth-
brown cutaway-
white waistcoat-
trousers pale gray
cloth with braid-
tucked shirt-
spotted green
cravat-black
silk hat-
black shoes-
chamois
gloves-
1856

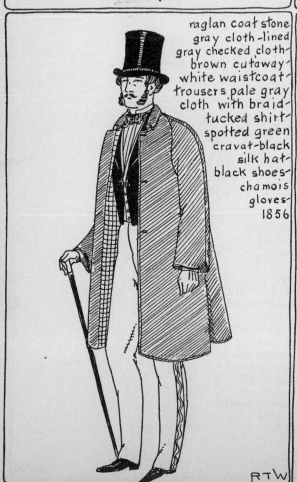

black cloth
overcoat-self
buttons-brown
trousers striped
black-brown
silk "flat
scarf" with
jewelled pin-
black silk
hat-black
shoes-
1858

RTW

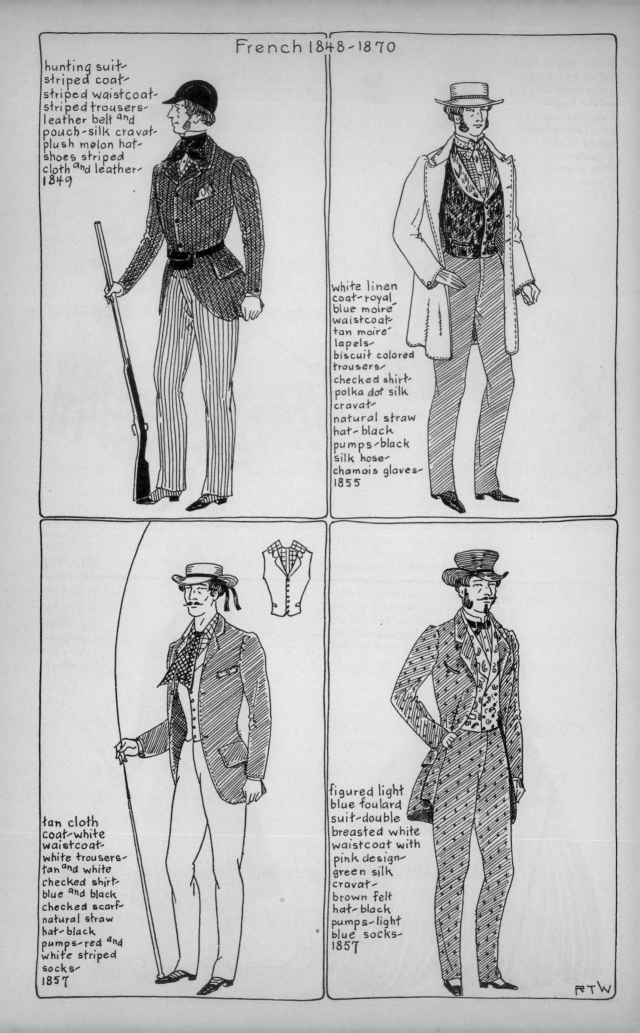

hunting suit-
striped coat-
striped waistcoat-
striped trousers-
leather belt and
pouch-silk cravat-
plush melon hat-
shoes striped
cloth and leather-
1849

white linen
coat-royal
blue moiré
waistcoat-
tan moiré
lapels-
biscuit colored
trousers-
checked shirt-
polka dot silk
cravat-
natural straw
hat-black
pumps-black
silk hose-
chamois gloves-
1855

tan cloth
coat-white
waistcoat-
white trousers-
tan and white
checked shirt-
blue and black
checked scarf-
natural straw
hat-black
pumps-red and
white striped
socks-
1857

figured light
blue foulard
suit-double
breasted white
waistcoat with
pink design-
green silk
cravat-
brown felt
hat-black
pumps-light
blue socks-
1857

FTW

bridal gown-white
satin-self buttons-
embroidered
white satin
flounces-pleated
chiffon-short
white kid
gloves-veil
and orange
blossoms-
1858

"mannish" taffeta
costume-plain
and plaid-
braid, cord and
tassels-waistcoat-
tucked lingerie
blouse-bow tie-
Empress hat-
ostrich and
bowknot-
leather
shoes-
1860

"turkey back"
silhouette-faille
silk-self ruching-
braid trimmed-
shirred hood-
cords and tassels-
striped silk skirt-
straw bonnet-
lace ruffle-
ostrich tips-
1867

princess gown-
gray silk with
gray cords and
buttons-sheer
white collar-
yellow gloves-
blue ribbon
and grapes
in hair-
1867

RTW

French 1848-1870

black riding habit-
white lace collar
and undersleeves-
white muslin
petticoat with
lace insertion
and tucks-black
hat-velvet
crown-straw
brim-ostrich
tips-yellow
gloves-mauve
veil-
1857

burnous of white
cloth striped green-
green velvet band-
green silk tassel-
green velvet bonnet
with white frill-
green silk gown-
1850's

black plush pelisse-
beaver fur-green
silk gown with
lingerie collar and
puffs-green bonnet
of silk and
velvet with
ostrich tips-
1862

black lace
mantelet attached
to "old blue" silk
yoke-blue silk
gown-blue straw
bonnet-ribbon-
white roses-
green foliage-
1866

RTW

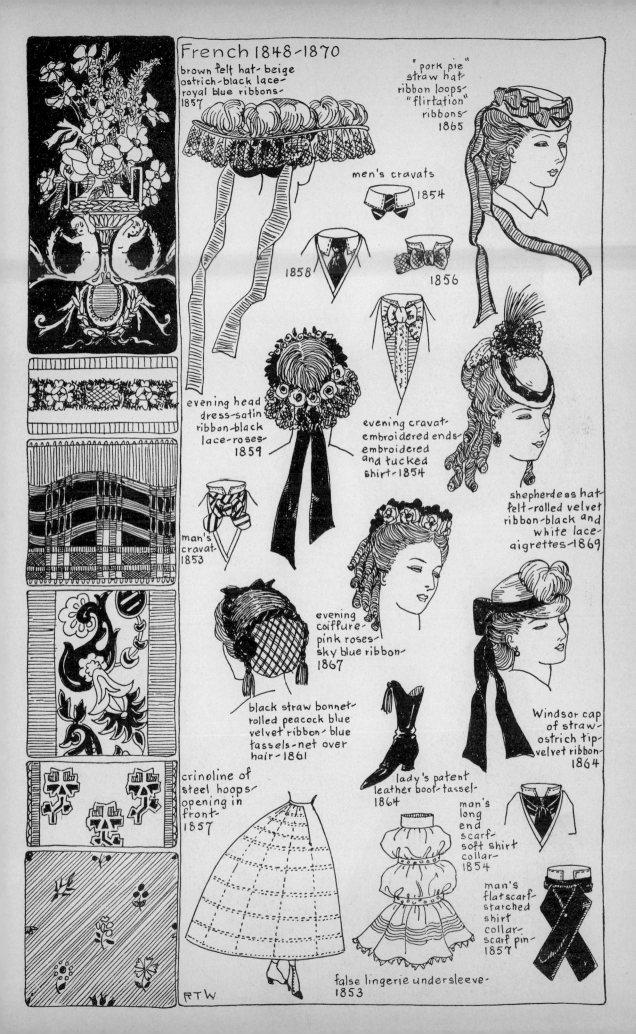

French 1848-1870

brown felt hat- beige ostrich- black lace- royal blue ribbons- 1857

"pork pie" straw hat ribbon loops- "flirtation" ribbons- 1865

men's cravats 1854

1858

1856

evening head dress- satin ribbon- black lace- roses- 1859

evening cravat- embroidered ends- embroidered and tucked shirt- 1854

man's cravat- 1853

shepherdess hat- felt- rolled velvet ribbon- black and white lace- aigrettes- 1869

evening coiffure- pink roses- sky blue ribbon- 1867

black straw bonnet- rolled peacock blue velvet ribbon- blue tassels- net over hair- 1861

Windsor cap of straw- ostrich tip- velvet ribbon- 1864

crinoline of steel hoops- opening in front- 1857

lady's patent leather boot- tassel- 1864

man's long end scarf- soft shirt collar- 1854

man's flat scarf- starched shirt collar- scarf pin- 1857

false lingerie undersleeve- 1853

RTW

Chapter Thirty=nine

Victorian England

1837–1901

IN THE MASCULINE COSTUME of the early part of this period, color, while more subdued than in preceding times, was still being worn, especially in day clothes. Colors were in various shades of brown, dark green, blue and violet. For evening wear, blue or black with white became the accepted mode. After 1850, the claw-hammer, or swallowtail coat and the frock coat were reserved for formal occasions. Coats were fitted at the waist with short flaring skirts. The double-breasted frock coat with silk-faced lapels and closed skirt front has always been known as the "Prince Albert," since it was worn by the Prince Consort of Queen Victoria. The pockets were placed in the back of the skirt and sometimes the coat had a velvet collar.

The morning coat, with rounded-off skirt fronts, appeared in the 'fifties, and about the same time appeared the short lounge jacket or sack coat, which became the coat for informal wear. It was called the *sakko,* a German contraction of sack coat, due, no doubt, to the nationality of the Prince Consort. The sack is any coat without a waist seam, that is body and skirt cut in one. Though originally considered eccentric, by 1870, the sack coat became generally worn.

Heavy tweed suits came into vogue for sportswear.

The dinner coat first appeared in England in the 'eighties and was called the "Cowes" or dress sack coat. It was described as a dress coat without tails, and was used for dinners and dances in country homes. It was not intended to take the place of the swallowtail, but to be worn on less formal occasions. In the United States, the coat was named the "Tuxedo," being first worn at Tuxedo Park. In France, it is known as the "smoking," its design having originated in the smoking or lounging suits of the 'forties. Berry Wall, a prominent society man and dress authority, was refused admission to a dance at the Grand Union Hotel in Saratoga, New York, because he wore "the latest English fad in dress coats." It later became more popular here than on the Continent, American men appreciating its informality.

Braid trimming on men's clothes came in about 1850, used as binding on coats and stitched down the side seams of trousers, surviving today on the trousers of the tail coat and the dinner coat.

Both trousers and black satin knee breeches remained the style for evening, breeches being the full dress for many British officials. Until the 'fifties, trousers were very tight, worn over the high boot with a strap passing underneath, from then gradually widening in the leg, the straps lasting into the 'sixties. Trousers were of striped, checked and plaid fabrics in various colors, the coat usually in solid color. The front closing flap gave way to buttons down the center front about 1845, with side pockets becoming general about the same time.

There were early attempts to introduce creases in trousers, but the style was not accepted. The Prince of Wales, later Edward VII, upon his visit to America in 1860 wore his trousers creased on the sides of the leg as well as at front and back. Creases down the front and back of the leg became general by the 'nineties, having first been introduced by army officers.

Cuffs on trousers, which began to appear with the turn of the century, were the result of Englishmen turning up their trousers on rainy days in the muddy paddock. An English nobleman, on his way to a wedding in New York, turned up his trousers for the same reason. He arrived late, neglected to turn down the cuffs and the fashion was on.

Waistcoats, until the 'eighties, were of colorful handsome fabrics and until the 'sixties, often embroidered. The white evening waistcoat was of brocade, satin, velvet, cashmere or piqué. Although the white waistcoat was first worn by Beau Brummel with his dark blue evening habit, the white waistcoat for day wear is noted as being made popular by Count Gabriel d'Orsay, a celebrated dandy who married Lady Blessington. He became successor to the "Beau" as fashion arbiter. He not only was a brilliant conversationalist but a painter and sculptor of talent and author of a book on etiquette. The white piqué fold which edged the neck of the dark vest from the 'fifties to the end of the century was the survival of the white waistcoat.

In the 'thirties and the 'forties, neckcloths and cravats were tied in front and mufflers, which filled in the space above the waistcoat to the chin, were tied in back. Until the 'sixties, the white evening bow tie often had embroidered ends (see Page 293). The jewelled stickpin appeared. The collar points which showed above began to turn down over the cravat in the 'forties, becoming a real turndown collar in the 'fifties. Also in the 'fifties appeared the stiff starched standing collar, with its narrow bow tie, to be followed, in the 'sixties, by detachable starched linen cuffs and collar. The round high collar came in in the 'seventies. Collars and cuffs of paper, to be worn once and then discarded, appeared for a short time.

The small cravat, tied in a bow in front, was worn from the 'fifties. It was stiffened by an inner lining and often the bow was sewn on, the scarf fastened in back by means of a strap and buckle, the original ready-made scarf. The scarf with long ends was first worn in the 'forties. It passed round the neck twice, was loosely tied in front and held in place by a scarfpin.

The flat scarf with wide crossed ends appeared in the 'fifties, and was the origin of the Ascot puff of the 'seventies. The Ascot, first worn at the

Ascot Heath races, was responsible for the great vogue of the ready-made cravat and was made of heavy colorful silks and novelty weaves. Variations of the style were the de Joinville, named after Prince de Joinville, and the four-in-hand or Teck, named after the Prince of Teck. The four-in-hand gained in popularity, replacing the made-up scarf by the end of the century. The bow tie continued in fashion to the end of the period.

Shirts of light colors, line checks and stripes, were worn with casual clothes past the middle of the century, but the fine white shirt for day and formal wear appears to have been the mark of the gentleman to the end of the century. An innovation, in the 'thirties, was the separate shirt front, or "dickey," which was replaced in the 'forties by the shirt with an inserted, tucked, pleated or embroidered bosom, of finer linen than that of the body of the garment.

Travel over the country, made easy by the railroads, carried people to "country, seaside or watering place," so that, by the 'fifties, country clothes came into existence. Men's casual clothes were in light colors, of fabrics such as nankeen, alpaca and foulard. Heavy tweed suits appeared for sportswear. The coat of the Duke of Norfolk's hunting suit, known as the Norfolk jacket, appeared in the 'eighties with knickerbockers, a first revival of knee breeches for day wear. Velveteen or corduroy breeches were for winter use and those of dark waterproof English cloth were preferred for autumn wear.

A fashion note of November, 1886, describes a "shooting jacket of strong plain or striped sail-cloth, gaiters of gray linen and a linen hat with cork lining."

There were many styles of topcoats. The short box coat dates back to the late 'thirties (see Page 277). It was single or double-breasted and has always been of fawn-colored cloth. An amusing fashion in the 'nineties was the use of the box coat over the evening habit, the tails hanging below to five or six inches. The burnous appeared in the late 'forties (see Page 289). The raglan, which is shown on Page 289, is of the 'fifties. It was named after the hero of the Crimean War, Lord Raglan, the loose armscye no doubt the result of his having lost an arm. There was a short sleeveless coat with cape, a flaring coat with straight sleeves and the MacFarlan, with its separate sleeve capes. In the 'eighties appeared the sleeveless Inverness cape coat of Scotch origin, the ulster of Irish origin, also the short double-breasted reefer adopted from the coat of the British Navy. The pall coat, or paletot, of the 'sixties was a heavy overcoat with a slight repression at the waist, a three-quarter-length garment. The Chesterfield, named after the Earl of Chesterfield, that classic dress overcoat of the twentieth century, also appeared in this period. Overcoats often had velvet collars, were fur-trimmed and fur-lined and were fastened by heavy braided loops.

There was also a vogue for shawls in masculine costume, that accessory being worn from 1840 to 1860. They were folded across the shoulders and were in wool in plaids and dark colors.

Until the 'sixties, the hair was worn moderately long and curled, usually parted at one side with side whiskers or beard all around the face. Whiskers separated by a shaven chin were called "Dundreary whiskers." Past the middle of the century, the mustache and the "imperial" appeared. Beards and whiskers disappeared in the 'eighties, but the mustache retained its popularity. At the same time, the hair was flattened on the top of the head and parted in the middle, sometimes from front to down the back. The preference appears to have been for straight hair in the 'nineties. The hair was dressed with Macassar oil all through this period, whence the vogue of the antimacassar, a tidy or doily which protected the back of the chair.

In tall hats, the fashion of fawn, gray or white beaver lasted until the 'nineties, with the black silk hat the headgear for formal dress. The invention of a machine for the manufacture of felt, in 1846, brought many new styles into vogue. In 1850, a round hard hat with straight brim and low round crown made its debut. It was designed by an English hatter, William Bowler, and was the original model of the bowler or derby. Another English name was the "billycock," a contraction of the name William Coke, the first Englishman to sponsor the style. Derby, the American name, had its origin in the fact that the Earl of Derby popularized the style by wearing the hat to the English races. His hat was gray with a black band. It was quite generally adopted in the 'seventies. A soft felt hat with wide brim and low flat crown appeared in the 'fifties, also the same model in straw and hats of woolen plaid for country wear. Caps had always been worn, but, with increase in travelling and sports, they now took a definite place in the wardrobe of the well-dressed man.

It seems well established that soft felt hats for men originated in Germany or Austria in the mountains of the Tyrol. After considerable British styling, these hats emerged as the Homburg or the fedora. The Homburg was named after Homburg, Germany, the place of its first manufacture. This hat was made fashionably important by being worn by the Prince of Wales (Edward VII), at Bad Homburg. The fedora took its name from the heroine of the drama by Sardou and was worn by both sexes in the 'eighties and the 'nineties.

The machine for sewing straw was perfected in 1870 and, by the 'eighties, the "boater" or hard straw hat was being worn when punting on the Thames. The Panama hat had been made for nearly three centuries in Ecuador and has always been in use by the Britisher in tropical countries. It was marketed at Panama, thus acquiring its name. The hat is known to have been worn in America in the eighteenth century.

Short Wellington boots worn under the trousers with straps lasted to the 'sixties. The laced-up shoe appeared in the 'fifties, followed by the side-buttoned shoe in 'sixties and the gaiter shoe in the 'seventies. The gaiter shoe had inserts of elastic at the sides or over the insteps and was known in America as the "congress shoe." In the second half of the century, black patent leather became fashionable for shoes. With the successful manufacturing of shoes, styles began to change often and special shoes were made for special occasions, such as dress shoes, evening shoes and sport shoes. Cloth spats and the gaiter halfway up the leg were fashionable throughout the period. Toward the end of the period came the cloth-top buttoned shoe.

A startling novelty in the early 'eighties were sleeping pajamas of Oriental origin, supplanting for many the long nightshirt with slashed sides.

Handsome gold-headed canes were carried, but were shorter than those of previous periods, being now cut to measure to reach from the man's hand of his slightly bent arm to the ground. Rings, scarfpins, heavy gold watches with heavy gold chains came into fashion about the middle of the century. Watches were carried in the vest pocket in the 'forties, when the shorter vest acquired the small watch pocket.

Buttons on suits and coats matched the cloth in color, often cloth-covered. Horn buttons were used and, by the middle of the century, buttons of dyed vegetable ivory were most popular, continuing in use today.

Cloth-covered buttons were first manufactured in the United States in 1826 and pearl buttons about 1885.

In women's clothes, the period known as "mid-Victorian" is the mode of the crinoline with its many flounces and ruffles, Queen Victoria living virtually in retirement after the death of the Prince Consort in 1861. The Queen attended the Paris Exhibition in state in 1855, thereby bringing about an acceptance of French ideas and feminine fashions into England.

The general style of the costume was that of the contemporary French, but it lacked the Gallic flair for lightness in clothes and, while it was definitely a period of ornamentation of all kinds, it was truly overdone in the English mode.

Boys' clothes became much simpler, with a leaning toward the peasant style of smock and trousers. An interesting fact is that, while the costume of the little girl followed closely, in design and trimming, that of her grownups, the design of the small boy's clothes appears to have been based upon the various European national costumes.

In 1851, Mrs. Amelia J. Bloomer of Seneca Falls, New York, attempted a reform in women's dress by appearing in full Oriental trousers with a very short skirt or tunic, not unlike Paul Poiret's minaret costume of more than half a century later. The event is noted here, because of her visit to London, where she met with some success, and because of the reappearance in the 'eighties of "bloomers" worn by women when bicycling.

Victorian England

sack coat-
one button-
shawl
collar-
same
period

black sack coat-
satin collar-
brown checked
trousers-green
flat scarf-
standing collar-
beige felt bowler-
black shoes-tan
cloth tops-
chamois gloves-
1850's

black sack
coat-braid
edge-white
piqué edge to
vest-turn-down
collar-black
scarf-tan
felt hat-black
ribbon-chamois
gloves-monocle-
black shoes-
tan spats-
1870's

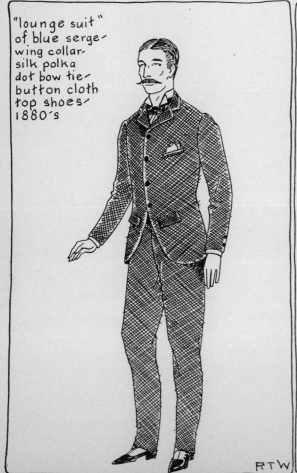

"lounge suit"
of blue serge-
wing collar-
silk polka
dot bow tie-
button cloth
top shoes-
1880's

dress lounge suit-
black coat-
trousers striped
gray and black-
black shoes-
gray spats-
1890's

RTW

Victorian England

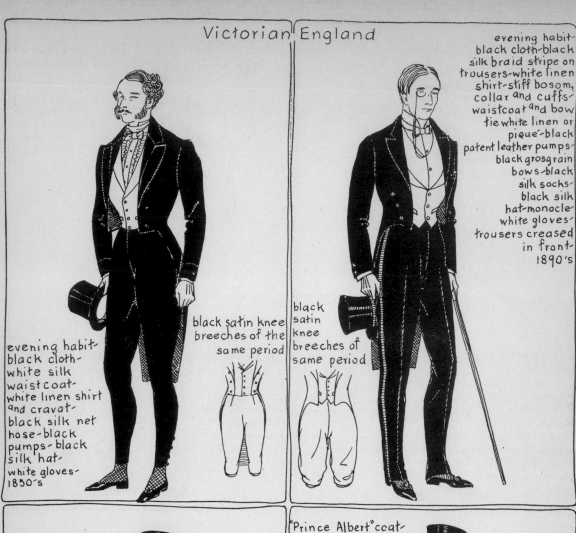

evening habit-
black cloth-
silk braid stripe on
trousers-white linen
shirt-stiff bosom,
collar and cuffs-
waistcoat and bow
tie white linen or
pique-black
patent leather pumps-
black grosgrain
bows-black
silk socks-
black silk
hat-monocle-
white gloves-
trousers creased
in front-
1890's

black satin knee
breeches of the
same period

black
satin
knee
breeches of
same period

evening habit-
black cloth-
white silk
waistcoat-
white linen shirt
and cravat-
black silk net
hose-black
pumps-black
silk hat-
white gloves-
1850's

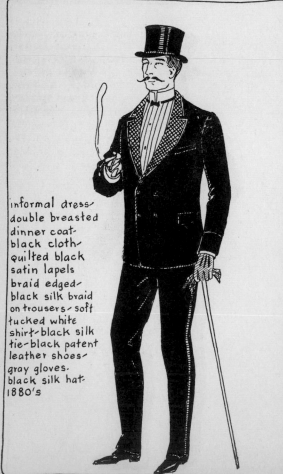

informal dress-
double breasted
dinner coat-
black cloth-
quilted black
satin lapels
braid edged-
black silk braid
on trousers-soft
tucked white
shirt-black silk
tie-black patent
leather shoes-
gray gloves-
black silk hat-
1880's

"Prince Albert" coat-
black cloth-black
satin facing on
lapels-waistcoat
pearl gray covert-
pearl buttons-
trousers darker
gray cloth-
blue silk
scarf-heavy
gold watch
chain-black
shoes-gray
spats-gray
gloves-black
silk hat-
1890's

FTW

Victorian England

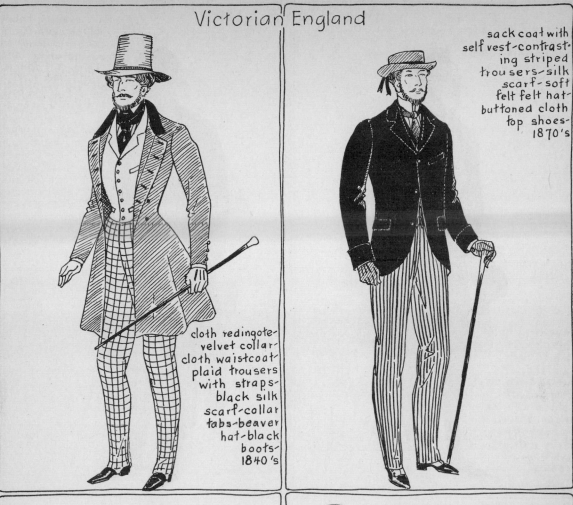

cloth redingote-
velvet collar-
cloth waistcoat-
plaid trousers
with straps-
black silk
scarf-collar
tabs-beaver
hat-black
boots-
1840's

sack coat with
self vest-contrast-
ing striped
trousers-silk
scarf-soft
felt felt hat-
buttoned cloth
top shoes-
1870's

"seaside"
costume-
flannel coat-
flannel trousers-
woolen sweater-
straw boater-
with striped
band-shoes
of sailcloth
and leather-
1880's

Norfolk jacket
and knickerbockers-
heavy woolen
cloth brown
plaid on tan
ground-yellow
and brown
knitted socks with
cuffs-white
linen spats-
brown shoes-
1890's

RTW

Victorian England

MacFarlan coat-
plaid trousers
over black
boots-silk
cravat-
standing
soft collar-
black silk
hat-
1850's

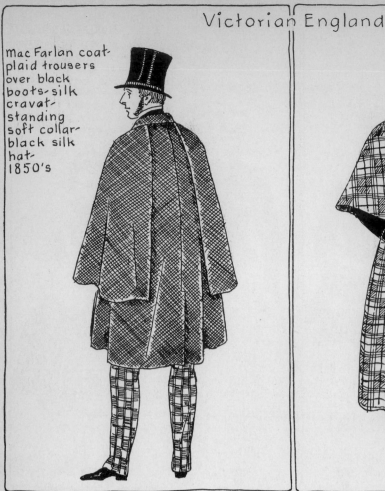

Inverness coat-
sleeveless-plaid
woolen-belt
with leather
covered buckle-
checked woolen
cap-cloth top
shoes-
1880's

dress overcoat-
heavy tan
broadcloth-black
velvet collar-
machine stitching-
horn buttons-
wing collar-
four-in-hand
scarf-black
shoes-tan
spats-black
silk hat-
1890's

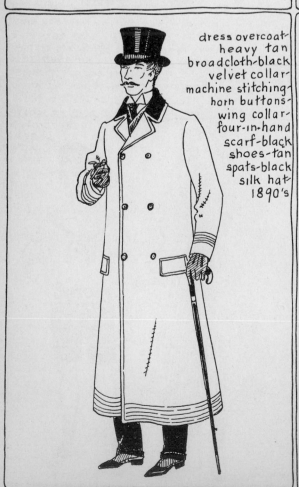

Chesterfield overcoat-
black cloth with
velvet collar-
fly front-Ascot
scarf striped
red on black-
gray and black
striped trousers-
gray spats-
black shoes-
black silk
hat-
1890's

RTW

Victorian England

girl's cambric dress and pantalettes-self frills-ribbon-cambric bonnet-white stockings-black slippers-mittens····
boy's tunic pleated to yoke-neck frill-bow tie-leather belt with buckle-nankeen trousers-white stockings-black slippers-straw hat-ribbon and tassel-1830's

plain jacket-checked trousers-white waistcoat-bow tie-felt hat ribbon band and edge-black shoes-short stick····
velveteen coat and dress-shirred ribbon band-lingerie undersleeves-ermine tippet and muff-embroidered muslin pantalettes-white stockings-laced cloth shoes-leather tips-shirred silk bonnet-1850's

cloth suit with braid edges-striped stockings-black shoes-felt hat with feathers····
wine red silk with beige velvet trimming-vestee of shirred ivory lace-red stockings-black slippers-gold buckles-1880's

"seaside dress"-striped light and dark blue surah-white jersey with dark blue embroidery-white straw hat-white ribbon blue ostrich tips-dark blue stockings-black and white "seaside shoes"···
sky blue tam and knee pants-white cambric blouse-colored scarf-white socks-brown shoes-1890's

RTW

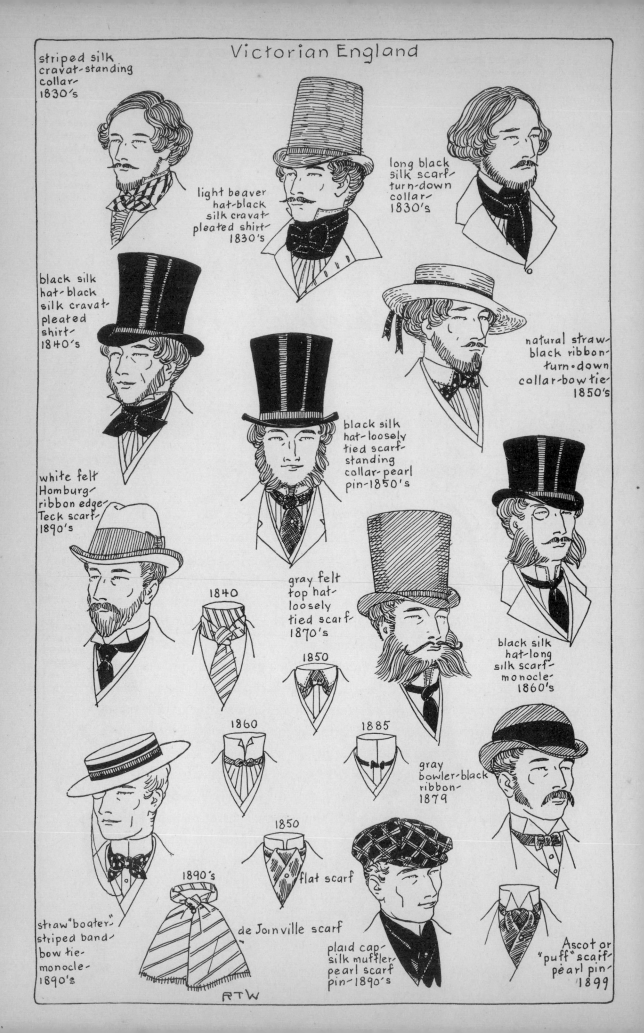

Victorian England

striped silk cravat-standing collar-1830's

light beaver hat-black silk cravat-pleated shirt-1830's

long black silk scarf-turn-down collar-1830's

black silk hat-black silk cravat-pleated shirt-1840's

natural straw-black ribbon-turn-down collar-bow tie-1850's

black silk hat-loosely tied scarf-standing collar-pearl pin-1850's

white felt Homburg-ribbon edge-Teck scarf-1890's

gray felt top hat-loosely tied scarf-1870's

black silk hat-long silk scarf-monocle-1860's

1840

1850

1860

1885

gray bowler-black ribbon-1879

1850

flat scarf

1890's

de Joinville scarf

straw "boater"-striped band-bow tie-monocle-1890's

plaid cap-silk muffler-pearl scarf pin-1890's

Ascot or "puff" scarf-pearl pin-1899

RTW

Chapter Forty

French

1870–1880

IN THIS DECADE, the feminine interest was centered in the back of the costume. The pannier, or overskirt, of the late 'sixties was now bunched up in back, necessitating the tournure, or bustle. The style is known in England as "tied-back time." The skirt proper was long, usually ending in a train, even for street wear. The short-waisted bodice was lined with silk or muslin and shaped with inserted whalebones, fastening in front. Toward the end of the decade, the tunic, or peplum, descended over the hips, the bunched-up drapery in back dropped down, leaving the upper part of the costume quite sleek and in basque style. Sleeves for day wear were long, generally flaring at the lower edge. Evening-gown sleeves were tiny caps and the décolletage was square.

The design was most elaborate, several fabrics and trimmings employed in one garment. For winter, materials used were cashmere, satin, taffeta, moiré, velvet, faille, and, in the summer, surah, mohair, foulard, and lace, jet, tulle for evening with much bead and jet ornamentation. Pale blue was a favorite color, but bright colors were predominant, among them verdigris, royal blue, purple and garnet. Very much of the period were checks and stripes. Ribbons, braids, tassels and knotted fringe continued fashionable. A new style note was the pleated flounce, Black lace motifs were applied to velvet, silk and net. It still was a period of ribbon.

Coats, mantles and dolman wraps were of heavy silk trimmed with jet and passementeries edged with lace or fringe. For winter, there were sealskin coats in three-quarter or full length. Sealskin was dyed brown, not black as in the twentieth century, changing to a golden brown near the skin. The secret of the process disappeared with the death of the London furrier who discovered it. Silk plush was also smart, either sealskin or plush, edged with a band of beaver, and finished with collar and cuffs of the fur. Sable, mink, martin and chinchilla too, were fashionable.

In this period lingerie took on importance with drawers, petticoats and the chemise of fine cottons, ornamented with filmy lace and delicate embroidery. Wrappers and dressing gowns for wear at home were of transparent muslin and sheer nainsook, lace-trimmed.

High-heeled shoes were of fine kid or fabric, laced or buttoned and, toward the 'eighties, a narrow pointed toe came into fashion. Women also wore a congress boot, a shoe with elastic inserts at the sides, which proved unsatisfactory, the elasticity quickly disappearing. Rich fabrics were still used for evening slippers. Stockings, which were never seen, matched the evening gown and, for day wear, the silk petticoat. Purple and red, in petticoats and stockings, were great favorites.

In the first half of the decade, the hair, like the costume, was drawn up toward the back away from the face, exposing the ears, with the ends cascading down the back in cadogan fashion, in ringlets or looped braids. The thickness of the braids was exaggerated by being dressed loosely and over a cushion. A fringe or bangs often softened the brow, and long earrings were worn. By the end of the decade, the hair was dressed up the back in simpler fashion.

Bonnets were still elaborate but very small and worn high on the head, ribbons occasionally tied under the chin. Toward the end of the period, the hat replaced the bonnet, but ribbons, flowers and ostrich plumes continued as ornamentation. The short tightly tied face veil appeared.

Much attention was given to parasols, or sunshades, and to fans, which were of lace and chiffon, embroidered and spangled. Gloves were of kid in light colors, short and long, the latter buttoning to the elbow.

There was a marked trend toward a more active life, with young women taking to sports or "games," such as fencing, boating, tennis and bicycling.

French 1870-1880

gray cashmere
over pleated royal
blue silk skirt-
narrow royal blue
velvet ribbon-
blue buttons-
white ruching
at neck and
sleeves-
1871

plum purple velvet
jacket and skirt-
lilac velvet drapery-
mink fur bands-
buttons-self ruche
on skirt-lilac
silk bonnet-béret
crown-purple ribbon-
white roses-green
foliage-black shoes-
beige gloves-
1873

heavy tan faille silk
gown and bowknots-
pointed train-white
taffeta drapery with
pearl embroidery-
white ostrich tips and
aigrettes in hair-
white slippers-
1875

front and
back

black satin-accordion
pleated ruffles-jet
beaded cording-velvet
loops-wisteria blossoms-
white chiffon vestee and
sleeve caps edged with
rhinestones-velvet
neckband-jet
jewelry-
1879

RTW

French 1870-1880

natural straw-
black velvet
band and
ruching-
1871

natural straw-
mixed flowers-
old blue
ribbon-
1876

gray felt-French
blue velvet
ribbon-gray
ostrich-back
bandeau-
1872

bottle green
velvet-shaded
gray and brown
plume-pink
roses-green
foliage-green
bow-1875

brown velvet-
brown satin
loops-beige
plumes-
1875

pleated
pink
ribbon-
yellow velvet
bow-pink and
yellow flowers-
green foliage-
1876

buttoned fabric
top-patent leather
heel and toe

laced shoe-
kid or fabric

satin shoe-
elastic sides-
rosette

laced shoe-
kid with rosette

corset and
whalebone
petticoat

purple satin hat
and ribbon-shaded
purple and pink plume-
1878

whalebone and
silk

whalebone and wire

satin slipper

whalebone and tape

whalebone and shirred silk

RTW

Chapter Forty=one

French

1880–1890

[handwritten annotations: bustle + train disappeared / Cloth jackets were close fitting / bodice more close fitting than ever / point in front was adopted by bow / with high neck / like with / patter]

HE TOURNURE, or bustle, really a slim crinoline of the early 'seventies, grew less important in the latter part of that decade, to become again a definite feature of the mode of the 'eighties and to disappear by the 'nineties.

The costume was still complicated in design and composed of several fabrics and trimmings. Although short dresses appeared for dancing, street and country wear, the long train gown held its own. The straight foundation skirt continued to be superimposed by a shorter overskirt or draperies caught up in back. The pleated flounce of the underskirt developed into a real pleated skirt in this period.

The fitted, boned basque bodice, always made separate from the skirt and worn over the tightly laced stays or corsets, still reigned. The basque gradually shortened but the bodice retained its long waist, by the middle of the decade, dipping into a point in front. The silhouette was shaping into the "hour-glass figure" of the 'nineties. Forms of fine braided wire were used to enhance the curves of undersized breasts. Stockinet, or jersey, a cloth manufactured in the Isle of Jersey, was the fabric usually employed for the basque bodice.

The bodice often had an inserted front, a full shirred or pleated vestee of soft silk, chiffon or lace. The folds of this bloused front often fell five or six inches below the waistline or, again, hung peplum-like below a short "jacket bodice" and were called a "jabot."

The high neck prevailed in day gowns and, by the middle of the decade, high standing stiff collars and starched linen collars and cuffs became the fashion. The décolletage of the evening gown was moderately low, and sleeves were usually of elbow or cap length. The slim day sleeve was generally long or "bracelet length."

History making in the mode was the tailored suit of cloth, comprising coat, skirt and bodice brought out by Doucet of Paris. That event occurred near the end of this period and has survived over half a century. Doucet, originally founded as a house of lingerie in 1824, became a *maison de couture* late in the 'seventies. This couturier also originated the coat with "fur sides outside," conceiving the idea of using fur as a fabric.

Winter materials were heavy in velvet, satin, poplin, damask, serge and brocade. Summer fabrics consisted of light silks, foulard, muslin, tulle and such laces as Chantilly, Mechlin, English, Valenciennes and blonde. Appliquéd motifs of black, écru or cream-colored lace and passementerie were employed with velvet, ribbon and jet.

Lingerie and petticoats were of silk in delicate colors lavishly ornamented with embroidery and lace. In winter, an underpetticoat of woolen or flannel was always worn and edged with colored crochet woolen lace. The top petticoat was usually reinforced with stiff muslin below the waist in back, to accent the silhouette of the tournure or bustle.

Wraps were indeed varied in shape with long loose coats, long and short mantles, dolman wraps, long circular capes lined throughout with squirrel. Sleeves were flaring, cape-like or cut in one with the body, pointing the way to the all-out revival of the cape in the next decade. Tightly fitted jackets or long coats were known as paletots. Winter wraps, usually full length, were of velvet, sealskin, plush and cut velvet and often

trimmed with bands of beaver. For summer, there were mantelets of cashmere, faille silk or heavy lace edged with lace frills and trimmed with
passementerie. Very small round muffs of fur or fabric were carried and
the feather boa reappeared.

Bonnets tied under the chin and called "carriage bonnets" resembled
the fontange headdress of the latter part of the seventeenth century, even
to the curled fringe of hair over the forehead. The ribbons were attached
farther back on the bonnet, coming down behind the ears. Hats were being
worn more and more, a favorite shape being the recurring postillion hat,
now named the Rembrandt hat. It was ornamented with ostrich plumes
and the brim was usually turned up at one side. To all the usual millinery
trimmings in vogue, a new one was now added, that of stuffed birds.

The hair was drawn back off the ears, sometimes low in a chignon,
cascading curls or dressed high in a bun. The front hair was often cut
short and curled into a mass on the forehead. Flowers, velvet bows, small
ostrich tips and aigrettes adorned the evening coiffure.

Long white kid gloves were *de rigueur* for evening, with delicate
colors worn in the daytime. Sunshades were of chiffon and silk finished
with lace and ruffles, a large ribbon bow tied on the handle. The use of
jewels, especially diamonds, was extravagant. Onyx and black cut jet were
very fashionable, dull jet being reserved for the mourning costume.

Mourning was strictly observed in dress, the entire costume of gown,
coat and hat trimmed with heavy, dull black crêpe.

The fashionable woman's footwear consisted of heavy English shoes
for morning, button or laced shoes of kid or a combination of kid and
cloth for afternoon, while "opera slippers," of plain satin or kid to match
the gown, were worn for evening. Stockings were mostly cotton thread
instead of silk, hidden by trailing skirts. The vogue of the colored stocking continued, bright red stockings being noted in contemporary fashion
plates of young women.

Large embroidered silk and feather fans were carried. Two styles of
folding scented fans, of violet wood, are described as a Parisian novelty in
a fashion journal of October, 1886. One was entirely of wood spotted with

silver dots, the other, a wooden frame covered with Swedish leather and embroidered with birds, flowers and other motifs.

Small fabric bags with metal and jewelled mounts were in fashion and the knitted-silk beaded bag returned to favor.

The vogue for aprons was revived in the "tea apron" of sheer white lingerie fabric trimmed with lace, colored embroidery and colored satin and velvet ribbon.

That famous English dressmaker Redfern founded his Paris house in 1881, maintaining also a branch in London, and later, one in New York.

parsoles became larger

folding fans, low neck time with short sleeves, full bloomers + bathing suits with large sleeves

French 1880-1890

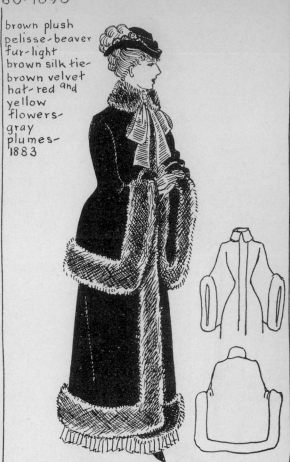

brown plush
pelisse-beaver
fur-light
brown silk tie-
brown velvet
hat-red and
yellow
flowers-
gray
plumes-
1883

pink satin
and cream
lace-white
ostrich and
aigrettes in
hair-painted
silk fan-
1882

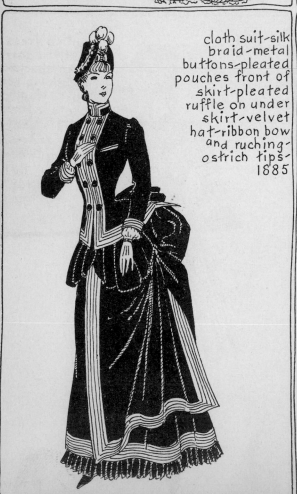

cloth suit-silk
braid-metal
buttons-pleated
pouches front of
skirt-pleated
ruffle on under
skirt-velvet
hat-ribbon bow
and ruching-
ostrich tips-
1885

Venetian red
cloth gown-
dark gray fur-
self color silk
embroidery-
velvet toque-
Venetian
red-gray
birds-
1889

RTW

French 1880-1890

traveling paletot coat checked brown and tan cloth- brown velvet collar-metal buttons-brown cloth hat- brown feathers- 1886

riding habit- light gray cloth- jacket edged silk braid-dark gray silk embroidered horseshoe and monogram-gray silk stock- brooch-gray felt hat- gray veil-white gloves-black patent leather boots- 1885

yachting costume- white flannel "princess polonaise"- woolen braid- blue embroidered motifs-pleated white homespun skirt- blue and white striped jersey jacket- cap white cloth and leather- white linen shoes- 1886

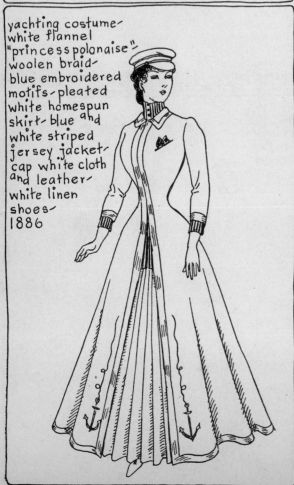

hunting dress- light and dark brown checked cloth-velvet collar, cuffs and pockets-leather waistcoat- leather gaiters- brown tweed hat- 1887

RTW

French 1880-1890

lace fichu-pleated crêpe-yellow and black velvet ribbon

black silk bonnet-jet leaves-white lace-yellow ribbon-black lace veil-jabot lace and lawn-pearls

black lace bonnet-black satin ribbon-pink roses-green foliage

brown velvet bonnet-pearls-brown ribbon-three birds

evening gloves painted in color

jet and gold comb

parasol-striped red and blue silk-red ribbon

straw sailor-grosgrain band

velvet bows

Rembrandt hat-felt-ribbon and ostrich

fan-ebony frame-shaded red feathers

evening petticoat-pale blue surah-scalloped flounces-lace flounce-pleated under frill

bag of velvet and nickel

silk "jacket bodice"-edged chenille-jet bead embroidery-white gauze "jabot" and sleeve frills

braided wire bustles

kid evening slipper

satin house slipper

lawn apron-lace-velvet ribbon and belt-cord and pompoms

RTW

Chapter Forty two

French

1890–1900

huge balloon sleeves— large at top and from elbow down is fitted

1894

ITH 1890, the bustle disappeared, along with tied-up skirt drapery, though occasional folds and shirred peplums were still seen on the hips. The general design in costume became less complicated, albeit that two or three fabrics were combined in one garment. As a rule, skirts fitted snugly over the hips, flaring to the floor in bell shape and ending in a train, which was worn all hours of the day, even when walking. In the streets, skirts were held up to one side, the proper handling of which became an art and a gesture, very characteristic of the period.

The skirt was cut in many gores and not only lined from waist to hem with silk, cambric or sateen but also interlined with stiffening, the whole hanging from a narrow belt. In fact, in this period, even washable fabrics were silk-lined, stiff taffeta being the most desirable because of its rustling sound or "frou-frou." Added to which were the beruffled taffeta petticoats of all colors, snug-fitting to the knee and flaring below. The sleek "hourglass" silhouette caused the elimination of petticoats down to but one, and that well fitted over the hips.

petticoats tied at back

The leg-of-mutton sleeve, stiffened with tarlatan, buckram and lining, reappeared and grew to enormous proportions. The puff reached to the elbow with the forearm section tightly fitted, followed in 1899 by the long slim tight sleeve. Evening gowns were sleeveless or had short puffs. The breadth of the shoulders was further enhanced by short capes, deep lace ruffles from neck to shoulder and wide circular bretelles. The deep-pointed bodice was reinforced with whalebone and lining.

The soft, full overhanging blouse, either separate or part of the gown and always finished with a belt, is definitely of the 'nineties. It was fashioned of any soft, sheer fabric and ornamented with embroidery, beads, braid, lace and insertion.

The collar of the day dress was high, sometimes edged with ruching, sometimes finished with a large tulle or lace bow placed either front or back. Small neck ruffs of tulle or ribbon loops were often worn with the low round décolletage.

The tailored suit, with jacket, skirt and "shirtwaist," took firm hold and has survived half a century. The appearance of coat, skirt, waistcoat and lingerie shirt for sportswear in the feminine world dates back to the middle seventeenth century of Louis XIV and Charles II, when women took over the masculine design for their riding habit. The short jacket, with skirt of walking length, first appeared in the 1850's. In its strictly English, mannish design and fabric, the suit dates from the 'eighties, but its whole-hearted acceptance took place in the 'nineties. The blouse of lingerie fabric had been making intermittent appearances since the 1830's, but now followed the masculine model in having shirt length instead of being fitted and sewn to a belt.

The princess silhouette of glove-like fit, gored from neck to hem, appeared in the 'nineties in tailleur, tea gown and ball gown, and, in 1899, the striking black-spangled evening gown, followed later by colored spangles. Of the period was the fitted bolero jacket worn over the princess gown or the full blouse.

The influence of the Maison Callot increased the vogue for costly lace, a novelty being bands of black lace insertion. Necks, wrists and fronts of blouses were finished with lace frills and voluminous jabots were in fashion. There were evening gowns made entirely of lace over taffeta. The chemise and drawers of fine linen, batiste, pale silks and satinet were lavishly lace-trimmed and beribboned. The lace-edged, beflounced petticoat in silk, linen or nainsook created a pretty effect, typical of the period, held to one side when walking.

Flounces were concentrated upon and accordion pleating was much favored, sometimes the whole gown being thus pleated. Materials were tucked, quilted, smocked, and laces were threaded with silk or velvet ribbon. Embroidery in silk or wool extended to tailored dresses and suits. Added ornamentation consisted of embroideries in silk and gold tinsel, pearl and crystal beads and gold lace insertion. The textiles of the decade were foulard, moiré, figured satin, damask, poplin, serge, muslin and tulle. Cloth was trimmed with rows of machine stitching.

As to wraps, for which fawn and gray were the favorite colors, there were Eton jackets and finger-tip length capes. Capes were two or three tiered, severely tailored or elaborately trimmed. Winter wraps were of velvet or cloth bordered with fur, while summer mantles were of silk and finished with embroidery, lace and pleated ruffles. Characteristic of the period is the full-length redingote of mastic-colored cloth with wide lapels and flaring collar.

The specialization of costume for the specific occasion began to take shape in the 'nineties, sports clothes following the English style. Yachting, "lawn tennis," bicycling and golf became popular, necessitating more practical clothes. The smart woman wore the "shirtwaist" and separate skirt with golf cape or Norfolk jacket for golf, and when bicycling, a short skirt or full bloomers with a fitted jacket. The tailored separate skirt of walking length was called the "rainy day skirt."

Such sports clothes were made of homespuns, coarse masculine tweeds and double-faced Oxford cloths. Colors were somber in dark blue, brown, Oxford gray and plaids. The tailored shirtwaist which accompanied such a suit was mannish with stiffly starched collar and cuffs, the collar either standing or turned-down. A small felt fedora, cloth tam-o'-

shanter or sailor completed the costume. By this time, the long riding skirt had been replaced by a shorter one, below which showed the mannish English leather boots.

The corset of firm heavy satin, in black or color, while lower than that of preceding years and only just covering the hips, was straight in front and decidedly fitted in at the waist, producing the "wasp-waist" effect. The entire garment was heavily boned with steel and whalebone. An eighteen-inch waist was the desired and admired size of that day. "Kangaroo walk" was the name given by humorists to the movement resulting from the figure encased in the straight front corset. The chemise was worn next to the body, the corset over and the drawers over the corset.

Small hats in toque form and hats with brims of moderate size were perched high on the head, invariably worn with the lace veil tied in back. Ornamentation comprised paradise plumes, aigrettes, ostrich plumes, wings, ribbon, jet, artificial violets and roses.

The former sleek effect in hairdressing was discarded in favor of a fluffy effect in which tiny curls softened the neckline and framed the face. The hair was simply dressed, drawn up into a knot on the top of the head and done in the new Marcel wave invented by the Parisian coiffeur. Small black and white ostrich tips with short aigrettes were added for evening wear.

A touch of rouge and a dash of rice powder sufficed in cosmetics, although, before the end of the period, cold cream was being used and "costly" perfumes were introduced.

The fashionable furs were chinchilla, Russian sable, seal and Persian lamb, of which scarfs, capes, jackets and small round muffs were made. Bands of fur trimmed the velvet or cloth costume, while revers and flaring collars were faced with it.

The fashionable shoe wardrobe contained walking boots and plain Oxford shoes, which were heavy in the English manner, and high button boots of kid to be worn under the trailing gown. Dressy slippers were of black or brown kid, black patent leather, also bronze slippers with stockings to match. Stockings were black in cotton thread or silk. That style note of the gay 'nineties, the open-worked black silk stocking, made its appearance.

Accessories were fans, suéde gloves, parasols and umbrellas. Small gold watches worn on long fine chains were tucked into the belt or concealed at the waist. Purses were small and of fabric or leather, the favorite style being the "pocketbook," a flat folding book-shaped purse with compartments.

The bathing suit was of serge, alpaca or flannel in dark blue or black and usually trimmed with white braid. The fitted bodice, high neck and elbow-length leg-of-mutton sleeves were of the prevailing mode. Bloomers were worn under the knee-length skirt with black stockings and low canvas shoes.

Fresh violets were very popular, worn in the evening and on coats, suits, dresses and muffs. The vogue of violets lasted through the first decade of the twentieth century. Here, in America, an admirer presented his lady-love with dozens of the showy, long-stemmed rose of bluish red called the American Beauty rose. Orchids in those days were sent only to actresses and were considered flowers of the *nouveaux riches*.

French 1890-1900

evening gown-
slate gray velvet
and brocade-
silver lace collar
and belt-cream
satin folds on
bodice-cream
suéde gloves-
lace fan-
gray slippers-
1890

princess evening gown-
white satin-dark blue
velvet ribbon-sleeves
black lace net over
white satin-black
lace ruffles and
bib-white embroidery
on skirt-ruche
velvet ribbon
points-white
slippers-blue
wings in hair-
painted silk
fan-amber
sticks-white
suéde gloves-
1895

princess gown-
French gray cloth-
black Persian
lamb-shirred
bodice front-
gray toque-fur
band-black
velvet ribbon-
black aigrettes-
white gloves-
black shoes-
1892

peacock green
cloth gown-
black soutache
braid embroidery-
violet satin under
bodice and belt-
black felt
hat-draped
black satin-
black ostrich
plumes-slim
black silk
umbrella-
1899

RTW

French 1890-1900

gown with separate double cape-old blue velvet and black velvet-mink bands and muff-black felt hat-black and blue ostrich plumes-1893

princess gown with jacket-old rose cloth-white soutache embroidery on white-gored skirt-batiste and lace jabot-lace frills-black felt hat-black ostrich-rose silk rosettes-white satin loops-white face veil-mink and lace muff with lace bowknot-1895

changeable brown checked taffeta-ivory lace bolero-brown velvet ribbon-pearl buckles-accordion pleated white blouse-white neck bow and frills-turban of red roses-green foliage-white lace-black silk umbrella-1897

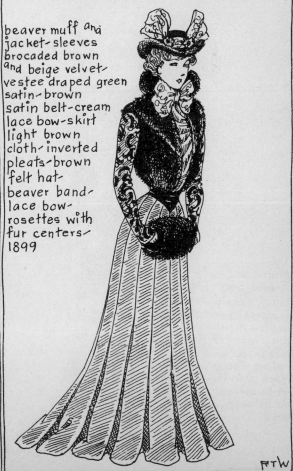

beaver muff and jacket-sleeves brocaded brown and beige velvet-vestee draped green satin-brown satin belt-cream lace bow-skirt light brown cloth-inverted pleats-brown felt hat-beaver band-lace bow-rosettes with fur centers-1899

RTW

French 1890-1900

redingote-mastic
colored
broadcloth-
bone buttons-
muff and toque
black Persian
lamb-black
wings-blue
brocaded
ribbon-
white
gloves-
black shoes-
1894

summer cape-
black taffeta-
accordion pleated
frills-white lawn
collar and jabot
with lace-
taffeta rosettes-
straw hat-
pleated
taffeta
fans-
light cloth
dress-
white kid
gloves-black
shoes- black
silk umbrella-
1895

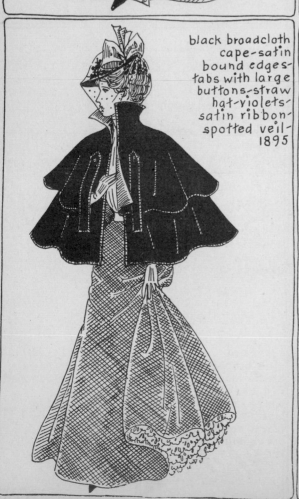

black broadcloth
cape-satin
bound edges-
tabs with large
buttons-straw
hat-violets-
satin ribbon-
spotted veil-
1895

evening cape-
black velvet lined
and trimmed with
mink-black
embroidery on gold
cloth-black silk
tassels-white
satin gown-
lace and roses-
white ostrich
fan and
headdress-
aigrettes-
1897

RTW

French 1890-1900

yachting costume-
heavy white linen-
self bands-shirtwaist
navy foulard white
polka dots-navy
blue belt-cravat
pale blue silk
striped navy-
stiff white
collar-navy
and white
cap-white
linen
oxfords-
1895

bicycling costume-
brown tweed-white
lingerie shirtwaist-
leather belt-
gray green felt
hat-black ribbon-
green gaiters-
black oxfords
. . . .

black
bloomers-
white
shirtwaist-
stiff collar-
black
stockings-
tan slippers-
1896

tennis costume-
striped chambray
and white linen-
pearl buttons-
tam-o'-shanter
of red flannel-
white linen
oxfords-
black
stockings
1895

corset of
pink brocaded
coutil-lace
frill-chemise
white nainsook-
lace and ribbon-
black stockings-
black slippers-
1892

RTW

Chapter Forty-three

Masculine Costume

1900–1942

B Y THE twentieth century, masculine costume had become thoroughly standardized, with a distinct code of rules as to the wearing of it. The cut of the garment, length of coat, breadth and shape of the shoulders, shape of the lapel, width of trousers and number of buttons vary, but the changes are barely perceptible from season to season. Directly after the First World War, there became evident some slight influence of Italian tailors presenting a military expression, and occasionally also a Hollywood note is brought to our attention, but it can be definitely stated that thus far in the twentieth century, as in the nineteenth century, London is the style source for men's fashions in clothing.

In the first decade appeared the concave shoulder, very broad with considerable padding in the shoulder head, creating a dip in the shoulder line. This extreme style was responsible around 1910 for the introduction of a natural shoulder without padding, which is still worn by conservative men. A straight-sided, straight-back short jacket originated in the 'twenties in a college town, a revolt against the nipped-in waist and spiderlike silhouette of the ready-made.

An attempt was made in the middle 'twenties to accentuate the chest and straight-line shoulder, by means of a high waistline which necessitated high-rise trousers. The high waistline was further accentuated by the use of a double-breasted vest with horizontal bottom. (See Page 343). The idea originated in London but was of short duration. In the 'thirties, London designers set up a straight military shoulder and found it advisable to break the line on the chest with folds. This is the drape idea. Through the use of dynamic principles of design, in the last ten years, it has been possible for the tailor to make a short man appear taller and a corpulent man slimmer.

The slim trousers of the late nineteenth century took on fullness in the first decade of the new century; in fact, a very exaggerated form appeared in the "peg-top" trousers. This style did not last. The slim silhouette persisted until the early years of the 1920's, when "Oxford bags" came into vogue. They were sometimes as much as twenty-four inches in width at the bottoms. The very wide trousers lasted through the 'twenties, then were cut narrower with a taper toward the foot. Pleats at the waist appeared in the early 'thirties.

The sports costume in the first half of the period consisted of the Norfolk jacket, knickerbockers and heavy woolen hose with deep turned-down cuff. The cap with wide visor and ample crown accompanied the outfit. In the latter part of the 'twenties, knickers became voluminous in width and length and were known as "plus fours." That term originated in the British Army, when breeches were measured as reaching to the knees, plus four inches. White linen knickers were much in evidence in the summer. The sports coat with pleated back and half belt stitched on or in, appeared in the middle of the 'twenties.

A revival was the dress sack or formal lounge, sometimes braid bound, which came in, in the 'twenties. It is worn with formal striped gray and black trousers and has either a peaked or notched lapel.

Early in the 'thirties, the white mess jacket, copied after that worn by the British officer on tropical duty, appeared. It was worn during the summer with black tie and the cummerbund of East Indian origin, which often took the place of the waistcoat. Then came the white dinner coat either single or double breasted, also worn with black tie. Black mohair breeches trimmed with braid accompany the white dress coat. The white shirt with soft turned-down or fall collar and soft bosom of piqué or linen is usually worn with the summer dinner coat, either black or white. The introduction of summer evening clothes was due to the popularity enjoyed by many semitropical summer resorts in the Bahamas, along the Mediterranean and the coast of Florida.

After the First World War, the summer suit for day wear in the States came to the fore and is worn not only to business in the South but in the North as well. Materials consist of heavy linen, seersucker, tussah, shantung, tropical worsteds and a fabric of cotton and mohair which is popular. Smart suitings of good texture woven with synthetic yarns as the base are also employed. Wool gabardine was developed for wear in the summer months in tans, grays and blues. The fabric derives from the famous East Indian gabardine with a red back known as suncloth.

The English walking coat was a style which met with acceptance by the middle class in that country. It enabled one to dress differently from the clerk and yet was not formal attire. (See Page 338.)

Black or midnight blue continues *en règle* for evening clothes, but the classic dark-blue business suit of the early part of the period has been supplanted by the wearer's own choice of fabric and color. Woolen textiles for suits consist of tweeds, shetlands, serges, flannels, gabardines and worsteds, in beautiful grayed color mixtures. After years and years of black, gray, brown and dark blue, we now have suits of French blue, blue-green, pinkish beiges, while in sports clothes much liberty in color is permitted. In patterns, there are diagonals, pin stripes and checks, herringbones, glen or "glenurquhart" plaids, the pin dot or sharkskin pattern.

The hand-stitched or "hand-pricked edge," instead of machine-stitching of collar and lapel of the informal suit, was a new feature which appeared in the 'thirties.

The crudely woven but artistic Harris tweed of heather colors, originally made in the Isle of Harris in the Hebrides, enjoyed a great demand in the early half of the period. Great advances have been made in the last twenty years in the styling of fabrics. German manufacturers, in the 'twenties, made an unsuccessful attempt to gain a portion of the American woolen cloth trade and undersold the British weavers to such an extent that, for a time, there was an influx of cloth fair in quality but poor in design.

The great advance in the weaving and dyeing of synthetic fibers or yarns has largely supplanted the use of silk as lining in men's clothing.

Definitely of the twentieth century is the polo coat of natural-color camel's hair. It appeared in the first decade, is still good and was evolved from the cricket "wait coat" thrown over the shoulders between periods of play.

The successful attempts of cloth processors to produce a water-repellent cloth are attested by first, the raincoat and then the trenchcoat of the First World War. These coats, both in England and the United States, are well designed, smartly tailored and some of the British makes are world renowned.

The following overcoats of the preceding century, with style variation, are still with us, namely, the raglan, the Ulster, the Inverness and the Chesterfield. The paletot, or paddock, of the early years of the century was a fitted overcoat with waist seam and skirt pleats in back, headed with the two buttons. It was the evolution of the original English riding coat, or redingote. The Chesterfield seems to have established itself as the classic dress overcoat. In the list of overcoatings are vicunas, thibets, friezes, chinchillas, undressed worsteds, Meltons and Montagnacs.

The huge racoon coat for winter wear was the result of riding in the open car and was considered proper equipment for attending football games. In the late 'twenties its popularity was challenged by another coat of deep-pile camel's hair.

The dress shirt continues to be made of fine white cotton or linen with stiff or pleated bosom of linen or piqué, while the informal white shirt is usually of cotton broadcloth, poplin or a basket weave. Other fabrics are figured silks, plain, plaid, striped cottons and flannels in all colors. An innovation in the 'thirties was the dark-colored shirt in navy, wine red or brown, with light-toned coat and trousers.

The backless evening waistcoat of white piqué, cooler for night club wear and dancing, has been popular for several years.

A detached soft collar, wrinkle-proof and requiring no starch, was introduced by some shirtmakers in the 'twenties. Later on, the soft collar was still further improved by the use of a rayon fabric in the lining, collar and shirt being now attached. Of the 'twenties and the 'thirties is the pin collar, in which the turned-down collar points are held by a long gold pin passing under the scarf knot.

The polo shirt, with long collar points which lay over coat or sweater, is popular and much in evidence in the summer. To conceal the bare neck, a brilliantly colored bandeau scarf is loosely tied around the neck, filling in the V.

The predominant note in neckwear for the period is the four-in-hand, with the occasional appearance of the bow tie. All fabrics, weaves, patterns and colors hold with club and regimental stripes, the favored of the whole period.

In the early years of the twentieth century and contemporary with the "shirtwaist girl," men, in the summer, discarded their vest and carried their coat over the arm. This fad created the vogue of the leather belt, which has been worn since. Buckles are of leather, gold, silver or other metal. Gallowses or suspenders continue to be worn with evening clothes and are still preferred by many in place of the belt.

The derby and the black or blue fedora or Homburg vie with each other for day town wear and with the dinner jacket. The collapsible opera hat of black grosgrain silk accompanies full dress and the silk top hat is worn with the cutaway or formal day clothes. The gray top hat is still seen in England at the races.

The hard straw hat, sailor or boater is still with us for wear in town, although a lighter style of the Homburg type in coarsely woven straw, jute, hemp or other exotic material is usurping its place. The newer hat is bound with a wide, pleated, brightly colored silk puggree, originally tied about the East Indian helmet. Panama hats in the hands of stylists have taken on a more acceptable shape.

The open-air activities of men in the late 'twenties brought into existence for use on the golf course, at the races and for country wear generally, a light-weight, paper-thin felt hat which could be rolled up and packed into a suitcase. The cap, though still used for sports in England, gave way to the soft felt in the United States.

The derby and hard straw hat of the first decade retained the black silk cord of English origin to about 1915. It was wound round the ribbon band, one end formerly used in anchoring the hat to the buttonhole in the coat lapel. English hats often had eyelets in pairs at the side of the crown for ventilation.

A noteworthy style of dressing the hair occurred in the first decade, when men wore their hair straight, parted in the middle, the side pieces reaching to the ears in length.

The turtle-neck sweater of solid color, which first appeared in the 'eighties with the fad for bicycling, football, lawn tennis and yachting, lasted through the first decade of the twentieth century. Then the gay, colorful sweater of Fair Isle, England, completely changed the trend in this garment. The V-neck appeared, also the coat sweater in varied color designs. In the wake of the V-neck came the soft shirt and the colorful scarf.

Negligee or house robes became general, and here masculine taste was permitted to indulge not only in plain silks, flannels or velveteens, but in the most colorful of figured silks. Beach robes are of bright-colored cottons and flannels in bold patterns, stripes or solid color. The blazer, a separate unlined sports jacket, originally of navy blue flannel bound with white braid, also took on very gay stripes.

From the 'nineties, men's underwear experienced a radical change. Until then, the long union suit of lisle or cotton was worn for summer, changing to one of wool for winter. The great vogue for sports brought in an entirely new fashion. Founded upon the athlete's running pants and skeleton shirt, undergarments changed to sleeveless lisle shirts and shorts of fine cottons, first white and later to highly colored stripes, plaids and prints. Union suits of lisle or silk, form-fitting, often knee length, continue to be worn, principally by horsemen.

Hose or socks are of silk, lisle and wool, of varied colors and clocked. Plain brown, blue and black in ribbed weave are the most popular.

Pajamas are made of many different fabrics, either cotton or silk, plain colored or striped. The tunic either buttons jacket-like or slips on over the head. There is also a knee-length coat with long lapel, buttoned and belted and worn without trousers.

In the early years of 1900, high shoes, either laced or buttoned, were worn in the fall and winter and low shoes, also either laced or buttoned, in the summer. They were to be had in tan, brown, gun-metal calf or patent leather. By 1930, high shoes had disappeared from the wardrobe of the well-dressed man. Blucher, signifying the style of lacing, originally designated the half boot named after the Prussian General Blücher.

The fringed leather piece which drops over the lacing of the sports Oxford was originally intended as protection to the laces when tramping over the Scottish moors.

Sports shoes were fashioned of white buckskin or a combination of white buckskin and black or brown leather saddles, but, with the late 'twenties, came various styles in pigskin, followed by sandals of interlaced strips of colored leather. A popular sports style is the moccasin type of low shoe, slipperlike, made with a firm leather sole. The very thick crêpe rubber has become a staple. The black-waxed calf Oxford is worn with formal day clothes and the black patent-leather Oxford with tails or the dinner coat.

Spats have been worn throughout the period with the low shoe or Oxford, always of gray or beige and usually of broadcloth, though occasionally of linen for summer.

Colored handkerchiefs, striped or plaid or in deep rich colors, and of fine cottons and linens, are used only with informal clothes. The fine white linen or batiste handkerchief with exquisite hand-turned or hemstitched edge and monogram continues in demand.

The walking stick, much used in England and on the Continent is but occasionally seen in the States. Gold or silver headed sticks of rare and exotic woods gradually gave way to those of heavy Malacca with a crooked handle. Gloves are of white buck or kid for dress and chamois, mocha or pigskin for informal wear. The wrist watch, a small watch attached to an adjustable bracelet of leather, silver or gold became more popular after its use in the First World War. It was worn as early as 1910 by the British officer. The heavy gold watch in use for centuries has been replaced by one, wafer-thin, of gold or platinum with a very fine chain. Another gadget of the twentieth century is the tie clip of gold holding the scarf to the shirt when the vest is dispensed with.

The fashion in boutonnières is a dark red carnation, either fresh or artificial, worn on the lapel of the dinner coat and a white carnation with "tails."

Englishmen continue to demand custom-made clothes, or, as they term it, "bespoke tailoring." English ready-to-wear clothing has never achieved the excellence of design and tailoring that has, since the middle of the 1890's characterized the product of the best American manufacturers. The only ready-to-wear used extensively by the well-dressed Britisher is confined almost exclusively to certain overcoats and raincoats or utility sports topcoats of outstanding design.

In the first quarter of the present century, American designers of the ready-made endeavored to evolve a real American style, but, with the exception of a few so-called university styles, the manufacturers are willing to follow the custom tailors, deriving their ideas and design from London.

In the first decade of the twentieth century, the small boy, who had been wearing straight knee-length breeches, changed to knickerbockers with the accompanying Norfolk jacket. His overcoat followed the style of his elders. Again, copying his seniors, he changed to slacks in the 'thirties. The vogue for sports clothes has fitted in beautifully with the youngster's way of life.

In this year of 1942, the designers of England and the States have brought out clothes which will conserve materials for the armed forces.

The fabric is composed of synthetic yarn, using sixty-five per cent or less of wool. The suit is shorn of cuffs, pleats, buttons on sleeves, and patch pockets. The jacket is shorter, trousers are narrower and the vest is eliminated from the double-breasted. The British model is called "the Utility Suit," while we have named ours "the Victory Suit."

Formal evening wear: Tail coat, black or midnight blue, unfinished worsted; trousers same, braided side seams, uncuffed bottoms; waistcoat, white washable piqué, single-breasted; white shirt, stiff bosom plain or piqué; bow tie, to match bosom; wing collar; pearl studs; white buck or kid gloves; shoes, patent leather Oxfords or pumps; hose, black or dark blue silk with or without clocks, also lisle; silk top hat or opera hat; overcoat, black or dark-blue Chesterfield, single or double-breasted.

Informal evening: Dinner jacket, black or midnight blue, unfinished worsted; trousers same, braided side seams, uncuffed bottoms; waistcoat, white washable piqué or black silk, single or double-breasted, or black cummerbund; white shirt, stiff bosom, piqué or wide box pleat; wing or fold collar; silk bow tie, black or midnight blue; gloves, white mocha, buck or chamois; shoes, patent leather, low shoes or pumps; studs, pearl, mother-of-pearl, enamel or colored stones or plain gold; hose, blue or black silk, plain or clocked; overcoat, single or double-breasted Chesterfield, belted guard coat or box coat in black, Oxford or midnight blue.

Formal day: Cutaway, black or Oxford cheviot or unfinished worsted; waistcoat, same or light-toned washable fabric, as linen, single or double-breasted; trousers, black and gray, striped worsted, uncuffed bottoms; silk top hat; white shirt, stiff bosom, plain or pleated linen or piqué; wing or fold collar; cravat, Ascot or four-in-hand, gray or conservative stripings; gloves, white or gray buck, mocha, fawn calf or white chamois; pearl or jewel scarf-pin; hose, plain or ribbed, silk or lisle, black or dark blue; shoes, black or gun-metal calf Oxfords; overcoat, blue, black or Oxford Chesterfield.

single breasted
sack suit-
gray striped
worsted-
modified
peg-top trousers-
black leather
shoes- brown
capeskin
gloves-gray
fedora hat-
wing collar-
polka dot
bow tie-
1905

single breasted
sack suit-
herringbone
shetland-striped
silk four-in-hand
scarf-white
collar attached
shirt- snap
brim felt fedora-
tan Oxford
shoes-
1941

double breasted
sack suit-
plaid over
diagonal-high
turned-down
collar-very
narrow four-in-
hand scarf-
black shoes-
1906

double
breasted
sack suit-
blue sharkskin-
fabric-white
collar and
shirt-striped
four-in-hand
scarf-black
Oxfords-
1941

RTW

formal day dress-
Prince Albert frockcoat-
satin faced lapels-
silk buttons-pearl
gray silk Ascot
scarf-high white
collar-trousers
striped gray and
black-black
patent leather
shoes-white
spats-black
silk top hat-
black
stick-
1906

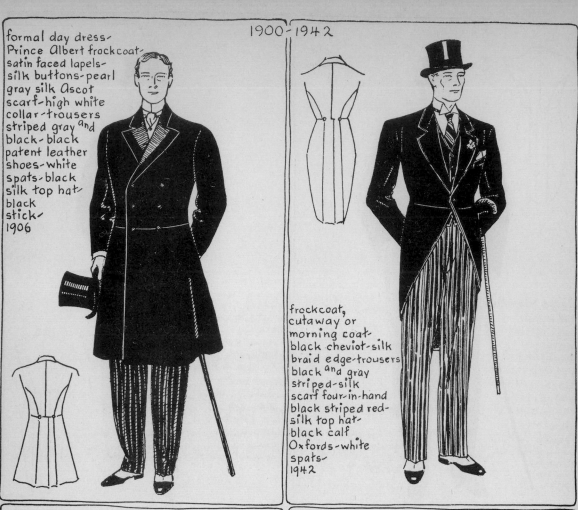

frockcoat,
cutaway or
morning coat-
black cheviot-silk
braid edge-trousers
black and gray
striped-silk
scarf four-in-hand
black striped red-
silk top hat-
black calf
Oxfords-white
spats-
1942

English walking
suit-tan worsted-
white piqué
waistcoat-white
figured brown
four-in-hand scarf-
mocha
gloves-brown
derby-black
calf shoes-
tan spats-
1906

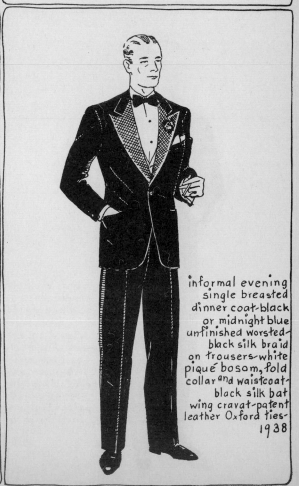

informal evening
single breasted
dinner coat-black
or midnight blue
unfinished worsted-
black silk braid
on trousers-white
piqué bosom, fold
collar and waistcoat-
black silk bat
wing cravat-patent
leather Oxford ties-
1938

RTW

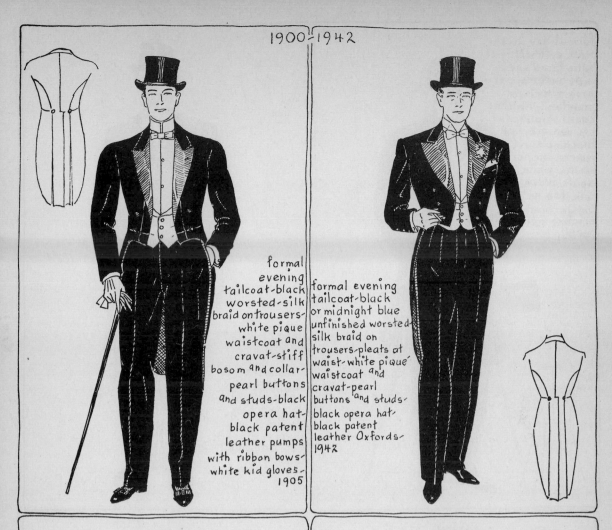

formal evening tailcoat-black worsted-silk braid on trousers-white pique waistcoat and cravat-stiff bosom and collar-pearl buttons and studs-black opera hat-black patent leather pumps with ribbon bows-white kid gloves-1905

formal evening tailcoat-black or midnight blue unfinished worsted-silk braid on trousers-pleats at waist-white pique waistcoat and cravat-pearl buttons and studs-black opera hat-black patent leather Oxfords-1942

informal evening single breasted dinner coat-black worsted-satin shawl collar-black silk braid on trousers-stiff bosom-gold studs-black silk cravat-black patent leather pumps-ribbon bows-1910

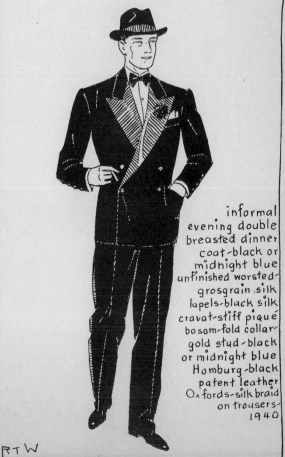

informal evening double breasted dinner coat-black or midnight blue unfinished worsted-grosgrain silk lapels-black silk cravat-stiff pique bosom-fold collar-gold stud-black or midnight blue Homburg-black patent leather Oxfords-silk braid on trousers-1940

RTW

golf suit with
"plus fours" vest
self material-
gray toned
shetland-knitted
plaid woolen golf
hose-fringed
brogues heavy
tan leather-
striped silk
four-in-hand
scarf-hat
beige feather
weight felt-
1927

casual clothes
golf and
country wear-
shirt wine red
cotton basket
weave-varied
colored silk
muffler-beige
flannel slacks-
pleats at waist-
tan leather
mocassins-
1941

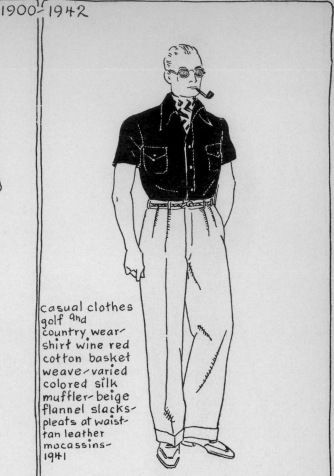

country clothes-
Norfolk jacket-
blue serge
jacket and vest-
gray whipcord
breeches-white
washable stock-
heavy knitted
golf hose-
heavy tan
blucher shoes-
checked
woolen cap-
1901

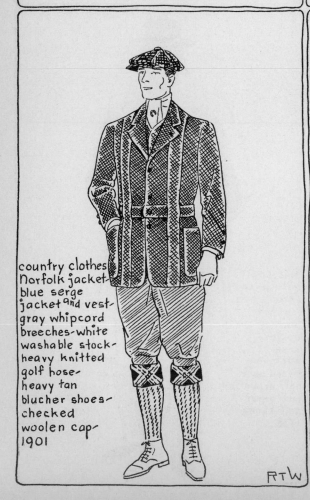

golf suit-
sports coat
checked worsted-
slacks light
colored flannel-
hat light brown
coarse woven
straw-draped
striped silk
puggree band-
shoes turned
calf-dark silk
handkerchief
in pocket-
1940

RTW

sack suit-
natural shoulder-
soft roll lapel-
checked flannel-
plain silk
four-in-hand
scarf-stickpin-
brown calf
shoes-
1912

raglan
overcoat-
tan whipcord-
tweed suit-
collar pinned
under scarf
knot-soft
felt hat-tan
grained calf
Oxfords-
1939

overcoat-
dark blue
chinchilla-
gray suit-
gray spats-
black calf Oxfords-
black derby-
chamois gloves-
1924

polo coat
natural color
camel's hair-
long belt-
leather
buckle-
horn
buttons-
tweed suit-
soft brown felt
hat-brown
calf shoes-
1936

RTW

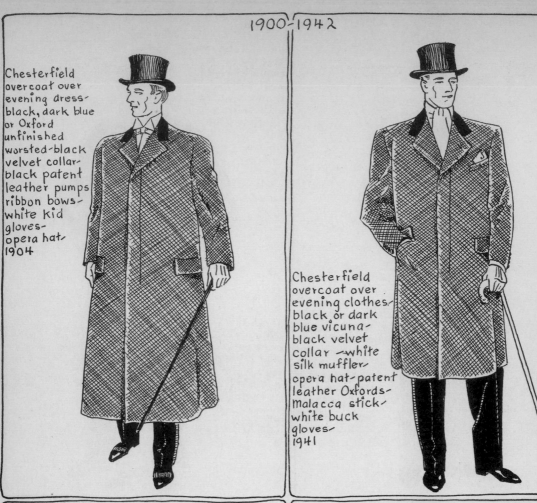

Chesterfield
overcoat over
evening dress-
black, dark blue
or Oxford
unfinished
worsted-black
velvet collar-
black patent
leather pumps
ribbon bows-
white kid
gloves-
opera hat-
1904

Chesterfield
overcoat over
evening clothes-
black or dark
blue vicuna-
black velvet
collar -white
silk muffler-
opera hat-patent
leather Oxfords-
Malacca stick-
white buck
gloves-
1941

dress overcoat-
double breasted
black, dark blue
or Oxford
Montagnac-
black velvet
collar-black
derby-black
patent leather
button shoes-
calf tops-
1905

dress overcoat-
on British Guard
lines-double
breasted-dark
blue melton-
dark blue suit-
black derby-
white silk
muffler-black
calf Oxfords-
1942

RTW

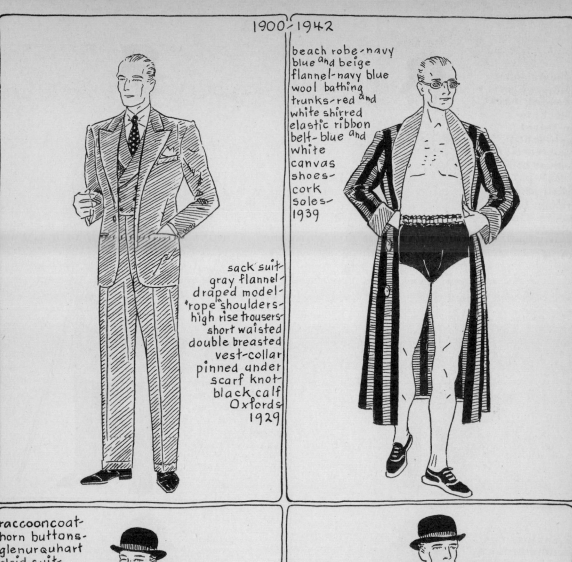

beach robe-navy
blue and beige
flannel-navy blue
wool bathing
trunks-red and
white shirred
elastic ribbon
belt- blue and
white
canvas
shoes-
cork
soles-
1939

sack suit-
gray flannel-
draped model-
"rope" shoulders-
high rise trousers-
short waisted
double breasted
vest-collar
pinned under
scarf knot-
black calf
Oxfords
1929

raccooncoat-
horn buttons-
glenurquhart
plaid suit-
striped scarf-
black derby-
tan calf
Oxfords-
1928

fur-lined
overcoat-
black broad-
cloth shell-
nutria lined-
otter collar-
gray suit-
black derby-
black calf
Oxfords-
1918

RTW

trench coat-
waterproofed cotton
gabardine-putty
color-convertible
collar-leather
buttons and
buckle-long
belt-gray
flannel suit-
brown felt
hat- tan
Oxfords-
1924

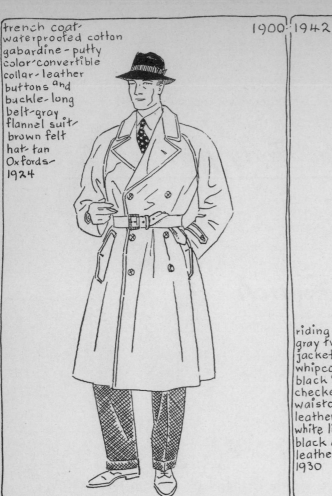

riding habit-
gray tweed
jacket-gray
whipcord breeches
black and white
checked flannel
waistcoat-
leather buttons-
white linen stock-
black derby-tan
leather field boots-
1930

summer suit-
oyster white linen-
vegetable ivory
buttons-navy blue
basket weave cotton
shirt-collar
attached-scarf
white silk
blue dots-
navy blue
handkerchief-
sport
shoes
white
buckskin
black calf
trimmings-
1938

summer
single breasted
dinner coat-
white synthetic
fabric-soft
white pique
shirt- collar
attached-black
silk tie-black
grosgrain
cummerbund-
black mohair
trousers with
silk braid stripe-
1936

Chapter Forty-four

French

1900–1910

IN THIS DECADE, a great change took place in the shape of the corset. In the early years, it retained its very small waist but grew longer in the hips and had a straight front. In 1907, the curve of the hips was reduced, a less tight lacing widening the waist. Curves almost entirely disappeared in the following year, the corset became straight and long over the hips and lower under the bosom. With the added length of hip, attached garters appeared, replacing the round garter worn above or below the knee.

In the first part of the decade, skirts fitted in molded form over the hips, flared out in bell fashion to lie on the ground with a train at the back. To the flounces of evening and summer gowns of lighter materials were added pleatings and ruffles of chiffon and lace. Petticoats were much beflounced and ruffles of silk, called "dust ruffles," were added to the under side of cloth skirts.

Trains persisted on the skirts of tailored suits until the middle of the period, when the skirt, straight of silhouette appeared, a decidedly new note. It cleared the ground, had a raised waistline and was made with groups of side pleats or wide inverted box pleats. Linings were dispensed with in the new straight skirt.

Short fitted jackets and boleros were worn with the flaring skirt, but with the straight skirt, jackets became longer, semifitted and usually had the mannish collar and lapels. The tailored suit became the accepted street costume, of navy serge or black broadcloth. For resort wear in the summer, tailored white suits of mannish fabrics were made, after the English style with Norfolk jacket. Shirtwaists were severely tailored and blouses were soft, sheer and filmy. Stiff starched collars with a small bow tie or the four-in-hand were worn with the shirtwaist. In general, collars of day dresses and blouses were boned and often reached up to just behind the ear.

The sleeve of the tailleur was fairly straight, but that of the gown widened into fullness over the forearms, by 1903 falling over a tight cuff. It was known as the pouch or bishop sleeve. Another style was the full drooping elbow-length sleeve finished with a deep ruffle of lace or self material. The dropped shoulder line of 1905, in which the collar, yoke and shoulders were in one flowing line, was very pleasing. The next move, in 1910, was the kimono sleeve or kimono-sleeve construction, of Japanese origin.

In the second half of this decade, the waistline rose higher, the silhouette straightened and narrowed, culminating, by 1910, in the style inspired by that of the First Empire. Evening gowns became tubelike and trainless. When trains were worn, as for full dress, they were only narrow slithering tails. The tube-shaped skirt of the suit, but a yard in width, necessitated a slit at the side to the knee. Another style had a wide band placed just below the knees, suggesting the much-used expression "hobble skirt."

Separate coats were in dressmaker style, semifitted, either seven-eighths or full length, with straight sleeves and made of black satin, broadcloth or navy serge in winter or of black taffeta or natural pongee for summer wear. The dolman sleeve was revived for coats near the end of the period. There were long coats of rich furs, such as chinchilla, ermine, mink and sable. A newcomer in fur coats was ponyskin, in rich black. Stoles, boas, long neckpieces and very large muffs were in vogue. Evening wraps in dolman style were of heavy brocades and velvets ornamented with fur bands, lace and passementerie.

The fabrics of the period were velvet, satin, foulard, poplin, mousse-line-de-soie, surah, damask, crêpe de Chine trimmed with silk or bead embroidery and appliquéd lace motifs. In cloths, there were serge, cashmere and mohair, but broadcloth was the most popular. Rows and rows of shirring were used and lace insertion and beading threaded with ribbon continued in fashion. Among the many laces, a particular pattern was that of Irish crochet, of which jackets and coats were made, even entire dresses.

The coiffure of the period was the pompadour, drawn up high over a pad or roll of false hair (a rat, it was called). The chignon at the neck was worn also. There were ornamental combs of amber or tortoise shell decorated with gold filigree work and jewels. These combs were worn in pairs and a third was the back comb, all three holding the hair in place.

Hats, fairly large, were perched on the top of the head, a bandeau underneath to set them up still higher. The large black velvet hat trimmed with ostrich plumes was a revival of the "Gainsborough." A black straw sailor, with very wide straight brim, was known as the "Merry Widow," after the popular operetta by Franz Lehar, the Viennese composer. From 1907, both crown and brim grew in size, the hat settling down on the head and attaining huge proportions by 1909. The brims that had flared off the face, now drooped over the face. Heron and bird-of-paradise plumes, and willow plumes which were ostrich feathers with added tied flues, were the favorite ornamentation. Such dressy hats were worn with street clothes at any hour of the day, accompanied by the flattering face veil of lace or spotted net tied in back.

High button or laced shoes of kid were worn in the winter and Oxford shoes or slippers in the summer. Pumps of patent leather or calf, with flat bows of grosgrain ribbon, resembling the man's evening pump, appeared in the middle of the decade. Day shoes were either black or brown, matched by lisle or silk stockings, with the black silk stocking becoming general. A popular combination was the black stocking worn with a tan Oxford. Dressy slippers were of bronze kid, and evening slippers were of satin or brocade, with stockings to match the gown. Silk stockings, with cut-out lace inserts over the instep, were very smart.

Long suède or kid gloves, in white, black or brown, were always worn with short sleeves and gloves of silk in the same colors in the summer. Parasols, too, were carried in the summer, fashioned of silk, lace or chiffon, edged with ruffles or trimmed with velvet ribbon.

In this period, white batiste and the finest linen, embroidered, beribboned and lace-trimmed, gradually usurped the place of fine muslin and nainsook for lingerie. "Umbrella drawers," with a full skirted leg did away with "open drawers." Undergarments consisted of a chemise, over which the corset was worn. Then, a "corset cover," to which were added rows of narrow ruffles, if the bosom were too flat. The pantaloons were trimmed with lace and ribbon and the petticoat was of nainsook, fine linen or changeable taffeta, embroidered, frilled or lace-edged.

Small leather bags and "pocketbooks" were in use until the Empire mode brought in the large handbag of "saddle-bag style," the sabretache, of a century back, that same bag that accompanied the Directoire costume. It was of tapestry or brocade, with long gilt or silk cord rope which hung from the arm or shoulder.

The "dog collar," composed of several rows of small pearls held together by bars of diamonds or brilliants, was a definite style feature in this period of high collars. Earrings with screw fastenings appeared.

The automobile was responsible for the long coat, or "duster," of natural pongee or linen and the chiffon veil two to three yards long, worn over the large hat and tied under the chin. Then followed many styles of "automobile bonnets," designed especially for riding in the open cars. Unpaved, dusty roads made these enveloping garments and goggles or colored spectacles for the eyes very necessary.

Riding breeches were becoming popular for horseback, the habit retaining its draped side-saddle skirt for dress.

The bathing suit was still dresslike in design, but dispensed with its high collar and long sleeves and the skirt reached only to the knees. Bloomers and black stockings continued part of the ensemble. Silk suits, of colors other than black or navy blue, were making their appearance.

The indulgence in cigarette smoking among women was on the increase.

French 1900-1910

tailored suit-blue
serge and black
satin-bolero
jacket-tailored
shirtwaist-black
silk bow tie-
natural straw
sailor-black
ribbon band-
1902

tailored suit-tan
broadcloth-black
velvet collar and
cuffs-lace blouse-
tan felt hat
faced with
black velvet-
bright green
bird-
1905

bolero and skirt-
dark red cloth-
inverted box pleats-
high waist line-
black braid on
jacket-tailored
shirtwaist-
green straw
hat-flowers-
black
aigrettes-
1906

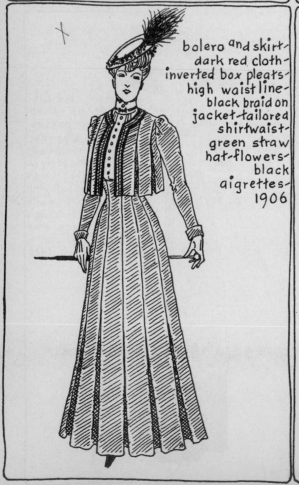

midnight blue
charmeuse-
dolman wrap-
knife pleated
skirt-satin
cording-lace
collar and jabot-
long suéde gloves-
black velvet
hat-willow
plumes shaded
rose and blue-
leather
hand bag-
1908

RTW

French-1900-1910

rose silk with
Irish crochet lace-
black velvet bows
and belt-bertha-
bishop sleeves-
fitted hip yoke
edged self cording-
inverted box
pleats-lace hat-
black velvet
band and bow-
1903

emerald green
satin-cream
lace-yoke of
tucks and lace
insertion-lace
bow with long
ends-rose colored
velvet hat-green
ostrich plumes-long
white kid gloves-
hair in marcel
wave-
1904

princess gown-
white batiste-
Valenciennes lace-
embroidery-fine
tucks-black
straw hat-black
aigrettes-white
parasol-chiffon
and lace-white
kid slippers-
1909

French blue silk-
and black velvet-
kimono sleeves-
cream lace yoke
and collar-silk
embroidery on
skirt-black
straw hat-pink
roses-blue silk
parasol-chamois
gloves-blue
slippers-
1910

RTW

French 1900-1910

evening gown-
yellow satin-
deep lace bertha-
black velvet
ribbon-fitted
shirring over
hips-crushed
self belt-pearl
"dog collar"
1904

evening gown-
coral velvet-
turquoise blue
chiffon fichu-
bead embroidery-
black velvet belt
and bow-jewelled
buckle-fox fur-
self colored
embroidery-pink
rose and black
velvet ribbon
in hair-
1908

evening wrap-
mauve velvet-
black velvet
collar-gold
passementerie,
cord and tassels-
paradise in hair-
black velvet
gown-
1909

black silk coat-
black silk braid
on collar and lapels-
lace blouse with
jabot-cloth skirt-
pleated chiffon
hat-pink rose-
black silk
umbrella-
1902

RTW

French 1900-1910

satin corset-insertion threaded with ribbon-1901

brocaded satin corset-lace top-shirred ribbon garters-1905

satin corset-lace top-bowknot-1910

black calf or patent leather pump-grosgrain bow

patent leather-white kid top- black buttons

satin opera slipper-rhinestone buckle

chemise-white nainsook or crêpe de chine-tucks-lace-colored ribbon

soft brown kid or patent leather

umbrella drawers-nainsook-lace-beading-ribbon

corset cover-nainsook-beading and ribbon

black or brown kid Oxford

combination corset cover and petticoat-nainsook-lace-tucks-ribbon threaded through insertion

colored changeable taffeta petticoat

petticoat-white nainsook or crêpe de chine-tucks-lace-colored ribbon

RTW

Chapter Forty=five

French

1910–1920

TWO IMPORTANT EVENTS took place in this period; first, the return to the natural figure; and second, as a result of the First World War, the adoption of the simple tailored, unadorned frock for day or informal wear. Another influence of the war was the all-black costume relieved only by jewelry.

This decade found the straight silhouette with raised waistline definitely established in the mode, with Paul Poiret the first couturier daring enough to place the belt just under the breasts in true Empire style. He was also responsible for the open-neck kimono waist, which did away with high collar and set-in sleeves for many years to come. Another striking departure was his use of brilliant color in emerald green, cerise, vermilion, royal blue and purple. Startling at first was his combination of cerise and purple.

The long tunic hanging over a narrow underskirt appeared in 1911. Sometimes a wide band or sash finished the edge of the tunic or was tied around the underskirt at a place below the knees. This narrow skirt of suits, dresses and evening gowns was called the tube, or hobble skirt.

354

It was one and a quarter yards in width, though often but a yard around. As walking thus became almost impossible, a slit at the side or front remedied the situation.

The tunic shortened and became fuller, turning into panniers or draped fullness at the hips in 1912. Next, the fullness dropped halfway down the skirt length, sloping in to the ankles. This was the peg-top silhouette.

An attempt was made to introduce a divided or trouser skirt into the mode under the name of "harem skirt." Though worn by mannequins in public, it did not meet with success.

In 1912, Poiret designed the Persian costumes for "Le Minaret," creating a belted tunic, knee-length, with wired flaring edge over a slim silhouette. The minaret tunic shared honors with the peg-top silhouette until the First World War.

Then appeared the short full skirt, "eight inches" from the ground. The skirts of evening gowns were given added flare by two or three flounces with whalebone edge. This fashion, for which Lanvin became famous, is known as the *infanta style,* or the *robe de style,* and the skirt length, changing from period to period, is still good in evening dresses.

1914 saw the birth of the chemise frock of medieval origin, but it was not taken up until 1916, and did not become general until the following year. At first, it was a straight slip, over which was worn a straight tunic or overblouse with long tight sleeves. Then the tunic lengthened, took on a belt placed low at the hips and the underslip disappeared.

In 1917, came the "tonneau silhouette," which met with little success. The skirt widened at a place halfway between waist and hem in barrel shape.

In 1918 and 1919, the skirt of the chemise gown shortened to just below the knee. Its shortest length was still to come in 1925, when it frankly reached the knee. The day frock was a scant affair, with fairly low round neck and sleeveless. The evening model, as short and sleeveless, had no back and often, a long narrow trailing panel which acted as train.

Vionnet, in 1919, created a sensation with her tubular frock of crêpe de Chine which slipped on over the head. She made unlined gowns of fabrics cut on the bias. Noteworthy, too, was her handkerchief tunic, with its corners hanging to the hem of the underskirt.

Navy blue and black were the colors for day dresses in such fabrics as foulard, satin, charmeuse and serge. Materials became soft in finish like duvetyn, suède cloth, chiffon broadcloth, soft twill gabardine, and there were crêpes of every description, crêpe de Chine, georgette crêpe, crêpe marocain and Canton crêpe.

Chanel, in 1918, introduced jersey cloth to the mode which jumped to the fore for the chemise frock and the dressmaker suit. The evening version of the chemise frock was of silk crêpe or georgette embroidered with beads, crêpe lamé, metal brocade or gold or silver cloth. Gold and silver fringe edged the tunics. Picot-edged and grosgrain ribbon became great favorites. Ostrich fringe was a novelty for gown and hat.

As far back as 1915, Chanel displayed models at Deauville made of artificial silk. Artificial or glazed satin was used for sports skirts.

Soft woolens in novelty weaves were used for sports clothes. The tailleur of dressmaker style usurped the position of the strictly tailored suit. Late in the period, the white piqué waistcoat worn with the blue or black suit was a smart accessory.

Dress coats had dolman sleeves and wrap-around fronts with but one fastening. Evening cloaks were a combination of cape and coat design, with large, standing, fold-over collars. The raglan was favored for the separate sports coat, made of such cloths as chinchilla and camel's hair. Along with the same sports coat for men, appeared the raccoon coat, which enjoyed a great popularity.

Fur coats and capes followed the lines of cloth dress coats and were trimmed with contrasting furs. Muffs were very large, soft and flat. Bands of fur not only ornamented suits but even chiffon gowns. The scarf of large skins and the long stole were worn also in the summer over light dresses. The most lowly skins were now dressed into pliable pelts, such as muskrat, skunk, rabbit and lamb. Other furs were chinchilla, ermine, sable and mink principally for evening, and caracul, Persian lamb, broadtail, ponyskin and kolinsky.

The Spanish shawl returned to the mode, with the revival of fringe, tassels and the dolman type of wrap.

The sweater acquired new styling in lovely colors, not only of wool but of spun silk and artificial silk worked with metal threads. The cardigan with knitted sash was smart. Another sports jacket was of black velveteen worn with colored or white wool or silk skirt.

Brims of hats were large, flaring, drooping or turned-up and, as the crown settled down to the eyes, it too grew very large. The automobile, especially the open car, had much to do with the change of style in millinery. It necessitated the crown fitting the head, and long chiffon veils, tied over hat and under chin, held the headgear secure. Then hats became small, hugging the head. A revival of the sailor occurred in the second half of the decade; another revival was the tricorne. A forerunner of the cloche of the next decade was the pillbox shape.

Trimmings were confined to feathers or wired wings of silk or velvet. Hats were weighted down under great quantities of plumes. So devastating to bird life was this fad for fine plumage that, through the efforts of the Audubon Society of America, protective measures were passed, bringing about the passing of the craze.

Face veils of lace or net, spotted with chenille dots or velvet disks, were worn, also large veils of silk lace or net draped over the hat. The "harem veil," leaving the eyes exposed and fastened to the brim in back, was a summer fashion. (See Page 364.)

The hair was dressed off the face and over the ears, wrapped or swirled close to the head, paving the way for the universal bob of the next decade. Occasional bobbed heads were seen toward the end of this period, but the style did not become the mode until the 'twenties. The "beauty shop" now made it possible for all women, regardless of wealth, to enjoy the services of a hairdresser. All women could have curly locks by means of electrical machines which produced a "permanent wave." Auburn, the favorite color of hair of the twentieth century, was responsible for the fad of dyeing locks a reddish hue with henna. Cosmetics of natural tone and artfully applied were less frowned upon than formerly. Lipstick was added to rouge and powder.

The new mode required very little corseting, that garment becoming a soft girdle of tricot or knitted elastic, waistline-high and just covering the hips. The breasts were held firm and flat by a soft bandeau, camisole or brassière. An entirely new carriage or posture was adopted. The hips and abdomen were thrown forward, helping to produce the much-desired flattening silhouette of the bosom. The pose of arms akimbo or hands on the hips, which had always been avoided by the "lady," was now à la mode. This new figure was called the "boyish form" and the "debutante slouch."

Simple lingerie, with just a touch of lace or embroidery of white batiste or fine handkerchief linen, was worn until 1918, when crêpe de Chine and silk jersey came in for undergarments. Silk met with huge success and delicate shades of pink, blue and mauve became popular. The petticoat disappeared entirely and sheer silk slips were worn under only such evening frocks as required them. Often, just a bandeau and a pair of silk knickers sufficed under the chemise frock. Many women took to wearing silk pajamas instead of the nightgown.

Footgear for day wear consisted of shoes with high-laced or buttoned tops of gabardine, kid or suède, the buttoned Oxford, the plain pump, the slipper with cut steel or rhinestone buckle, all with the slim French heel and long, pointed toe. With the short chemise frock came a great change in footwear. The long, pointed shoe, conservative in style and color, was supplanted by the so-called French last, with short vamp and round toe, the slender curving Louis XV heel or the lower, "baby Louis" heel. Shoes were cut in intricate strap-fastening designs, ornamented with buckles, even to jewelled heels. Day shoes were beige, sand, taupe, gray or black, while evening shoes matched the gown in color, made of satin, gold or silver brocade. Sports Oxfords were of white buck, with black or brown leather trimming for summer and of brown leather for winter.

The black or tan silk stocking of the earlier part of the decade gave way to gray, taupe, Cordovan and sand tones matching shoes of like colors. Gray stockings were general. Beige stockings matched beige spats worn with black pumps. Nude or blond hosiery was first worn in Paris in the second half of the decade. It was introduced by a small French shop where stockings were dyed to order. Black was rare by the end of the period. White was the color for summer sports wear. The instep of the evening stocking was often decorated with embroidery or a lace insert.

There were bags of very fine beads in exquisite design and color,

from Louis-Philippe
Sec. R.p.
1880 –1890
1890 – 1900
1900 –1910
1910 – 1920

bags of gold and silver mesh, also those of tapestry, while the leather handbags became the accessory for street and sports. From this time, the fittings of the bag were given as much thought as the bag itself. Still with us are the several inside pockets containing small change purse, small mirror and comb, and these articles are to be found in the lowliest bag. Jewelled cigarette holders and cases were among the contents of the bag, the habit of smoking having become general in the feminine world.

Bead necklaces of all kinds and all lengths came into fashion. The short pearl necklace, with the accompanying button pearl earrings, became especially popular. Large ornamental hairpins, usually worn in pairs, were of amber or tortoise shell, often studded with brilliants. The simple untrimmed frock was the beginning of the craze for costume jewelry which exists today. Pieces effective in design and color were used with certain gowns, the intrinsic value being unimportant.

War work proved the great convenience of the wrist watch, which became very popular. While the practical model was worn on a leather-strap bracelet, the dressier timepiece was attached to a matching jewelled bracelet or a black grosgrain ribbon. The watch became unbelievably small, and an exquisite ornament in gold or platinum set with tiny jewels.

The bathing suit followed the dress design with high or low neck and shoulder cap sleeves. Skirt and knickers grew shorter, about five or six inches above the knee. American women wore long stockings with sandals. French women did not wear stockings either with the one-piece knitted maillot or swimming suit or with the conventional suit with short skirt. Various new fabrics were employed in its making, such as silk jersey and awning-striped materials.

The "pencil umbrella," a long, slim affair of black silk, was carried in this period. Raincoats of waterproofed gabardine were usually tan in color.

With the "robe de style" came a vogue for the small old-fashioned bouquet of fresh flowers set in a frill of lace. The craze for violets had passed but roses were as popular as ever. Orchids or gardenias worn singly or in a corsage of two or three were very "swank."

tailored suit-
tan cloth-
self covered
buttons-lingerie
blouse with
jabot-brown
straw hat-brown
willow plumes-
white stockings-
black strap
slippers-green
silk parasol-
1911

peacock green
velveteen suit-
black fox
bands-black
plush hat-
beige cloth
brim-amber
ball pin-
black leather
shoes-beige
cloth uppers-
1916

X

sports ensemble-
burnt yellow
cloth-stitching-
blouse yellow and
green silk plaid-
green neck
embroidery-green
suède belt-
green felt hat-
black facing-
black ribbon
band-gold
buckle-black
leather shoes-
sand suède
uppers-
1917

tailored suit-
blue cloth-
white piqué
waistcoat-black
velvet hat-
black lace veil-
black suède
purse-sheer
black silk
stockings-black
strap slippers-
1919

RTW

French 1910-1920

kimono bodice-
stand-away
collar-peg-top
skirt-slate
blue charmeuse-
cerise straw
hat-slate blue
ribbon and plume-
cerise velvet
bag-white
stockings-
black slippers-
1913

kimono
sleeve
treatment-
"minaret"
tunic shape-
peg-top skirt-
purple taffeta-
white batiste frill
and undersleeves-
cerise straw hat
and ostrich-white
stockings-black
slippers-
1914

midnight blue
taffeta-kimono
sleeve treatment-
short peplum-
crushed self
belt-white
organdie collar-
black felt
hat-wired
lace wings-
laced shoes-
black
leather-
beige
suède uppers-
1916

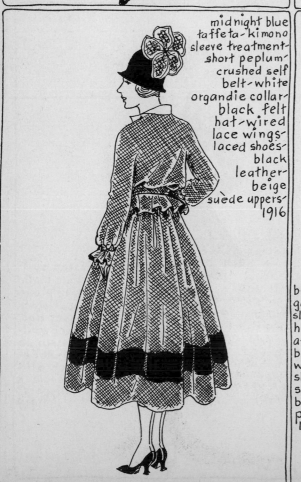

beaded
georgette frock-
slipped on over
head-fastened
at neck in back-
beaded sash
with tassels-
sheer black
stockings-
black
pumps-
1920

RTW

evening gown
by Poiret-
chiffon with
fur bands-
metal and
wool embroidery
on cloth-
cord girdle
with tassel-
1910

ivory lace
over old blue
taffeta-
"hobble skirt"
with taffeta
sash-pink
roses-green
foliage-girdle
of brilliants-
blue taffeta
headband-
pink ostrich
fan-
1911

crimson velvet
skirt and
crushed belt-
beaded black
chiffon bodice-
turquoise blue
ostrich fan-
silver slippers-
pearl gray
stockings-
jewelled
comb-
1914

gold cloth and
black velvet-
train panel
lined gold cloth-
blue silk
embroidery on
bodice and panel-
gold bead
shoulder straps-
sheer black
silk stockings-
black velvet
slippers-
1920

RTW

French 1910-1920

dolman wrap-light brown cloth with mink- black velvet hat-light brown willow plumes-black stockings- black slippers- 1912

dolman wrap- red and black velvet brocade- white fox- peg-top skirt amber satin- white beaver hat-black aigrettes and bow-black velvet bag- black pumps- black stockings- 1912

raglan coat- green cloth- skunk trimming- single large button-gray felt hat with black velvet-taupe suède laced shoes-black leather heel and toe- 1915

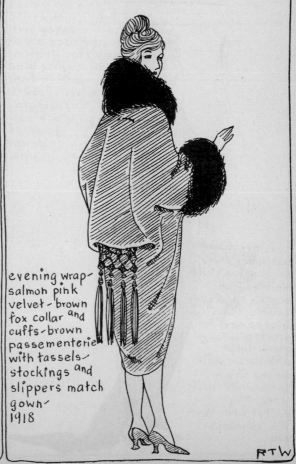

evening wrap- salmon pink velvet-brown fox collar and cuffs-brown passementerie with tassels- stockings and slippers match gown- 1918

RTW

golf costume-
tweed skirt-
knitted cardigan-
tailored white
washable shirt-
felt hat-white
buck shoes
with leather
fringe-
1913

tennis costume-
lingerie blouse-
silk scarf-
awning
striped cotton
skirt-panama
hat with
striped ribbon-
white buck
shoes-brown
trimming-
white
stockings-
1915

summer sports
costume-white
satin glacé skirt-
knitted tan
woolen cardigan-
knitted and
fringed sash or
scarf-black
straw sailor
with harem veil-
striped ribbon
band-white buck
shoes-black
leather trim-black
silk stockings-
1918

"country suit" of
tweed-leather
buttons-black
silk sailor-
white Ascot
scarf-tan
leather gauntlets-
fringed woolen
scarf-woolen
stockings-
beige suède
shoes-
1919

RTW

French 1910-1920

pink satin corset worn over chemise 1914

beaded bag 1918

corset-silk brocade-elastic waistband 1918

green gold mesh bag 1919

square toe-short vamp-brocade and velvet 1919

"slipover" corset-silk tricot mesh-worn over knickers-brassière on georgette bodice 1914

patent leather and kid 1912

gray spat over black pump 1917

satin slipper-velvet frill-rhinestone buckle 1917

button shoe-gray or beige suède-black patent leather heel and toe 1915

embroidered nainsook combination 1911

laced shoe-white kid-black patent leather 1916

combination with knickers-crêpe de Chine 1918

Oxford-black or brown kid 1918

cothurn-brocaded silk 1916

envelope combination-crêpe de Chine 1918

fan-green ostrich-amber stick-silk tassel 1916

brassière-pink satin-embroidery-Cluny lace 1919

black satin slipper-jewelled buckle-black silk stocking-lace insert 1918

black velvet bag-bead embroidery-silk tassels 1916

RTW

Chapter Forty-six

French

1920–1930

THE LONGER SKIRT arrived by 1921, having been eased in by the uneven hemline with panels and drapery hanging below the short skirt. Then the hemline started back upward, growing shorter and shorter until 1925, when it reached the knee. Never before, in the history of the mode, was so short a skirt worn by the fashionable woman. That lasted several years, when the hemline again began its descent, by 1930 touching the floor in evening gowns, with day dresses ten to twelve inches off the floor.

Since this time there have been two distinct hemlines, a long one for evening wear and a short for day dresses.

The uncorseted figure was definitely established, with its low-waisted girdle of satin or knitted elastic practically boneless. For the first time in the history of the corset, that garment was worn next to the body. The "foundation garment" of brassière and "panties" in one, well fitted and fashioned of firmly woven or knitted fabric, was as generally worn as girdle, brassière and knickers. The petticoat or slip was eliminated under the day or evening gown unless the transparency of that garment necessitated an underpiece. The few undergarments worn were simple, usually unadorned, and of crêpe de Chine or silk jersey. Lace when used was blond or deep écru in color.

The straight silhouette prevailed throughout the period. The belt line placed low on the hips lasted until the last few years of the decade, when it began to creep slowly up, reaching normalcy in 1930.

In evening gowns, a continuation of the *robe de style* was the long straight basque, with very full skirt of ankle length. The décolletage was round, square or straight across, to the waist in back and with narrow shoulder straps. The low waistline was marked by embroidered motifs, cockades, sashes and belts of all fabrics and widths, finished with sash ends or drapery. Too, floating panels and gathered sections of chiffon hung from the hips.

Evening gowns revealed an Indo-Chinese influence in ornamentation and color, also in the gold and silver turbans often worn with them. The all-white costume for evening became fashionable. There were dull crêpes in all varieties of weaves. Lace dyed in dark colors was employed for entire dresses. Bead embroidery continued in fashion for both day and evening. Transparent velvet became the vogue, a lustrous sheer velvet of artificial silk with beautiful draping quality.

While synthetic fabrics had been in use for some time, it was not until the late years of the decade that the French couturiers frankly employed artificial silks and velvets for their creations. The rich colors and lovely folds of these materials account for their success.

The navy-blue dress and the "little black dress" in either jersey, crêpe or crêpe georgette became standard for day wear in town. Over it was worn a black coat of the same length, fur-trimmed in winter. Necks were high, round or in *bâteau line,* straight across from shoulder to shoulder. There was also the "cowl neck," with loosely draped front.

With the exception of the hunting suit, sports clothes lost their severely tailored cut. The former was of rough tweed with belted jacket and a simple skirt which unbuttoned down the center front, revealing tweed knee breeches. Heavy knitted woolen stockings, brogues and a simple hat completed the outfit. The tailored suit and coat have always been of English origin, but it remained for Paris to create, for sports wear, the three-piece *ensemble* of dressmaker type, consisting of dress and coat or overblouse, skirt and coat.

The overblouse was the result of the low waistline, necessitating wearing the blouse outside the skirt, even the lingerie blouse. The blouse was usually of crêpe de Chine, but the knitted silk or woolen sweater or jumper, heretofore worn only for active sports, enjoyed great popularity. With this style originated the fashion of wearing a single short string of pearls with the sweater. Colorful woolens in soft lovely weaves and patterns, suède cloth, knitted and angora fabrics were used, the most popular material being wool jersey, especially in beige and brown. Awning stripes for skirts were smart.

The *ensemble* finally eclipsed all other styles for daytime wear. A wardrobe composed of evening clothes, the indispensable "little black dress" with accompanying long coat and the three-piece ensemble, proved adequate to fill the requirements of the well-dressed woman.

In the second half of the period appeared the low-necked, sleeveless sports dress, with gaily colored handkerchief or scarf tied loosely about the shoulders. A cloche, or tied headband, and short gloves were worn with it.

Coats were in wrap-around style, one side fastened underneath on one hip, the other either fastened or simply held in place with the hand. Scarfs of self material were part of or attached to the coat or jacket, one end thrown over the shoulder.

Bobbed hair of the beginning of the decade evolved into the "shingle" by 1922, lasting several years. A shaggy cut like the Titus headdress of the Directoire, but called the "wind-blown bob," was a popular style. Tinting gray hair with bluing originated in this period. Before the end of the 'twenties, the hair was worn a little longer, making an arranged coiffure possible, but always retaining the small head shape.

Bobbed hair revived the use of the wig or transformation, a skillfully made caplike coiffure which entirely concealed the wearer's own hair. In the early 'twenties, there was a short-lived fad for transformations of orange, red, green and purple for evening. While the transformation is not generally worn, it is still in use by many women with unsatisfactory hair. The wig of today has reached such perfection that it seldom reveals its artificiality.

With the short hair appeared a new metal hairpin, fashioned, like the cotter pin, of machinery, and called a "bobby pin."

Hats grew smaller and shed their trimmings, evolving into the cloche or mushroom shape about 1923 and surviving through 1930. It was a simple round crowned hat with tiny brim, usually of beige or black felt, winter or summer, enveloping the head to the neck in back and to the eyes in front. Reboux produced this hat, which became classic, often with no decoration but the ornamental shaping of the felt. Sometimes the simple hat was relieved by a grosgrain ribbon band or a single jewelled brooch or buckle. The béret, especially the Basque béret for sports, took firm hold and in its many variations continues in style. Veils of all kinds disappeared.

In furs there were long enveloping capes and coats with wide standing collars in moleskins, squirrel, gray and dyed kolinsky, beaver, Hudson seal, broadtail, caracul, mink, sable and ermine. New were babylamb, honey beige-sheared goat, honey beige or summer ermine. Furs were used on suits and dresses in very wide bands and a novelty was monkey fur. Fox skins of one to four skins in length were worn, a costly one being silver fox.

The high shoe disappeared, replaced by the pump and slipper. The low shoe became the "all-year-round" foot covering, protected in bad weather by galoshes or *arctics,* overshoes of rubber. Shoes had rounded toes, French heels, spike heels, straps crossed in every conceivable manner, upstanding tongues or frills with large buckles of metal, cut steel, marquisite or rhinestones. Street slippers were of patent leather, kid or suède. A newcomer for day wear was the dark-blue kid pump or slipper. Turned calf, resembling suède but much more durable, also appeared.

Oxfords or brogues in white buckskin for summer sports wear had brown or black leather trimmings, the winter model in brown leather. Gillies, sports shoes in brown leather or white buck with laces tied around the ankles, were also smart.

The white buckskin with high heel and brown leather trimming became standard for summer wear in the country, accompanying frocks or suits. Heels were either moderately high Cuban or the very high spike heel.

Evening slippers were of satin, brocade shot with gold or silver, while those of plain gold or silver took the place of the former bronze slipper as the "go-with-everything."

The light-colored stockings led the way to the flesh-colored, nude or blond stockings which fashion decreed. Woolen or lisle stockings were worn with sports shoes.

The buttoned glove was replaced by the "slip-on" glove of chamois, suède or doeskin, wrist-length or reaching halfway up the forearm. White, black or beige were the preferred colors with beige or brown for sports. With the growing casual feeling in clothes came the elimination of gloves for evening. The long glove disappeared, not being seen even upon formal occasions. It became the fad to wear one's gloves a size larger than formerly, giving the desired loose wrinkled effect.

Pajamas of crêpe de Chine, in brilliant colors, became the fashion for boudoir and lounging on the beach.

The use of cosmetics became general, powder, rouge, lipstick, eye shadow and eyebrow pencil over a make-up base being employed by young and old, the lady of leisure and the business woman. The vanity case was carried as generally as the purse, and could be had in beautiful design, regardless of its price. Repairs to the make-up, such as powdering the nose or adding lipstick, were calmly made in public with the aid of a small mirror. The vogue for "sunbathing" brought in the sun-tanned or very brown complexion.

Parasols disappeared and the umbrella grew smaller, gave up its long handle and took to colored silks instead of the former black. When closed, it was a stubby affair of about twenty inches in length. Raincoats also changed to gaily colored waterproofed silks.

Much attention was given to handbags, which became fairly large. After the war, travelling increased, especially to and over Europe, with the passport a requirement. That, with vanity case, the cigarette case and holder and the usual articles to be found in a woman's bag, made the larger container a necessity. The flat envelope design predominated, staying with us to date. Evening bags of both envelope and pouch shape were in costly fabrics with jewelled clasps and mounts. Every possible leather was employed for the more practical bag, beautifully lined and fitted with "gadgets."

It was in this period of simple unadorned dress necks, that costume jewelry settled down for a long stay. Pieces were designed for certain gowns, furnishing an effect or a color note, the intrinsic value of the bauble being of no matter, so that silver and gold plated metal with semi-precious stones sufficed. The slave bracelet of links appeared and long earrings were important for day and evening. The clip, a jewelled ornament which fastened to the garment by a clip, was newer and smarter than the brooch.

The lovely feather fan of the previous decade continued as a decorative evening accessory. A revival of artificial flowers in this period brought the nosegay and corsage into fashion. The nosegay, or boutonnière, was worn with the tailor-made as well as with the gown.

Because of the fashionable slim figure, exercise was scientifically taken up, necessitating a "play suit," which was of washable cotton, resembling the rompers of the youngster.

Many horsewomen adopted *jodhpurs* for active riding, long breeches tight from the knees to the ankle, with low boots worn underneath.

Bathing suits, in the first years of the period, were still accompanied by long stockings. They disappeared by the middle of the decade, the dressmaker type of suit being replaced by the French style of knitted woolen one-piece swimming suit or a combination of knitted maillot or jumper with flannel or knitted shorts of contrasting color.

The use of colored spectacles as a protection for the eyes, which originated with the automobile, was becoming popular for both winter and summer sports.

Winter sports grew in popularity and the fluffy angora type of knitted sweater, tam-o'-shanter and socks worn with knickerbockers early in the period were replaced by the simple tailored dark-colored mannish costume. It consisted of long trousers and jacket of jersey, gabardine, whipcord or flannel with the tailored flannel shirt or knitted sweater.

Madelaine et
Madelaine-
Directoire suit-
bottle green cloth
braided skirt-
black satin cravat-
lingerie blouse-
black velvet
bicorne-sand
colored pumps
and stockings-
envelope bag-
1920

tailored suit-
black
broadcloth-
silk braid-
lingerie blouse-
black velvet
bicorne-black
patent leather
shoes-silver
buckles-sheer
black stockings-
black suéde
bag-
1921

Molyneux-
ensemble-brown
wool with beaver-
tunic blouse with
bias jabot-cloth
belt and buckle-
beige felt hat-
beige suéde
slippers-blond
stockings-tan
leather bag-
1928

Servais-
ensemble-red
woolen coat-
lining and dress
red and white
printed crêpe-
accordion pleating-
red suéde belt-
red felt hat-
black suéde
pumps-blond
stockings-
1930

RTW

French 1920-1930

navy wool
jersey-self
sash in
back-self
covered
buttons-dark
blue leather
pumps-blond
stockings-
shingle bob-
1925

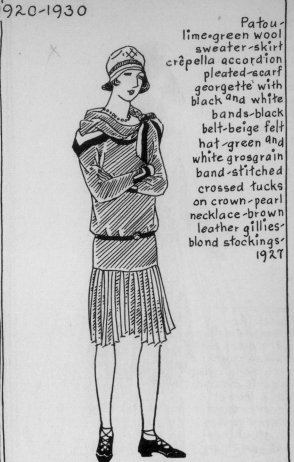

Patou-
lime-green wool
sweater-skirt
crêpella accordion
pleated-scarf
georgette with
black and white
bands-black
belt-beige felt
hat-green and
white grosgrain
band-stitched
crossed tucks
on crown-pearl
necklace-brown
leather gillies-
blond stockings-
1927

printed voile-red,
yellow and green
on black ground-
cowl neck-skirt
and drapery one
piece, length of
fabric-black
velvet sash-
beige straw hat-
red and yellow
grosgrain-
beige leather
envelope bag-
black suéde
pumps-blond
stockings-
1928

Suzanne Talbot-
sleeveless sports
frock-white
and yellow
silk-belt
with buckle-
béret shirred
yellow silk-
white doeskin
slip-on gloves-
grège silk
stockings and
shoes-brown
leather trim-
brown suéde bag-
1929

RTW

French 1920-1930

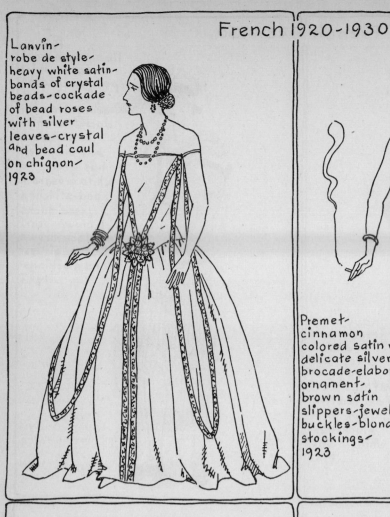

Lanvin-
robe de style-
heavy white satin-
bands of crystal
beads-cockade
of bead roses
with silver
leaves-crystal
and bead caul
on chignon-
1923

Premet-
cinnamon
colored satin with
delicate silver
brocade-elaborate
ornament-
brown satin
slippers-jewelled
buckles-blond
stockings-
1923

Chéruit-
black moiré
with circular
design-green
taffeta scarf-
drapery with
green taffeta
lining-silver
slippers-pearl
straps-blond
stockings-
shingle bob-
1926

Augustabernard-
black satin-
draped scarf
knotted to shoulder
strap-faced with
rose satin-
jewelled buckles-
black velvet
pumps-blond
stockings-
short slip-on
white doeskin
gloves-
1930

RTW

Madelaine et
Madelaine-
cape of monkey
fur mounted
on black chiffon-
muff of monkey
fur-draped
black velvet turban-
taupe suede shoes-
gun metal buckles-
taupe stockings-
1920

day coat-
tan kasha cloth-
embroidery in
bright peasant
colors-hat tan
cloth-black cloth
facing-peasant
embroidery-black
patent leather
shoes-sand
colored stockings-
1921

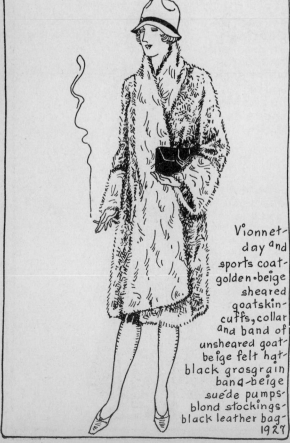

Vionnet-
day and
sports coat-
golden-beige
sheared
goatskin-
cuffs, collar
and band of
unsheared goat-
beige felt hat-
black grosgrain
band-beige
suede pumps-
blond stockings-
black leather bag-
1927

Chanel-
evening wrap-
white velvet-
white fox-
fine stitched
tucks-white
velvet bag-
jewelled
mount-
white gown-
white slippers-
1930

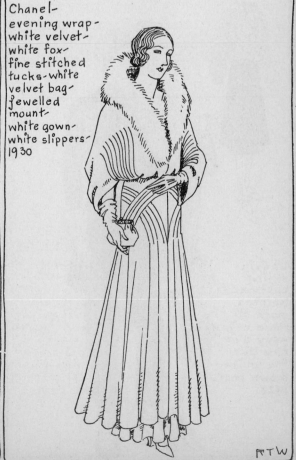

FTW

French 1920-1930

cross-saddle habit of whipcord-brown coat-tan breeches with suéde reinforcements-brown field boots-white shirt-club striped scarf-tan felt hat-crop with ivory handle-1925

formal habit-black melton cloth-black velvet collar-buff cloth waistcoat-white shirt-white stock-white buckskin or chamois gloves-black patent leather boots-silk hat-1925

Lanvin-skiing costume in knitted cloth of three colors-navy blue, sky blue and white-brown boots-1928

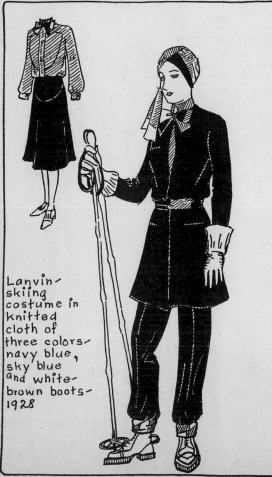

tennis frock-white crêpe de Chine-accordion pleating-striped silk headband-white socks-white buckskin shoes-1929

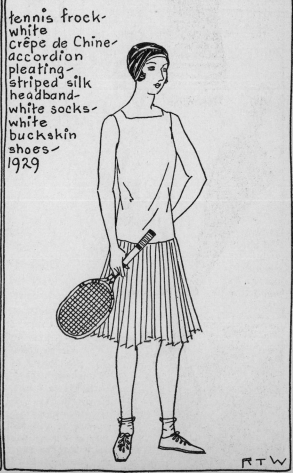

RTW

French 1920-1930

uncurled ostrich fan-ivory sticks

Reboux-red felt hat-red velvet bow and band-1927

Basque béret for sports

elastic girdle-back lacing-no bones-flounce net with crystals-1920

one piece black wool jersey swimming suit-white bands-1930

combination brassiere, vest and bloomers-silk jersey-1930

combination brassiere, girdle and drawers-pink silk jersey-ecru lace-1930

black and white knitted swimming suit-1929

beach pyjamas-white silk jersey-royal blue bands-1924

brassière and panties-pink silk jersey-colored applique-1927

bathing suit-silk jersey-top sulphur-middle orange-skirt and sash black-sheer black stockings-1921

brown and beige silk umbrella-amber and wood handle-1922

Perugia-cothurn of lamé or satin-1922

Perugia-black leather with red edge-1922

Perugia-evening slipper-velvet and lamé-1922

R.T.W.

Chapter Forty-seven

French

1930–1942

B Y THIS PERIOD, clothes had become so thoroughly specialized that the wardrobe of a well-dressed woman contained costumes suitable for all occasions. There were clothes for town, for the country, for tea or cocktail parties, the hostess gown for informal evenings, formal evening dress, for the various sports and if, at sports, she was only a spectator, then there was the "spectator sports" costume.

The waistline settled back into its normal position, but the figure retained its natural lines till the winter of 1937 and 1938, when the Paris couturiers presented the fashionable woman with a new corset or girdle. It was made of the same fabrics, but came up higher under the bosom and confined the figure by means of extra bones, producing the required smaller waist of the new mode.

The change is supposed to have been influenced by the appearance and success, both here and abroad, of the photoplays of Mae West, especially her first picture "Diamond Lil," in which she portrayed a siren of the 'nineties with all her voluptuous curves.

The "all-in-one," or foundation garment, now as generally worn as

379

the girdle and brassière, also took on more form by means of careful fitting and added bones. Instead of the flat silhouette, the shape of the breasts was enhanced by cuplike-shaped brassières, called "uplift style." Carriage and posture changed from a slouch of standing on one leg to a firm position on both feet, with chest out and shoulders thrown back. The corset, girdle and foundation garment were made of satin and elastic or knitted elastic. An improvement in knitted elastic fabric was the "two-way stretch" weave which did not ride up on the figure. It was also firmer, more elastic and eliminated the need of bones.

Hemlines of day clothes were from six to eight inches off the ground till 1939, when they again rose, reaching fifteen inches by the spring of 1940. Evening gowns still touched the floor or were ankle-length.

There were several evening silhouettes in the 'thirties, the long basque bodice with bouffant skirt, the gown with classic drapery and the slim, sleek gown with or without train. The bouffant gown was fashioned of such fabrics as taffeta, slipper satin, heavy velvet or organza with horsehair. The classic and the slim models took materials which fell in clinging folds, such as sheer velvet, jersey and crêpes.

New, in the beginning of the period, was the summer gown of cotton, appearing first in white piqué, then in organdie and that billowy synthetic fabric organza, in lovely designs and color. Crêpes and printed georgettes were also popular for summer. Other warm-weather fabrics were cotton denim and knitted ordinary cotton string. The former was used for play clothes and the latter for sweaters, turbans and gloves.

Lace, especially in black and jet came back as trimmings in the second half of the decade, and faille silk returned to the mode, especially for the dressmaker suit. The most unusual color of the period was Schiaparelli's "shocking pink," a fuchsia pink.

Lingerie consisted of panties worn over a girdle, a silk petticoat and shaped brassière, or a form-fitting silk slip, which eliminated petticoat and brassière.

Another change in the silhouette occurred in 1933 with the broad and exaggerated square shoulders of tailored clothes. Sleeves varied from the leg-of-mutton to the long, tight style and in all lengths. They were shirred or pleated into the armscye and padded into the square effect. In the second half of the period, the simulated bustle in tied-back drapery tried to assert itself, but the style was temporary.

A fashion of several years was the evening gown, high of neck in front and entirely minus back. There was also the "halter dress," of beach origin, with a bib for a bodice in front, drawn up, gathered and held at the neck by a cord or ribbon. The halter neck was adopted in summer day frocks too.

Dinner suits appeared, copying the man's summer informal evening outfit with white jacket, long black skirt and blouse. The masculine cummerbund was also imitated. Winter evening gowns of sheer wool crêpe or wool jersey became a fashion. Late in the period, the evening sweater came into the mode, of wool embroidered in silver and gold, silk and beads.

The remainder of the period was one of jackets accompanying evening gowns. Jackets either matched or contrasted with the dress and were of velvet, cloth or crêpe, embroidered with gilt or sequins. The "covered-up look" became the required effect for theatre or restaurant dining; in fact, the dinner dress came to stay.

A startling new idea in summer evening gowns appeared in 1939. It was the bare midriff which originated on the beach. The long skirt and the very short bodice were separated by an expanse of bare torso, which effect was often heightened by long tight sleeves. Sometimes, the bare midriff was simulated by a joining of flesh-colored chiffon between skirt and bodice.

The "little black dress" of crêpe, georgette or silk jersey retained its hold. A less formal, simpler frock was the "run-about dress" of wool jersey or flannel for winter, of colored silk or cotton for summer. The shirtwaist dress appeared with skirt and blouse joined together. The blouse was of shirtwaist design, and the skirt either plain or pleated, in silk, wool or cotton according to season.

With the return to the normal waistline, sweaters and blouses were worn under the skirt instead of outside.

The jackets of suits were short in reefer or semifitted style. In the second half of the period, the contrasting jacket and skirt appeared, a light jacket with dark skirt or the other way round. The country suit of color and novelty weave replaced the black or navy blue suit for town wear. Oxford gray became smart. Jacket and coat edges were finished with saddle stitching.

The long straight coat of the early years acquired a fitted body. The redingote appeared and the untrimmed dress coat, with which a fur scarf or short fur cape was worn. There were long coats over which fur boleros were worn. Sports coats were in several styles, the reefer, the redingote and that great stand-by, the loose coat of camel's hair. Much leeway in color became the vogue, with pastel shades to the fore for country wear.

Evening coats, in general, followed Victorian lines, long and fitted at the waist in redingote style, of woolen cloth or velvet and often untrimmed and collarless. The short jacket of silver fox, bulky and square, was worn both with evening and day clothes.

Hats varied constantly but seemed to agree on the shallow crown or no crown at all. There were sailors and huge cartwheels, the Eugénie hat with its drooping plume, the Watteau hat, the pillbox, the tiny pancake hat, or "doll hat." The calotte, with ribbon bow or flowers known as the pompadour hat, and designed by Talbot for the Duchess of Windsor, became very popular. The shape of the béret varied and we had Victorian bonnets, little flower hats and turbans. Large brims flared up off the face. Felt hats of Tyrolese shape were worn with sports clothes. Veils enjoyed a distinct vogue, especially the short one of horsehair and in wide mesh.

Cauls, filets or nets, now erroneously called snoods and made of chenille, appeared in the middle of the decade; in fact, it was by means of the net that the tiny hat was held to the head. The original snood was a ribbon tied round the head, and in this period small hats were attached to snoods. For casual dress or sports, there were the hand-tied turban and the peasant handkerchief tied under the chin.

Wimples, tiny medieval caps, gold nets and small lace mantillas were worn in the evening. Artificial flowers, ribbons and feathers were again worn in the hair, also jewelled ornaments or clips.

Every style of coiffure or hair-do was modish, providing it did not conceal the contour of the head. The hair was kept shoulder-length, making it possible to adopt any headdress. In general, the hair close to the head was not curled; only the ends were curled, usually by a permanent wave. The hair dressed high in the back, in the style of the 'nineties, returned to favor in 1937, with the pompadour following the next year. Coiffures had straight bangs or curled fringes over the forehead, puffs, rolls and cadogan loops, even lacquered curls dusted with gold flakes in the evening.

The short slip-on or pull-on glove, loose-fitting and with hand stitching, remained in fashion, made of all fabrics and combinations of fabrics. The staple glove was of beige doeskin or suède for street, pigskin for sports and cotton suède for summer. Gloves contrasted with the costume, light with dark and *vice versa*.

All furs, both costly and lowly, were smart in this period, according to the occasion. The most popular furs for the long coat were sable, mink, chinchilla, baum marten, broadtail, Persian lamb and caracul, with silver fox for the short coat and scarf. Fashionable also, were furs of lesser value, such as beaver, nutria and plucked muskrat. For sports, there were leopard and the various dressed goat and lamb skins in light colors; for evening, tailless ermine, coffee-dyed ermine, summer ermine and white broadtail. Small muffs and those of moderate size were carried.

In this period, many of the Victorian colors returned to the mode, such as garnet red, cabbage red, eggplant purple, chartreuse, lime yellow, gray pinks and raw vivid pinks.

Low shoes or slippers became elaborate and fantastic. The slim spike heel replaced the Louis heel. There were sandals fashioned only of narrow strips with high heels, sandals without backs or toes and slippers with open toes or a hole where the toecap should have been. They were of many fabrics and leathers. The shoe with the wedge sole, a revival of the Italian Renaissance, appeared in the middle of the decade. That was followed by the platform sole, a sole of great thickness, with high heel. Pumps, Oxfords and brogues were utility shoes in leather, kid, suède, alligator, lizard, toadskin, snakeskin, calf and turned calf. Bronze kid reappeared for afternoon wear in 1940. The blond stocking retained its hold, while, coinciding with the rage for the sun-tanned complexion, young women went stockingless in the summer.

Costume jewelry remained very important as a costume accent in gold and silver with semiprecious stones. Following the vogue for jewelled clips, tiny watches were clip-fastened and earrings were made with clips instead of screws.

The mechanical slide fastener was perfected and manufactured in all colors and was used to fasten girdles, foundation garments, dresses, coats, handbags; in fact, wherever a trim concealed closing was required.

The large handbag remained in vogue, of fabric or leather, of varied shape, with the smaller jewelled bag of precious fabric for evening use.

Play clothes consisted of the cotton dress, with skirt covering the thighs, or a knee-length skirt buttoned down center front, or the dirndl skirt of peasant origin, with shorts underneath. Shorts and slacks became very popular for sports. "Girdle panties" of elastic tricot confined the figure under the slacks. Generally worn was the one-piece swimming suit of knitted or elastic fabric in pleasing patterns and colors.

The tailored mannish costume of pants and jacket became standard for winter sports, especially for skiing. Navy blue, even black, were the favorite colors in gabardine, whipcord, jersey or flannel. A tailored knee-length skirt for skiing, worn with high knitted socks, appeared late in the period. The tailored knee-length dress with flaring circular skirt was the favored style for rink ice skating.

Cosmetics, powder, rouge, lipstick, eye shadow and eyebrow pencil were employed by all well-dressed women. Finger-nails were lacquered in all shades of red, varying from a delicate pink to that of mahogany red, the use of a certain color governed by preference. Gray hair, no longer dyed by the smart woman, was given a blue or mauve tint by a rinse in a tinted bath.

French 1930-1942

Schiaparelli-
black ribbed
wool-blouse
white crochet
string-S-clips-
pull-on gloves-
Eugénie hat-
blond
stockings-
black antelope
bag and pumps-
1931

Molyneux-
navy blue cloth
dress-jacket
fuchsia pink
cloth-white
flower at neck-
Tyrolese hat
black felt-
grosgrain band-
gloves and
pumps blue
antelope-
blond
stockings-
1937

Balenciaga-
jacket, café au
lait satin-
twisted black
buttons-black
crêpe dress-
circular pleating-
Suzy hat-fancy
straw-veil-
black antelope
gloves and pumps-
beige crocodile
bag-blond
stockings-
1939

Lelong-
black cloth
jacket-Persian
lamb-plaid
skirt of sewn
squares-Suzy
hat-cerise
beaver crown-
white felt brim-
black ribbon-
beige and black
feather-blond
stockings-black
patent leather
pumps-
1939

RTW

Marcel Rochas-
flowered
taffeta with
velvet
trimming-
black felt
hat-
blond
stockings-
black
suéde
pumps-
1935

Lucien Lelong-
black silk
crépe-bias
seams-self
bowknots-black
velvet Eugénie
hat-blond
stockings-
black antelope
pumps-
1931

Worth-
black satin-
shirred into
raglan shoulder-
pleats on hip-
self buttons-
velvet hat-
satin crown-
black
antelope
bag and
pumps-
blond
stockings-
1935

Alix-
brocaded
navy blue
silk-stand-
out panniers-
self buttons
and tie belt-
pleats in
front of skirt-
blond stockings-
blue kid
pumps-
1939-

RTW

Paquin-
coat of
pomegranate
red wool-
brown sealskin
bolero and
muff-
Maria Guy hat-
black taupé-
brown suede
slippers-blond
stockings-
1931

Vionnet-
coat of
soft red
woolen cloth-
Persian lamb-
velvet beret-
blond
stockings-
black patent
leather
pumps-
1932

Molyneux-
green wool
coat-green
straw hat-
ribbon bow-
chamois
pull-on gloves-
blond stockings-
copper colored
suede open-toed
sandals-
1936

Creed-
redingote
butter yellow
cotton whipcord-
black felt
sailor-black
silk muffler
and handkerchief-
black leather
shoes-blond
stockings-
1937

RTW

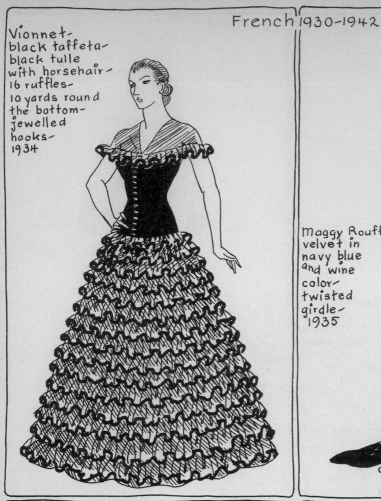

Vionnet-
black taffeta-
black tulle
with horsehair-
16 ruffles-
10 yards round
the bottom-
jewelled
hooks-
1934

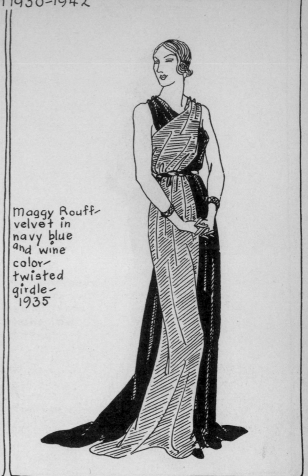

Maggy Rouff-
velvet in
navy blue
and wine
color-
twisted
girdle-
1935

Patou-
dinner suit-
black silk
crêpe-corded
pockets-green
chiffon blouse
and tie-
corded black
crêpe toque-
black gloves-
1939

Alix-
white
jersey-
shirred
at waist-
peplum-
colored
stockings-
white
sandals-
1940

RTW

French 1930-1942

Patou-
evening wrap-
two shades of
red-trimmed
with sable-
1931

silver fox
jacket
over black
crêpe gown-
late
'thirties-

Mainbocher-
evening greatcoat
red woolen
cloth trimmed
with blue fox-
red velvet
hat with
ostrich feather-
1938

Creed-
evening coat-
brown velvet
with black
passementerie-
1939

RTW

beach costume-
trousers of
natural linen-
brassière and
hat of plum
colored linen-
plum colored
felt sandals-
1933

play suit-
golf or
tennis-
cotton
fabric-
shirt,
shorts
and skirt-
buck shoes-
sunshade-
mid-'thirties

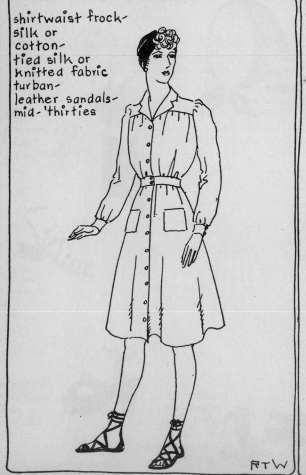

shirtwaist frock-
silk or
cotton-
tied silk or
knitted fabric
turban-
leather sandals-
mid-'thirties

winter play
costume-
yellow woolen
coat-beaver
collar-red suede
waistcoat-
beige slacks-
beige shirt-
beige leather
shoes-red
knitted calotte and
socks-
mid-'thirties

RTW

French 1930-1942

Schiaparelli knitted cap 1932

Maria Guy green velvet gold metal stripe 1934

"off-the-face" felt hat velvet ribbon 1936

Suzy black beaver black satin 1939

Schiaparelli black felt black chenille net 1936

J. Suzanne Talbot black velvet pink roses 1940

Suzy pink flowers green foliage 1940

Reboux sailor of East Indian scarf black velvet brim 1940

velvet calotte late 'thirties

pancake béret

peasant handkerchief style late 'thirties

colored silk umbrella

satin and elastic girdle lace brassiere 1934

seamless elastic foundation garment 1934

pink satin corset slide fastener 1939

knitted swimming suit 1940

empire sandal petunia satin 1936

gold sandals straps edged black 1935

beige calf crêpe rubber sole 1940

summer sandals red felt braided straw soles 1940

platform sandals red velvet 1940

RTW

Chapter Forty-eight

1947 and The New Look

THIS MOMENT appears of the greatest importance in the feminine mode. A new couturier, Christian Dior, said to be a former successful Paris art dealer, has turned his creative talents to women's clothes and therein has launched a breath-taking silhouette. Breath-taking to the lay public, because entirely opposite to the pencil-slim form of the past decades. It was not without warning, however, because those who know could sense some suspicious signs of the coming change in the late 'thirties. Even then the trend was toward a rounder figure, a smaller waist, snug bodices and, occasionally, full flaring skirts.

As ever, woman takes on a new allure which is laid at her feet by that goddess of changeable whims, Fashion. In these very whims lies the fascination of the mode, because fashion cannot and never does remain static for long. There is nothing new in fashion—it is only the modern interpretation of a given style that makes it so.

Milady has taken on a bosom, hips, stomach and derrière, all this happening despite a terrific wailing of the many opponents of the "New Look." We find ourselves giving up the broad, square, masculine look, a surprising distortion of round, feminine shoulders. We are slipping into a new form, requiring an hourglass corset, the guêpière or waist-clincher, with costumes boned, lined and padded; bustles, peplums, basques, tippets—in fact, all the blandishments of other days.

Call it what you will, guêpière (wasp), waist-cincher or waist-liner, the corset is back as the foundation of the mode. True, it is unlike the torturing garment of other days, being fashioned of lighter fabric and judiciously boned to control the figure. But the firm intent is to produce a small, tight waist, trim above and rounding below. Even the bathing maillot calls for some kind of girdle to give a defined waistline.

The vogue for bare shoulders, which has invaded day, country and play clothes, is responsible for a new engineering feat in brassières, a strapless wired "bra." This wired piece of structure does away with the binding shoulder strap for active sports, at the same time offering firm hold and support. A single wire arched over each breast and bent into a small loop between is the secret. Waist-length brassières with boned seams give a trim look to the tight bodice.

Aside from the stimulus it affords industry, the new style is a boon to many women who have been unable to display a slim silhouette. Of course the smaller waist offers a problem, but they can at least feel happy in possessing bosom and hips instead of the pads which the lithe young creatures must needs adopt.

The short, straight style in suit and dress was practical and fabric-saving during the war, but hemlines have been lengthening by half inches since. Then came the drop to fourteen and twelve, with a prophecy of ten for day wear. In England and in many sections of the United States, many women openly rebelled, but in spite of protests the long skirt is appearing in the metropolis and on Main Street.

The Dior or infanta silhouette is not fashion's ultimate dictum but by far the most important. Other contours are labelled the triangle which flares from neck to hem, back fullness with bustle drapery and the cocoon or wrap-around effect. One can choose between a narrow skirt and a full flaring model in suits.

A sensational circular skirt of Dior's is made with many seams, each panel reinforced with muslin and the hemline faced upward with calico for eight or ten inches. All of which makes the skirt stand away from the figure. And that quite naturally brings us to the subject of petticoats.

For nearly a half century but one petticoat has been worn, a sheath-like garment of silk and occasionally lace-trimmed. Now, all of a sudden, there are definite signs of "petticoat fever," with women wearing two and three at a time in taffetas of all colors, heavily flounced, and many crinoline-stiffened with horsehair or featherboning. White cotton ones are back, frilled with embroideries, and dainty organdy skirts have eye-let edging run with ribbons.

Beautiful lace again adorns slips and panties. Lingerie colors are peach, white, pale blue with black, a growing favorite, the latter further enhanced with black lace. Formerly only the demimondaine availed herself of such glamour.

Lace is once more in fashion; laces of all kinds and qualities. Lace for several decades has led a distinctively dimmed existence in the mode, but the devastation caused by the war in Europe made it imperative to restore and revive the industry to save the very lives of the lacemakers.

The long-sleeved nightgown of fine silk and lace-trimmed of the gay nineties is again worn for winter and not just by the lady of a certain age. This garment was re-introduced by gay, sensible young people. To them goes credit for a revolutionary feminine sleeping tunic, a knee-length affair resembling a man's nightshirt.

Dressing for the cocktail hour is a happy postwar custom, with the "five-o'clock-and-on" frock of ballet length fitting well into the picture. This short evening or dinner dress was an origination brought out in the early 'forties by the American couturière Valentina. The "ballerina," as the style is known, fills a woman's need for the dressy look when her escort is in business clothes. The tailored costume of jacket and skirt of handsome brocade is also meeting with decided approval.

One must note the much-publicized sensational décolletage of a Dior gown which he called "Cabaret." A wide V neckline opens to the waist and partially exposes the breasts. The bosom-baring décolletage is a revival of many appearances in the mode. The Cretan ladies displayed their breasts openly; the deep V neck appeared in the late fourteenth century worn with the hennin, and Agnès Sorel, "la Dame de Beauté" and favorite of the French Charles VII in the fifteenth century, had her portrait painted so.

A century later we find Marie de Médicis wearing the low neck at the French court, where it was designated as the "Italian Style," and 'tis said that it became really popular. In England it was worn, oddly enough, by maiden ladies, and Queen Elizabeth indulged in the low-cut front. We read that the French ambassador was deeply disconcerted during an audience with the English monarch, who was wearing her open-front gown.

After a period of "sans chapeau"—a casual fashion seen even on city streets—the smart feminine head is once again coifed, in a real hat. Dinner and evening gowns, too, are accompanied by chic little hats. There are berets, turbans, pillboxes, some large hats; but again we turn to Dior to mention his profile hats, made after his designs by Maud Roser. His is a new half-hat, half-hairdo idea, a modern version of the very jaunty soft hat which the dandy of the Renaissance wore over one ear. Some of those gentlemen attached the hat to a caul and thus kept the piece perched at the side of their heads but today's smart woman pins hers to a one sided up-hairdo.

The small soignée head with the hair dressed up in back is the fitting style atop the new figure. Many young women affect a medieval bob, an artistic headdress of beautifully brushed, swirled locks. Technicolor photography, which tinges all colors with a suspicion of red, has introduced a new shade in blonds. The color is lighter and pinker than Titian, rather like a pale tone of copper foil, a metallic but beautiful tint.

The greatcoat is with us, of heavy but soft cloth and with flaring skirt, also the coachman's cloak with its little capes. Attached to many a coat is an enveloping hood, the result of the hatless fashion.

Furs, which are still scarce in Paris, have adopted the rounded silhouette with softened shoulders. They are fashioned in jacket, three-quarter and full length with full sleeves. Sumptuous indeed are the new long capes of luxurious silver fox. Precious furs, of which there is a profusion in the United States, are given simple, casual treatment in design.

Successful ranch-raising of animals for their fur has augmented the supply of pelts in the world's fur markets, while successful experiments with mutation have produced new colors in valuable skins especially in mink and silver fox. From the ranch come deep-blue tones, black mink sprinkled with white, and, rarest and costliest of all, white mink.

Very popular for the modern way of life is the separate skirt, especially the dirndl of Tyrolean origin, worn with the tuck-in blouse. This style makes for many changes and offers a wide choice of color combinations and fabrics, in either long or short, for day or evening. It is also responsible for the very youthful and very American "mother and daughter" ensembles.

The world of fashion is enjoying the return of the many fabrics which had disappeared because of war priorities. Most worthy of note is the reinstatement in the mode, after an absence of some decades, of black broadcloth, a fabric of great elegance. There are sheer woolens, suède-surfaced woolens and wool jerseys, all of which tailor well and drape beautifully; also rare fleeces, tweeds and practically all the known cloths, silks and velvets. From our good neighbors to the south come Mexican and Guatemalan cottons, hand-woven and hand-loomed in brilliant color and interesting texture.

Suèded leather is not new for hunting clothes, the Spanish having made use of the soft, beautifully toned leather centuries back. But today, in this era of informal living, suède enters into every phase of costume, being carried into feminine evening dress. The chamoised leather, dyed in many subdued colors, lends itself to a simple unadorned mode.

Feminine footwear is inspired by the shoes of the peoples of all ages: the primitive fur boot, the alpargata, the moccasin, the sandal, the mule, the peaked toe, fashioned of all possible materials into models suitable to any and every occasion. In general, heels are of either extreme—that is, low and broad or high and spiked. The designers are creating footwear as simple or as extravagant as one might desire. Bronze slippers are staging a return. Suède, fancy and colored leathers, velvet and satin remain staple, and dress and weather shoes show signs of rising to ankle height. "Open-toed" shoes for day wear have been blacked out by the classic pump.

Time was when a pair of lady's rubbers covered any pair of shoes but the varied styles in any wardrobe have made overshoes a problem. The designers have got busy on that dilemma, and from California comes a protective boot to accommodate heels of all kinds. It borrows the clog idea of Colonial days, a flat sole of synthetic rubber cushioned with cork from which a bag rises to encase the foot. Strapped round the ankle, it is a modern contraption, with the uppers of transparent, sheer but sturdy fabric. The picture given on our accessory page will illustrate the result better than a description.

With the quantities of exquisite sheer nylon stockings again available, the bare-legged fashion has left us. The general color is darker and in many hues of muted tones of green, plum, brown and black, but so gossamer sheer are the stockings that such colors appear but as shadows over the flesh. There are lisles and wools for sportswear in knee-high or ankle socks, the latter called anklets. For spectator sports there is a very sheer lace mesh nylon, a flattering and almost indestructible stocking.

The beautiful white mousquetaire glove is back for evening wear in eight, twelve, sixteen, or twenty-button lengths, and the classic pull-on in black or brown doeskin is the preferred afternoon or cocktail glove. For street and casual wear we find slip-ons, one- or two-button shorties and wrist-strap gloves, the same styles for sportswear but of heavier leather such as pigskin, buckskin, goatskin and the like. White pigskin in the longer lengths, however, is a recent and truly chic addition to glove leathers for afternoon and evening dress.

One could devote many paragraphs to scarfs and mufflers, which are to be had in all possible lovely fabrics, printed, hand-blocked and hand-painted. The influence of the artist is evident today in all walks of life, because, regardless of the quality or price of the article, the applied design is artistic in motif and color—a statement which holds good for practically all of our modern materials.

We have passed through a period of bags in sabretache style with the long shoulder strap, a very convenient war fashion. The wrist strap seems newer and is attached to many different shapes which range from pouch to box forms. A novelty in this day is a chatelaine bag swinging from the belt. All styles are tailored and done in leathers and fabrics, a fairly new one being black broadcloth. Handbags usually bear some gilt or gold decoration in clasps, chains or monograms. The war left its mark in a trail of gilt insignia and other martial motifs.

Evening bags, smaller in size than the day pieces, are of satin, brocade, tapestry, embroidery or beading, making a featured note of the ensemble. It is possible for a woman of means to indulge her fancy in its wildest flight, so beautiful, extravagant, precious and costly are some of these receptacles.

There have been several attempts to bring back the long-handled umbrella, but the short, stubby model still holds its own. Designers have given much attention to clothes for inclement weather, creating rain-coats which are not only utilitarian but smart enough in appearance to wear on the sunniest day.

Touching upon the masculine mode, signs of a new trend are to be observed. Not to be outdone by Madame, the well-dressed man appears to be taking note of the feminine shoulder treatment by giving up the exaggerated square physique. High-class ready-mades are being prepared with narrower and rounder shoulders.

The popularity of the single-breasted fly-front topcoat for day wear is on the wane. Double-breasted overcoats are being made of handsome soft fabrics and accordingly are being tagged with very high prices. For instance, a coat of the South American vicuña, a small animal of the camel family with the finest and rarest wool in the world, can be had for approximately five hundred dollars. Guanaco, also of the camel species and of the same country, provides hair for a costly fabric similar to vicuña but slightly coarser in texture.

The topcoat of camel's hair or tweed and the raglan of light brown whipcord are staples for general use. Also to be noted for knock-about service are casual loafer coat of suèded cloth, the army coat of water-repellent cotton gabardine, sheepskin lined and collared, and the windbreaker of ponyskin.

The influence of battle dress is evident in civilian life, especially in sports clothes. The short battle jacket is of particular interest, a London tailor having designed an informal evening suit on the same lines in midnight-blue cloth for wear with the black tie. Its acceptance is a matter of conjecture—men do not as a rule like change (a woman's statement); and there is an objection to the outfit resembling too closely that of the uniformed attendant. The double-breasted Tuxedo or dinner jacket has definitely come to the fore in popularity.

The war, with attending curtailment of civilian manufacturing, followed by the army of returning veterans clamoring for clothes, created a dearth of all necessities. It has taken two years to reach anything near normalcy.

White cotton for shirts and underwear was simply unobtainable and so men wore what could be had. From California came the idea of shirts, shorts and robes done in bright-colored materials for sportswear. Necessity and the scarcity of woolen cloth put men into ensembles of light colors and combinations of colors. This latter scheme evolved a jacket in two colors, of a plain and a fancy weave, the front in one color or pattern and the sleeves and back in another. The latest tendency appears to be toward no pattern and cloth light in color for sports jackets.

Trousers continue to be made with pleats at the waist, affording some fulness in front. A new patented design in slacks, called "Daks," is a recent English contribution of importance in breeches that requires no belt.

There is a rise in the cut of some day shoes, a noticeably smart style founded upon the polo player's and army officer's boot and so named the "chukka" or "flight boot." The comfortable, casual Norwegian slipper, called the "loafer shoe," has become a staple. It is gradually working its way into the class for general wear, since shoe designers have given their attention to a dress version of the laceless slip-on.

The hats of the average man's wardrobe afford him a wide choice of what to wear, but pre-war rules still hold with the same insistence on when and where to wear a certain hat.

The well-dressed man likes a scarf of rich color but he also delights in a cravat gayly patterned perhaps with contrasting colors. According to his ensemble, it will be of silk, wool, cotton or synthetic fabric, in club or regimental stripes, weaves of small design or just plain. At the moment an incredible craze is current for garish colored neckties of truly startling motifs, very often hand-painted and for that reason costing a goodly sum. Such neckpieces are appearing not only with loafing clothes but with the town habit.

The notes given in Chapter Forty-three on men's robes, underwear, sweaters, hose and sleeping garments continue to appertain in this post-war period.

cat's-eye green
slipper satin-
black patent
leather belt-
black suède pumps-
Dior

black cloth and
accordion pleated
dark green taffeta-
black leather belt-
green velvet beret-
black suède
pumps-
Dior

pleated black chiffon over
pleated orange chiffon-
black leather
belt-Dior
black velvet béret
by Maud Roser-
black suède
pumps

black wool with
low décolletage-
black patent leather
belt-small black
hat with osprey-
Dior

RTW

1947

black wool suit-
turtle neck jersey
shirt-crushed fedora
of cinnamon velour-
Dior

beige cloth suit-
skirt pleated over hips-
plaid wool blouse,
béret and muffler-
Molyneux

black cloth jacket edged
with black serpentine
braid-green cloth
circular skirt with
gathers in back-
black velvet
béret-
Jacques Fath

gray herringbone woolen
suit- self-banded at
hip and hem-
embroidered
black velvet
pillbox-
Mainbocher

RTW

1947

evening gown of
black chiffon and dark
red taffeta-black
leather belt with
gun metal buckle-
Dior

evening ensemble of
cocoanut colored
satin and velvet-
velvet basque-gold
and silver embroidery-
sable fur-
Jacques Fath

white satin
and heavy white
cotton Venetian lace-
Maggy Rouff

black woolen
dinner suit-dress
worn with short
basque jacket-
black ostrich
trim and muff-
black béret-
Dior

RTW

1947

boulevardier greatcoat
of heavy woolen
cloth-
Balenciaga

Cossack coat of
bright blue cloth-
Persian lamb-
squirrel lining-
Dior

black wool redingote-
collar and fronts
faced with
pleated green
taffeta-
Dior

coachman's coat
of heavy woolen
cloth-
Grès

RTW

1947

circular capes
of gray flannel-
Grès

triangle silhouette-
greatcoat of thick
beige woolen cloth
with stitching-
Paquin

tweed greatcoat
lined with cloth of
contrasting color-
Creed

short hooded cape
of gray and gold
plaid cloth-
Grès

RTW

1947

Alaska sealskin
coat created
for Fredrica
by Dior

cape of
silver fox-
Fro ‖ ‖

coat of
champagne colored
nutria-coif of
Venetian lace-
Maximilian

coat of
dark ranch mink-
Esther Dorothy

RTW

1947

raincoat of
rain repellent
cloth with
detachable hood-
rubber boots

green suède leather
skeet jacket-
chamois patch
at shoulder-
bellows pockets-
tweed skirt-
calf gillie shoes

ski ensemble-
gray gabardine
jacket-dark blue
lining, hood,
mittens and
trousers

American
"mother and daughter"
design-of black
taffeta or velveteen
over white organdie
blouse

RTW

1947

for beach or sailing-
blue denim and
red and white striped
cotton- short slacks
or "pedal pushers"-
coolie jacket-
red and white
clogs

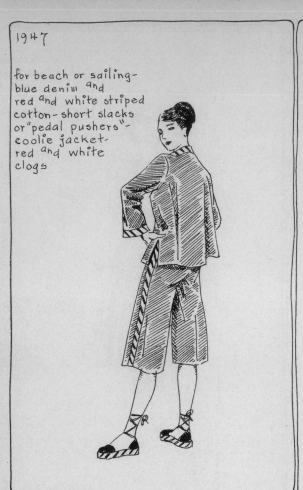

all-in-one beach suit-
beige wool jersey-
striped green belt-
wooden clogs with
green cotton straps

ranch or western riding
togs-whipcord frontier
pants and jacket-
wool shirt-colored
embroidery-leather
boots with heels
and colored leather
motifs-leather
and silver belt-
felt hat with
leather bride

for dinner at home-
black velvet slacks-
colorful silk
blouse-
ballet slippers

RTW/

1947

white sharkskin
bathing suit-
tucked body-
clogs of painted
wood and
cotton-
Brigance

black nylon elastic
swim suit-
zippered back-
Mabs

beach dress
of striped linen
worn over
pantaloons-
Molyneux

brown jersey one-piece
beach suit with full
bloomers-jersey skirt
striped green, brown and
black-striped
cotton clogs-
Jacques Fath

sun-dress in
culotte fashion-
printed batiste-
colorful cotton
wedge clogs-
De De Johnson

RTW

1947

modern farthingale
of taffeta with
ruffles

colored
taffeta petticoat
white cotton
ruffle-lace
edge-bands
of horsehair
braid

woman's
sleeping tunic
of silk
or batiste-
lace-edged

black chiffon
gown with
corselet of
black lace

lace-
trimmed
silk slip

laced and hooked
guêpière - black
satin-lace-
edged

long-sleeved
gown of silk
or batiste-
lace-edged

woman's
sleeping tunic
of silk or batiste

lace
and
satin
pantie girdle

removable wire

strapless brassière
with removable
arched wire

gartered
brassière
of nylon-
elastic-
black or
white

boned
"waist-liner"
of nylon
marquisette-
laced in front

RTW

1947

soft felt brimmed béret - Dior design made by Sygur

suède shoe with satin bowknot - Adrian

coiffure by Antoine

black suède pouch on leopard skin belt

pouch bag - black suède or fabric - Pichel

black felt or velvet toqué - black brush - Dior

suède or satin pump - moiré tie - La Valle

evening sandal - black velvet edged gold braid - yellow thongs tied in back

black suède bag - gilt decoration - Rosenfeld

wide girdle of pink antelope - Balenciaga

casual shoe - cocoa suède - Cobblers

gray suède and black patent leather - Drettas

silk umbrella - cobra handle case and shoulder strap

silk umbrella leather covered handle

California rain boot - transparent plastic - cork and rubber sole

sports glove - yellow crochet string with pigskin palm

tailored cloth hat with fantasy feather - Schiaparelli

return of the formal white glacé or suède glove

small suitcase - canvas and pigskin with silk umbrella Schiaparelli

black faille bag - silk umbrella in zippered compartment

RTW

sports jacket, green plaid-
green foulard scarf,
white polka dots-
beige flannel slacks-
brown reverse calf
shoes-crêpe
rubber soles

leisure jacket, rust gabardine-
colorful plaid wool sleeves and
collar-white shirt-
gray knitted pull-on
sweater-gray
gabardine slacks-
jippi-jappa hat-
brown and white
Norwegian
slippers

leisure jacket, camel's hair, natural
color- dark shirt-knitted scarf-
gold colored cotton slacks-
hemp hat with striped
puggree band-
brown and white
casual shoes

leisure jacket, brown suède
leather-beige corduroy slacks-
yellow flannel shirt-
maroon scarf-
brown and tan
casual shoes

RTW

1947-
ski costume-white processed cotton
jacket-elasticized waistband-
zippered front and pockets-
navy worsted gabardine ski trousers-
figured navy foulard neckerchief-
mitts, navy poplin and
tan leather-navy
poplin Swiss
ski cap-black
veal ski boots

hunting costume-
maroon and black plaid wool-
maroon wool shirt-
scarlet wool cap-
moccasin boot of
grained leather-
white wool hose with
maroon stripe

ranch costume-
tan wool gabardine-
Monterey jacket with
zipped front and pockets-
stockman pants-
dark green
gabardine shirt-
beige felt "ten
gallon hat"-
high heeled
cowboy riding
boots

active sports costume-
"bush jacket" of tan cotton twill-
bellows and pleated pockets-
tan twill shorts-white lisle
pullover shirt-
white knitted wool
hose-brown turned
calf shoes-
sun helmet, tan
cotton over
fiber

RTW

cotton or silk shirt of
brilliant colored
print - new English
slacks, patented
design - of fine
worsted -
canvas
beach sandals

brown and white
knitted shirt -
rust colored linen
shorts - blue
canvas beach
sandals

white knitted
swim trunks
in cable
stitch

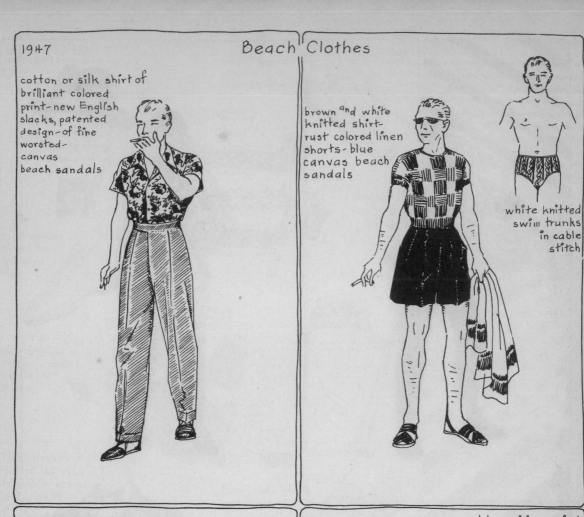

boating shirt, white
cotton with red stripes -
red cotton shorts -
white canvas
sandals

Hawaiian print
swim trunks

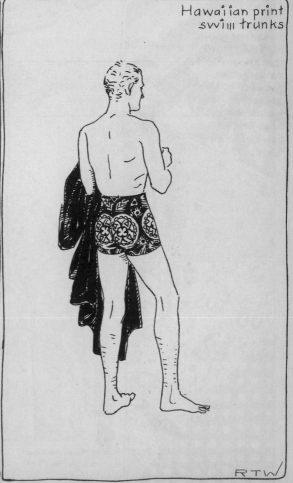

RTW

1947

thong laced to one side - reversed calf

the classic Homburg - dark blue and other colors

knitted ski sweater - navy or red on white

chukka boot of brown or black calf

cocoanut hat - polka dot puggree band

cotton shirt of two fabrics - white and colored check

scarf designs

dress version of the Norwegian slipper - calf or suède

English evening suit founded on battle dress - midnight blue with silk shawl collar

jippi·jappa hat with wide puggree band

cap for active sports - of straw or canvas

moccasin with platform sole - white buck · tan reverse calf

horsehide jacket for roughing it - wool lined

tri·colored straw with puggree band

RTW

1929-1946- 3rd period

Shirtwaist — inspired by man's shirt— centre front closing
introduced 1926- still popular in 1950)
Yoke gored skirt— natural waistline -
comfortable— made in all fabrics.
Princess and reefer coats unfurred were worn
with it. In N.Y.C. designs of Nettie Rosenstein,
Clare Potter gained attention. However paris still
reigned as centre of authentic fashion for retail store & dress
manufactures. WWII French importations
stopped making it nessecary for retail stores
to promote American designers. Adolesence
girl known as the Teenager became a person
of importance in clothing marts. As retailers,
editors + manu. catered to her whims a
wave of youthful fashions swept the country
producing mother + daughter outfits, boxcoat,
berets, shorts, slacks, boys shirts, low heeled loafers
saddle oxfords, mocassins sweaters + skirts, pinafores
and jumpers. The old women affected the young
look. Influence of childs sunsuits + evening
fashions were apparent in the dress market - neck-
lines became lower until the strapless with its
bolero, or cape
Cotton frocks previously considered appropirate
for day wear somber colors wools in sheer weaves for
Summer wear. Rayon was perfected in diff. weights
and textures.
L-85 restriction in dress wear

BIBLIOGRAPHY

ITALIAN —*Habiti Antichi et Moderni*—Cesare Vecellio—2 vols.

FRENCH —*Costumes français depuis Clovis*—Drawings by L. Massard.

Histoire du costume en France—J. Quicherat.

Le costume historique—A. Racinet.

Les arts—Moyen âge et la Renaissance—Paul Lacroix.

Vie militaire et religieuse—Moyen âge et la Renaissance—Paul Lacroix.

XVIIe siècle—Institutions, usages et costumes—Paul Lecroix.

Directoire, consulate et empire—Paul Lacroix.

The Eighteenth Century—Its Institutions, Customs, and Costumes—Paul Lacroix.

Un siècle de modes féminines, 1794-1894—Charpentier et Fasquelle.

Fashions in Paris—1797-1897—Octave Uzanne.

Mesdames nos aïeules: dix siècles à élégances—Robida.

Le costume civil en France du XIIIe au XIXe siècle—Camille Piton.

Histoire de la peinture classique—Jean De Foville.

Histoire du costume—Jacques Ruppert.

Histoire du costume—Librairie Hachette.

Le costume—Miguel Zamacoïs.

Les soieries d'art—Raymond Cox.

Cent ans de modes françaises—1800-1900—Mme. Cornil.

La mode féminine, 1900-1920—Éditions Nilsson.

GERMAN —*Die Trachten der Völker*—Albert Kretchmer.

Münchner Bilderbogen—Zur Geschichter des Kostüms.

An Egyptian Princess—George Ebers.

Die Mode im XVI. Jahrhundert—Max von Boehn.

Die Mode im XVII. Jahrhundert—Max von Boehn.

Die Mode im XVIII. Jahrhundert—Max von Boehn.

Die Moden des XIX. Jahrhunderts—Collection Geszler.

Modes and Manners of the XIX Century—Fischel-Von Boehn, 4 vols.

Le costume chez les peuples anciens et modernes—Fr. Hottenroth.

Kostümkunde—Hermann Weiss.

ENGLISH —*Manners and Customs of the English*—Joseph Strutt, 3 vols.

Everyday Life in Anglo-Saxon, Viking and Norman Times—M. and C. H. B. Quennell.

Everyday Life in Roman Britain—M. and C. H. B. Quennell.

History of Everyday Things in England, 1066–1799—M. and C. H. B. Quennell.

Life and Work of the People of England—16th Century—Hartley and Elliot.

Life and Work of the People of England—17th Century—Hartley and Elliot.

London in the Time of the Tudors—Sir Walter Besant.

Chats on Costume—G. Woolliscroft Rhead, R.E.

The Grammar of Ornament—Owen Jones.

Historic Costume—Francis M. Kelley and Randolph Schwabe.

English Costume—Dion Clayton Calthrop.

Dress Design—Talbot Hughes.

English Costume from the 14th through the 19th Century—Brooke and Laver.

AMERICAN—*Historic Dress in America*—Elizabeth McClellan.

Two Centuries of Costume in America—Alice Morse Earle, 2 vols.

Wimples and Crisping Pins—Theodore Child.

Accessories of Dress—Lester and Oerke.

The Psychology of Dress—Frank Alvah Parsons, B.S.

Economics of Fashion—Paul H. Nystrom, Ph.D.

The Ways of Fashion—M. D. C. Crawford.

Early American Costume—Edward Warwick and Henry Pitz.

A History of the Ancient World—George Willis Botsford, Ph.D.

Ancient Times—James Henry Breasted, Ph.D., LL.D.

The Fairchild Publications.

Vogue.

Harper's Bazaar.

British-American—*The Encylopædia Britannica.*